This is the full, exhilarating story of a journey as exciting—and as grueling—as any the Starship <u>Enterprise</u> has ever taken—from the birth of Gene Roddenberry's great idea to the completion of a great movie . . . a journey that carried cast, crew and hundreds of behind-the-scenes people as far as imagination, skill and the latest special optical effects technology could take them.

Never before in motion picture history had an undertaking of this magnitude been attempted, from the complex problems of reassembling the beloved stars of the original cast—a cast who had not performed in 10 years the roles they had immortalized—to the creation of extraordinary new film techniques untried in even the most spectacular of recent motion picture adventures. But then the millions of faithful "Star Trek" followers would have expected no less from the creator of their favorite TV show, and indeed, everyone involved felt a debt and responsibility to deliver something special to those millions who had helped make "Star Trek" a legend.

This is how it happened — the unexpected problems, the setbacks, the daily struggles and victories—from the reunion of Kirk, Spock, McCoy, Scotty, Uhura, Chekov and the rest of the crew to the final moments of triumph in . . .

THE MAKING OF

TREK ®
THE MOTION PICTURE

SUSAN SACKETT

GENE RODDENBERRY

Written by

SUSAN SACKETT

A WALLABY BOOK
PUBLISHED BY POCKET BOOKS NEW YORK

POCKET BOOKS, a Simon & Schuster division of
GULF & WESTERN CORPORATION
1230 Avenue of the Americas, New York, N.Y. 10020

Contents

2086047

Acknowledgments

So many people were of special help with the making of THE MAKING OF STAR TREK—THE MOTION PICTURE, and, as with the movie itself, nothing could have happened without these behind-the-scenes efforts that too often go unheralded.

Although the authors owe sincere thanks to many people, the following deserve this note of special appreciation:

Cheryl Blythe and Michele Billy for research, typing, and much needed moral support;

Director Robert Wise; costume designer Robert Fletcher; NASA technical advisor Jesco von Puttkamer; optical experts Doug Trumbull and John Dykstra; their assistants Mona Thal Benefiel and Mimi McKinney; Jim Dow and Carey Melcher of Magicam; publicists John Rothwell and Suzanne Gordon; and artist Andy Probert;

Still photographer *par excellence* Mel Traxel;

Leonard Maizlish and Howard A. Levine for advice and support;

Most especially, thanks to the STAR TREK Welcommittee, to Bjo Trimble, and to every STAR TREK fan everywhere for making it live—again!

THE MAKING OF

THE MOTION PICTURE

Preface

Thirteen years ago I was an eager new schoolteacher in Miami, Florida, wrestling daily with the minds of forty or so energetic nine-year-olds, trying to reach each child in some way, yet dissatisfied with the direction of my own life. I had *dreams*—dreams which seemed impossible, yet somehow compelling. The best ones centered around an intriguing new television program called *Star Trek,* and I desperately longed to somehow be a part of it all, or at least to live and work in the "magical city" that gave birth to such wonders. Someday . . .

Two years later, although some of the eagerness had worn away, I made the seemingly preordained move to Los Angeles. I secured a teaching job in my newly adopted state, but I hadn't really given up my fantasies of visiting the *Star Trek* sets, or of meeting, and possibly working for, a man named Gene Roddenberry—a name I saw each week on the show's credits and knew to be *Star Trek*'s creator and the person who inspired all these dreams.

But it was not to be. Paramount Pictures had a very firm "closed-set" policy, and I was routinely denied entrance at the front gate. Too bad there was no devil in sight who was interested in buying my disappointed and extremely inexpensive soul, since I would gladly have traded it for a glimpse of my favorite fantasyland.

With Hollywood beckoning all around me, I easily lost interest in the teaching profession. I dreamed of sets, lights, cameras, studios, and productions. There wasn't much demand for ex-schoolteachers in Hollywood, but nevertheless after adding my knuckleprints to all the doors in town, I did land a secretarial job at the National Broadcasting Company (thank you, Mom, for making me take typing in high school). I arrived there exactly the same week that *Star Trek* was handed its cancellation notice. So much for my incredible timing.

Four years later I left NBC, sensing it was time for a change. Perhaps I am gifted with some sort of ESP which lets each of us glimpse our own future without knowing it. Or perhaps I really was just lucky. But most likely it was the fact that I earnestly endeavored to apply the hope and optimism so often expressed in the *Star Trek* world to my own life. I never stopped hoping, never gave up dreaming that impossible dream. Eventually the puzzle pieces began falling into place on their own; on August 19, 1974, I found myself sitting across a desk from Gene Roddenberry, being interviewed for the job of his secretary. It was his fifty-third birthday that day, and in a way it was *my* birthday, too.

Since that day I've lived more of life than I had in all my previous years. Because of my involvement with *Star Trek*, I've met thousands of interesting people from many countries—scientists, statesmen, astronauts, business executives, writers, professors—and fans of every age and description. I've had opportunities to learn and grow in ways I never would have dared imagine could happen to me. But the greatest dream that has come true was to be a part of the making of *Star Trek—The Motion Picture.*

Of course, things have not always gone smoothly. There have been numerous frustrations and disappointments. Many times during the four and a half years Gene and I spent in our Paramount offices, we thought it was all over, that the movie would *never* happen. At times, Gene would be visibly suffering as he awaited the latest decision on the film, and I too would feel his pain.

Somehow, though, the good memories will always remain much more vivid. Like the first day I met William Shatner and didn't recognize him (after all those years of waiting!) because he was in disguise makeup for a recent television show called *Barbary Coast.* Or the time I dressed up in the British flag (and nothing else) to help celebrate one of our English scriptwriters' birthdays. They later were taken off the project, but we never forgot the fun they brought to these offices.

Without a doubt, working on this movie has been the most exciting thing in my life so far. When not needed back in the production office, I was usually on the set with my ubiquitous tape recorder, making notes and interviewing nearly every one of the hundreds of people involved in making this film. It's been an education, the kind that could never be taught in any classroom. The schoolteacher has at last become a pupil.

In writing this book, I've tried to give you some of my own newly acquired knowledge about how major motion pictures are made. If, as you read about *Star Trek*'s making, you find yourself longing, dreaming, and hoping that you could be a part of this world, then promise yourself that you will never give up that impossible dream. For it is *dreaming* that makes everything—movies and careers—possible.

SUSAN SACKETT
Hollywood, California
August, 1979

Introduction

As I write this, it is mid-October, 1979, and we are working anxiously around the clock to get the vital optical effects completed and into the *Star Trek* film before its December 6 premiere in Washington, D.C. We have about half of our optical footage delivered so far, and it looks spectacular. Our most difficult and complex opticals, however, are among those in work now, and my thoughts are increasingly on Robert Wise and Doug Trumbull who, with John Dykstra and the others, are spending seven days a week at twelve and fifteen hour work schedules in an effort to get every critical story-point optical delivered in time.

My other thought at this moment brings a pleased smile. It turns out that the *Trekkies* have been right all along—and on nearly everything they have tried to tell us. When they estimated that *Star Trek* fans numbered in the millions, their claim was ridiculed by experts at all the film studios. It turned out that Trekkie estimates were, if anything, on the conservative side. Trekkies were certainly right about themselves when they insisted that they were *not* simply a small group of shrill teenagers. Yes, there were teenagers among them, but more likely to be thoughtful and literate than shrill—and the other Trekkies with them included college professors, physicians, firemen, housewives, space engineers, and taxi drivers. Marvelous people with a strange, radical idea that the entertainment industry should listen to its audience—and who insisted to all willing to listen that the future is here *now*. At the top of the many things I owe them is my unreserved *respect*.

Finally, it is not possible to write an introduction to this book without acknowledging our debt to Stephen E. Whitfield (nom de plume of Stephen Poe) who, eleven years ago, wrote a paperback book entitled *The Making of Star Trek*.* It was the first successful book of its type and has astonished the publishing industry by having gone into its 24th reprinting to date. It was not only the model for this book but for many other filmmaking studies which have been written since.

As for the author of the book you now hold in your hands, there was no one available anywhere who had anything approaching Susan Sackett's knowledge and experience when it came to the more recent years of *Star Trek*. She is an author who had previously written two *Star Trek* books,† as well as scores of columns on science fiction and on *Star Trek* for several national publications. Over the years, she had become Paramount's "resident expert" on *Star Trek*, reading and commenting on most *Star Trek* manuscripts being considered for publication, as well as advising the studio on matters relating to fan activities and attitudes, and also on *Star Trek* format authenticity relating to merchandising. Before becoming an administrative assistant for *Star Trek*, she had worked as my confidential secretary for years before the movie began and knew my ideas and attitudes intimately, having handled all my correspondence, research and lecture material on that subject. During the actual production of the film, she carried the title *Assistant to the Producer*, which gave her constant and immediate access to all aspects of the filmmaking process.

In the beginning, the plan had been for me to co-author the book. It quickly became obvious, however, that this would be impossible. I was already committed to novelizing the *Star Trek* screenplay, a project which was consuming my evenings and weekends, and any further writing commitment might imperil my first obligation, which

---

*Ballantine, 1968.

† *Letters to Star Trek,* Ballantine, 1977 and *Star Trek Speaks*, Pocket Books, 1979, with Fred and Stan Goldstein.

was producing the film itself. In the end, the only choice was for me to supply information and comments (reflected in my name on the book cover) and leave it to author Sackett to be the actual writer. In retrospect, I am happy it worked out this way since it was clearly the best arrangement for this project.

Writing about one's self is an onerous and difficult task in which few if any of us can ever maintain any sense of perspective. Far better that one's part in a production of this complexity be written by a second party, with the studio and other involved third parties reviewing the text for completeness and accuracy. I am indebted to our director Robert Wise and to Paramount Pictures for their assistance in this. Finally, I am indebted to Susan Sackett for her writing skills which resulted in this very readable and informative account of how *Star Trek* happened all over again.

GENE RODDENBERRY
La Costa, California

1

Bon Voyage

INT. BRIDGE

A confusion of activity and VOICES. Pieces of equipment in a state of disarray: consoles open, fiber optic tubes unconnected, viewing screens dismantled. It's a frantic, desperate scene—a ship and crew totally unprepared. In the midst of all this: ALIEN ENSIGN is assisting UHURA (lt. comdr. stripes), deftly working her communications station, AD-LIBBING ". . . Hailing frequency four, check. Hailing frequency five, will someone please check me?" At the helm, sweat-soaked SULU (lt. comdr. stripes) has a service plate open, is peering inside to make delicate adjustments, AD-LIBBING ". . . Helm, now give me a reading on four point zero zero six of full." And at the Weapons Control, CHEKOV (full lt.) argues with TECHNICIANS who insist photon torpedoes read "ready" while Chekov argues the computer is not relaying that information.

By three o'clock in the afternoon of August 7, 1978, the first scene of *Star Trek—The Motion Picture* had not been taken to the satisfaction of director Robert Wise. The heat from the lights on sound stage 9 had all but melted the twenty-five or so people in front of the cameras who had been repeating the scene again and again since early morning. For the last hour, Bob Wise had been patiently attempting to get the actors, extras, special-effects people, and the rest of the crew into the perfectly synchronized tableau he had in mind. It was a tricky scene showing the bridge of the *Enterprise* being prepped for departure, involving everything from light panels, opening elevator doors, images on the main viewer (blue screen), last-minute checks at each bridge station, an extra suspended in midair on "antigravs" (by means of out-of-shot rigging), and ad-libbed, overlapping dialogue. On the screen, the scene appears randomly chaotic, although it had been planned by Bob and was now being directed by him with the kind of concentration and organizational skill shown by symphony conductors. Finally, after fifteen takes, Bob seemed pleased with what he had gotten on film. The entire crew burst into applause, and the first scene filmed for *Star Trek—The Motion Picture* was in the can.

In the early morning, the high-energy level charged the air with excitement, tension, and eagerness to begin. Everyone was due on stage at 9:00, although some of the cast had makeup calls at 7:00, and a few eager beavers were in at 6:00.

With the confusion of the last-minute checks on technical equipment before cameras could roll, the stage itself mirrored the scene to be shot. Actors were running lines, frantically learning new dialogue that had just been handed to them on blue (revised) pages—a procedure that would later become an almost daily practice. Camera and lighting checks were being made; people were congratulating one another; last-minute adjustments to costumes and makeup were being taken care of. Nearly a hundred people involved in getting this scene on film were crammed into the corner of stage 9, which housed the bridge set. With the blue screen in place behind the viewer, the only access to the bridge was through the elevator doors, and since one of these passageways was taken up with camera equipment, gaining admittance to the bridge was worse than a freeway rush-hour bottleneck.

There were brief, unrehearsed opening ceremonies: Producer Gene Roddenberry* presented Bob Wise with one of his personal treasures—a black cap with gold script lettering which read "Enterprise," given to Gene by the captain of the nuclear carrier *Enterprise* when he was invited on that ship for ten days of maneu-

---

*References to Roddenberry were written by Sackett and remain in the third person.

vers. It helped relax the mood a bit, and Bob continued to wear the cap throughout the day. Gene was presented with a specially prepared breakaway bottle of champagne secured by property master Dick Rubin, and together Gene and Bob cracked the bottle over the bridge railing, thus officially christening the starship. (The bottle was empty, as any liquid would have messed up the newly readied set.)

Although the first day's shooting did not involve the entire cast, nearly everyone was on hand for the first few moments. William Shatner, returning as James T. Kirk, brought along his three daughters, Leslie, Melanie, and Lizabeth. Leonard Nimoy dropped by to wish everyone luck, although Mr. Spock's first scenes were still a

Robert Wise *(left)* is welcomed aboard the *Enterprise* by Gene Roddenberry on the first day of shooting.

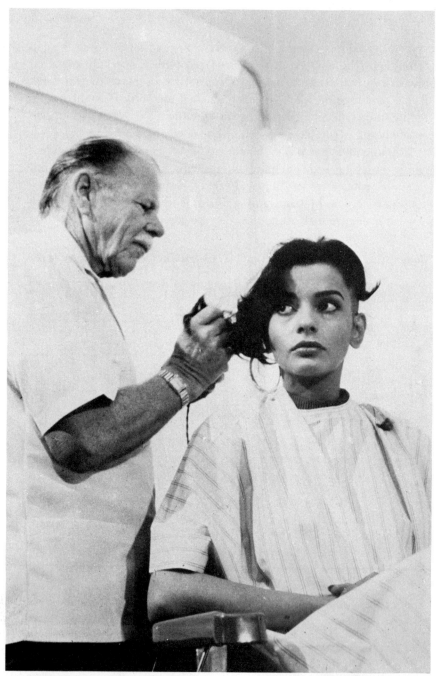

BEFORE: Persis Khambatta looks to makeup artist Fred Phillips for reassurance during her head-shaving ordeal.

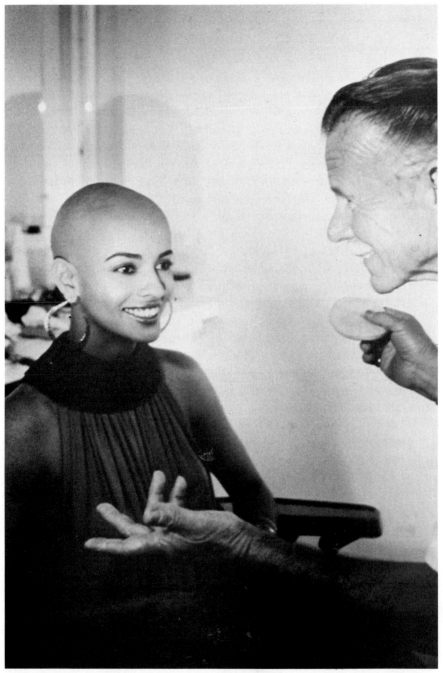

AFTER: Persis, transformed into Lt. Ilia, gets her newly shaved head powdered by Fred.

week away. DeForest Kelley (Dr. McCoy) came by to watch, although he also wouldn't begin for a few days.

The newest members of the *Enterprise* crew were a bit in awe of all this. The first day on a movie set is usually not like a big family reunion, and it was little wonder that the new kids on the block, Stephen Collins and Persis Khambatta, seemed more reserved. Steve had been cast only a week earlier, after a lengthy search for an actor who seemed right for the role of Decker. His strikingly handsome appearance attracted a lot of attention, though he preferred to sit quietly in a corner backstage and study his lines. But it was Persis, with her head smoother than a newborn baby's, who captured everyone's gaze.

Persis's character, Ilia, is from the planet Delta 4, home of a race of highly evolved humanoids who have no body hair—except for eyelashes and eyebrows. Roddenberry had warned her that she must shave her head for the part, and Persis had willingly agreed. On July 26, 1978, ten days before production began, Persis's locks connected with makeup artist Fred Phillip's electric razor.

That morning, with cameras on hand to record the event, Persis sat in Fred's makeup room, laughing and joking as he applied facial makeup, intensifying her naturally beautiful face. It seemed like some cruel practical joke that her shiny black tresses had been neatly set in curlers for the "before" shots, knowing that they would soon be lonesome for her head. She sat nervously chain smoking, chatting with the cameraman and others at hand, gaining moral support from those who had gathered to watch this almost virginal sacrifice. On the makeup table she had placed her treasured pictures of her family, along with some of her religious pictures. It comforted her to have this shrine, as she called it, nearby.

Fred and Persis seemed merely pawns in this event. Carl Barth, director of a film crew assigned to document the production, actually engineered the hairshaving scene. There was no "buzz, buzz, snip, snip, it's over"—that would be too quick. They rehearsed the procedure with Fred, Persis, and Fred's daughter Janna, also a makeup artist on the film. Persis's nerves were getting a bit tighter, and more cigarettes were lit, as Barth directed, "Now, snip a lock of her hair and put it in this box. . . . Janna, move the box in closer. . . . Fred, can you cross to the other side? . . . Hold the scissors the other way. . . ." Persis looked very small and very vulnerable.

After the first big locks were dramatically snipped for the cameras, Fred began in earnest with the electric razor. Persis smiled bravely, comforted from time to time by those around her, including Majel Barrett (Dr. Chapel), who had become a close friend. A few more poses for the cameras and Fred got down to business. As the razor whirred away, more and more bare head began to show. About this time the brave smile faded from Persis, and she grew quiet, and as more hair was removed, it became evident that she was fighting to maintain control. At one point some very large tears began to fall softly from those lovely eyes as she fully realized that it was actually happening. She refused to look in the mirror during the process, and Majel tried to cheer her with lighthearted comments like "You look like a dark peach." When she finally turned to look in the mirror, she quickly looked away again as if seeing someone else, then returned to gaze at her new self, which was rapidly emerging. She managed a smile, although there was still tension evidenced in her rigid hand clutching the chair. Her first comment: "I look like Hare Krishna. If you see someone at the airport handing out leaflets, it will be me!"

After all the hair had been removed and stored in a box, which Persis kept, Gene Roddenberry presented her with a gift—an electric razor (what else?). Touching a tentative hand to her scalp, Persis joked, "It feels like sandpaper." But once smoothly shaved, her head's true shape emerged—and it was wonderfully and strikingly lovely. Without her dark hair, she was, if anything, even more unusually beautiful, a unique face among the familiar ones on the first day of shooting.

As the first day's shooting wore on, the actors began to show signs of strain, and it was decided that Bill Shatner's close-up would be shot the following morning, when his face would look less fatigued. Of the 1,650 feet of film used on the first day, 420 feet were good, 1,070 feet were no good, and 160 feet were wasted, with one and one-eighth pages being shot for the day. Within two weeks, everything proved more complex than had been imagined, and production had fallen a week behind. The previous schedule had principal photography ending October 31, 1978, but this was revised within a short time to read December 22. Actually, principal photography ran slightly more than a month beyond that date—a costly delay but one not unusual on a technically complex film such as this. In all, it was an exciting day that had climaxed many long years of waiting but at last the *Enterprise* would fly once more.

2

The Resurrection

"If you can wait and not be tired by waiting . . ."
—RUDYARD KIPLING

STAR TREK—THE MOTION PICTURE
WAS FIFTEEN YEARS IN THE MAKING!

Hollywood hype? Not really, if you include the early years of its development as a television show from which it evolved into the successful film of today.

Star Trek (the television show) went off the air in 1969, and it wasn't until 1975 that it was awakened from its dormant state. But its path was constantly strewn with roadblocks. It was much like a trek through Wonderland, complete with Alices and Cheshire cats:

". . . Then it doesn't matter which way you go," said the Cat.
"—so long as I get *somewhere*," Alice added as an explanation.
"Oh, you're sure to do that," said the Cat, "if you only walk long enough."

It was a long walk, and eventually it did get somewhere, but the twists and turns in the road took several years to navigate.

The fifteen years of *Star Trek—The Motion Picture*'s making really began back in 1964 with a man with an idea and unparalled determination. The man was Gene Roddenberry, and his idea was *Star Trek*.

After knocking on all the doors in town, he eventually got Desilu Studios to put up the money for the first *Star Trek* pilot, "The Cage." It was rejected by all three networks. Later, an unprecedented second pilot was ordered ("Where No Man Has Gone Before"), and NBC added *Star Trek* to its fall lineup for 1966. It had taken nearly three years alone just to launch the television series.

A word should be said here about the creator of *Star Trek*. Throughout all those Wonderland years, Gene Roddenberry protected and cared for *Star Trek* almost the way a parent would care for a child. *Star Trek—The Motion Picture is* his child, nurtured through its infancy as a television show with parental guidance and love. He extends this love through the concepts he tried to convey in *Star Trek*—delight in the differences in people and things. Ever curious, there is a bit of Captain Kirk in him—or is it the other way around? He's somewhat of a Renaissance man—his interests extending from flying to sailing, from gem cutting to inventing, from reading anything and everything in print, to creating worlds of his own through his writing and producing. He hit Hollywood in the early years of television, writing for such shows as *Goodyear Theatre, The Kaiser Aluminum Hour, Four Star Theatre,* and *Naked City.* For two years he served as head writer for *Have Gun, Will Travel,* winning the Writers Guild Award for his episode, "Helen of Abiginian." In 1962 he created and produced his first television series, *The Lieutenant,* which starred Robert Vaughn, and Gary Lockwood (who later starred in *Star Trek's* second pilot, "Where No Man . . ."). In fact, *The Lieutenant* featured many actors he would later use in *Star Trek*—Leonard Nimoy, Majel Barrett, Walter Koenig, and Nichelle Nichols.

Now in his late fifties, he continues to attack new projects in the same way he tackled the long battle of getting the original *Star Trek* series on the air.

Star Trek was on the NBC network in prime time for only three seasons—1966 to 1969. It was never a favorite with most of the network brass, and they had the Nielsen ratings to back them up. Nevertheless, when NBC threatened cancellation for a second and again a third season, over one million fans wrote to the network to protest halting the *Enterprise's* five-year mission before completing her full tour of duty. The fans' leader was a perky redheaded lady—Bjo Trimble, a name that is practically a household word to every *Star Trek* fan in the world. She is responsible for creating *Star Trek* fandom almost singlehandedly, and wrote thousands of personal letters putting fans in touch with one another. "This is how fandom grows," she says.

Bjo does not look like a leader of the masses. She's petite, freckled, a Los Angeles housewife and loving mother of two daughters. She enjoys costume designing, book collecting, rock hounding, medieval culture, and herbology—all the usual things. She also likes to write and is the author of *The Star Trek Concordance* (Ballantine Books, 1976). But by far her most successful writing effort was the letter that started the million-letter "Save *Star Trek*" campaign.

According to Bjo, the mail campaign at the end of the first season (when NBC was only talking about the possibility of cancellation) was actually run by science-fiction writer Harlan Ellison.* The campaign was widespread—he wrote to all the known fan groups, the entire membership of two World Science Fiction Conventions (about seven thousand members), the members of the Science Fiction Writers of America (SFWA), NASA, scientists, and many others, urging them to keep this mature science-fiction program on the air:

December 1, 1966
It's finally happened. You've been in the know for a long time, you've known the worth of mature science fiction, and you've squirmed at the adolescent manner with which it has generally been presented on television. Now, finally, we've lucked-out, we've gotten a show on prime time that is attempting to do the missionary job for the field of speculative fiction. The show is <u>Star Trek</u>, of course, and its aims have been lofty. <u>Star Trek</u> has been carrying the good word out to the boondocks. Those who have seen the show know it is frequently written by authentic science fiction writers, it is made with enormous difficulty and with considerable pride. If you were at the World Science Fiction Convention in Cleveland you know it received standing ovations and was awarded a special citation by the Convention. <u>Star Trek</u> has finally showed the mass audience that science fiction need not be situation comedy in space suits. The reason for this letter—and frankly, its appeal for help—is that we've learned this show, despite its healthy growth, could face trouble soon. The Nielsen Roulette game is being played. They say, "If mature science fiction is so hot, howzacome that kiddie space show on the other network is doing so much better?" There is no sense explaining it's the second year for the competition

---

*The initial enthusiasm Harlan Ellison had for the show was terminated soon after his mail campaign. Because of a passionate disagreement with Gene Roddenberry over the rewrites of "The City on the Edge of Forever," Harlan withdrew his personal support of the series and frequently spoke with disenchantment of the show. Interestingly, Harlan's unshot manuscript and Gene's rewrite have *both* won major writing awards since then.

and the first year for <u>Star Trek</u>; all they understand are the decimal places. And the sound of voices raised. Which is where you come in.

<u>Star Trek's</u> cancellation or a change to a less adult format would be tragic, seeming to demonstrate that real science fiction cannot attract a mass audience.

We need letters! Yours and ours, plus every science fiction fan and TV viewer we can reach through our publications and personal contacts. Important: Not form letters, not using our phrases here; they should be the fan's own words and honest attitudes. They should go to: (a) local television stations which carry <u>Star Trek</u>; (b) to sponsors who advertise on <u>Star Trek</u>; (c) local and syndicated television columnists; and (d) <u>TV Guide</u> and other television magazines.

The situation is critical; it has to happen now or it will be too late. We're giving it all our efforts; we hope we can count on yours.

Sincerely,

Harlan Ellison

According to Gene Roddenberry, the letters that resulted from this campaign sent the network over the edge to renew *Star Trek,* and during the next season he invited a number of fans, including John and Bjo Trimble, to the set to show his appreciation.

"We were on the set," says Bjo, "in the middle of the second season—the week they got the word that *Star Trek* was going to be canceled. Everybody was so down, and John and I discussed this on our way home. We had hoped that by encouraging *Star Trek* we would be encouraging good science fiction to appear on television. John insisted there must be something we could do about this, and that's what set it all off.

"I went to Paramount* and got a lot of the fan mail, and I went to a couple of science-fiction conventions and got their mailing lists. In all, John and I mailed out around four to five thousand letters. We asked for a pyramid, whereby everyone would write to ten other people and copy this letter. I went to United Fan Mail, some people at Paramount, a banker I knew, and a big corporation secretary I knew, and I asked all of them, 'What is the kind of letter that you would throw away the minute you opened it? What is it about an envelope that makes you open it first? And what is the kind of letter you continue to read through?' If you open a letter which says 'Okay, Dummy!...' you're obviously not going to read much further. I put all of this together into

---

*Desilu Studios was bought out by Gulf and Western in 1967 and taken over by Paramount Pictures, one of their subsidiaries.

my 'How to Write a Letter' flyer." She not only told them to write, she told them *how* to write it—and it worked!

"I was amazed," says Gene Roddenberry. "I think you can't write and produce a show without hoping a lot of people out there will like it, but when I had heard they had received something over a million letters, I was stunned and delighted of course that they kept us on. The first reports from NBC were that they were not only going to keep us on, but they were going to put us on at a better time, although I think there were quite a few executives at NBC who felt that I was behind the whole campaign, as if I have a secret telephone somewhere from which I 'manipulate' fans and organizations. I tried to explain to them that if I could bring out Cal Tech on a torchlight parade at NBC, if I could have MIT picket Rockefeller Center, and do other things like that, I would get out of show business and into politics. But even today there are those still convinced that I am a Machiavellian publicity strategist. I suppose the fan campaign did cost the network a great deal of money. I understand they had to put on a lot of extra secretaries to handle the mail. Some of the fans did kind of funny things. During MIT's march against NBC in New York, I understand they snuck into the executive garage and put 'Save *Star Trek*' bumper stickers on all the executive limousines."

NBC and *Star Trek* again set precedence when, during the closing credits of the March 1, 1968, episode (second season), a soothing voice-over proclaimed:

> And now an announcement of interest to all viewers of *Star Trek*. We are pleased to tell you that *Star Trek* will continue to be seen on NBC Television. We know you will be looking forward to seeing the weekly adventure in space on *Star Trek*.

The million letters had overwhelmed them. What they were really saying was "Please, give us a break and stop writing already." Of course, the polite fans didn't know that. They immediately began to write nice little thank-you notes, giving NBC the added headache of having to process all of them.

However, at the end of the third season, Bjo just wasn't up to the effort, and the letter campaign failed to get off the ground again. This time, nothing was able to save the show for a fourth season, and when NBC aired its final new episode of *Star Trek* on June 3, 1969 ("Turnabout Intruder"), the network figured that was the end of that particular fling with fantasy. But the ghost of that "dead" program has continued to haunt them for ten years now.

By every network standard of the time, *Star Trek* was a failure. Yet it somehow achieved greater success *after* it failed than is true of most series that "succeeded." The network gave "poor ratings" as the reason for the cancellation. Nielsens told the story as far as they were concerned; demographics, which are a body-type count rather than a general head count (i.e., how many women eighteen to forty-nine watch? how many teenagers? etc.), hadn't been taken into consideration, which in *Star Trek*'s case were later determined to show a highly desirable audience profile.

According to Gene, "Had the network been in demographics then instead of just straight Nielsen head counts, we probably would have stayed on. Demographics recognize that young people about to have a family, about to acquire a car, washing machine, children, soap, diapers, can be sold many more products than the elderly retired widow. A year after *Star Trek* went off, I'm told that the head of NBC research came to them and said 'We've discovered the show with *perfect* demographics—it's the one you just threw off the air.' Had we been a year later, had they been a year earlier with demographics, we probably would have had a ten-year run."

Naturally Gene felt the cancellation keenly, as did the cast, which had become almost a family in the three years they worked together. "It was sadness—like a family parting," he said. "We didn't know what our future was. Certainly most of us did not envision any future for *Star Trek*. We knew from our fans there would be a lot of people who would remember it for a long time. None of us envisioned the new sort of audience phenomenon now that the show was off the air. We went on to doing other things. I think all of us definitely felt that a very interesting and in some ways significant part of our lives was over now."

Adding to the fact that *Star Trek* was never a Nielsen powerhouse was a third season which had its share of problems, no doubt contributing heavily to the low ratings responsible for cancellation. One of the main problems was the fact that *Star Trek*'s third-season time slot was Friday night at ten o'clock.

Gene went to NBC after the fans had mounted their campaign, saying if they would bring the show back for a third season, he would go back to personally producing the show, staying very close to it as he had done in the first season. He guaranteed them that he would give them superior quality and the best show possible. The only thing he asked in return was that they give it a good time slot. He felt Friday night was killing it the second season because, as he put it, "Friday night is a night out for young-minded people and a great TV night for things retired firemen's widows watch." The network promised *Star Trek* would have a 7:00 or 8:00 time slot one night Monday through Thursday. Under those conditions Gene promised he would personally produce the show.

After they picked up *Star Trek*'s option for a third season, NBC did two things—they decided to renew an option for only sixteen shows, which was half a season, and they decided to put the show on at 10:00 Friday night, the worst possible time for it. Gene told NBC, "I cannot go back and give twelve-hour days and seven-day weeks to a show that, going in, you folks are obviously intending to cancel. I cannot afford to personally produce this unless you give me a fair chance of keeping *Star Trek* on the air." They refused to do that, and he moved back completely to being executive producer.

With children nearing college age, Gene needed to look for sources of income after the cancellation happened. He met his contract requirements to serve as *Star Trek*'s executive producer, but he limited himself to that role. He, no longer rewrote or polished the scripts, which he had deliberately done in the first two seasons, giving each show his own personal touch.

On July 15, 1969, *Star Trek*, now in summer reruns on the NBC network for the last time, was pre-empted by the Apollo launch, which would culminate in the first moon landing by humans. (The show returned on July 29 with the rerun of an ironically titled episode— "That Which Survives.") Neil Armstrong took his first small step on the surface of the moon that month, and not only mankind, but *Star Trek*'s popularity was about to take a giant leap.

"*Star Trek* probably came along too early," Gene Roddenberry notes. "Had man landed on the moon during our first or second year the idea of space flight wouldn't have seemed so ludicrous to the mass audience. *Star Trek* probably would have stayed on the air. It wasn't until after we had gone off the air that the attitudes of scientists like Carl Sagan, concerning the probability of extraterrestrial life, began to appear in newspaper articles and in magazines. The eyes of the world did not turn to space seriously as a future probability until we were in our third year, and by then it was too late. That interest in space steadily grew over the first few years after we were finished and thus the episodes became more and more believable to the general audience. We were just a little ahead of our time, or NBC was just a little backward in the way they were using rating systems, or a combination of both. Space became a very legitimate thing. When we first went into production, my own father went around apologizing to the neighbors, saying, 'I know he's doing something crazy now, but he'll come back and write a good American western.' And this was a very general feeling.

"Today, you can walk into any gathering of any kind of people—real estate people, brokers, policemen, housewives, anything—and talk about space and extraterrestrial life, and you have many in your audience who believe in it. At the time we were making the early years of *Star Trek* that audience was just not there. The only audience that understood what we did was a very young-minded audience. Afterwards, when it got into syndication, by the time you'd had twenty reruns, college kids would come home, children or others would force nonviewers to look at it, or at least it would be on in the room. Interest grew and grew until today the majority of the American audience sees space travel not only as something desirable but also as something probably inescapable."

While Armstrong's footsteps were silently made in the vacuum of the atmosphereless moon, their echoes were loud enough to awaken interest in the sleeper owned by an unsuspecting Paramount Studios. As the world became increasingly conscious of the vast possibilities of outer space, *Star Trek* was quietly beginning its reruns in syndication. Anxious to recoup some of the money lost in the production of this program, Paramount hoped that the show might enjoy perhaps a few years in syndication.

The show went immediately into reruns in the fall of 1969, and by the late seventies it had been sold in over a hundred and fifty domestic and nearly sixty international markets. It has since rerun dozens of times, and shows no sign of abating, with some stations holding contracts for airing reruns well into the 1980s.

* * *

As *Star Trek* began to be syndicated to more and more television stations throughout the world, it soon became apparent that the show was not about to give up the ghost. A company handling the show's fan mail found itself deluged with requests for *Star Trek* photos and souvenirs.* The studio plainly had a hit on its hands, as mail continued to pour in by the sackful, urging the program to be revived. The earliest fans had never given up hope even after the program had been canceled, and new blood was being transfused daily into the cause of revival. It became something of a cultlike phenomenon which has continued to escalate for nearly ten years. Some of the reasons for its popularity in syndication are given by Gene Roddenberry:

"In the last ten years the future has suddenly come upon us. People are beginning to realize that the future is happening *now*. Whereas ten or fifteen years ago the future was something a quarter century or half century ahead, the rate of human development is moving so fast now that the future has finally caught up with us. Today you can't risk *not* thinking about the future, because many of the things you take for granted today may not even be here tomorrow."

He believes a lot of the unusual success of *Star Trek* is due to the fact that science fiction, when written properly as the legitimate drama that it is, is a very powerful way to introduce new concepts to people. He also insists that fiction has always been much more powerful than fact in discussing real issues, since the very essence of drama-fiction is to make the audience actually *become* the characters in that drama and feel all the pain and puzzlement and triumph that is happening in the story. He wanted the *Star Trek* audience to *become* the people in the starship *Enterprise,* to feel fear when they felt fear, to hurt when they hurt, to exalt with each winning of a new challenge. Gene believes that it is emotion that makes drama a powerful and meaningful experience, whereas a straight factual presentation of information is more likely to be merely a cerebral experience dealing with things always a bit removed from yourself.

But even *Star Trek*'s varied drama couldn't continually captivate its own loyal following. The fans' appetites were unsated by the Möbius-stripped program. They began to organize. Fandom caught revival fever, and the *Star Trek* fans ("Trekkies," "Trekkers," "Trekfen"—the terminology varies but not their ardor) gathered in groups and clubs to honor their heroes, to continue writing letters to Paramount and NBC, to view umpteen reruns of episodes until they were able to quote whole

*Lincoln Enterprises, P.O. Box 69470, Los Angeles, Calif. 90069.

passages verbatim, to swap film clips and photos, and to dream about the new world of love and peace and friendship and growth for all promised by *Star Trek*'s future. Eventually enough interest resulted in a small group of New Yorkers planning the very first *Star Trek* convention.

Conventions were nothing new to science-fiction buffs. They had been a way of life for them for thirty-eight years, but there had never been one honoring a single television show, science fiction or otherwise.*

The first all–*Star Trek* convention was held in January 1972. It was conceived by Al Schuster, who, with friends and associates Joanie Winston and Elyse Pines, hoped to gather three or four hundred fans. They planned to show the fifteen *Star Trek* television episodes, offer a chance for conventioneers to rap with Gene Roddenberry, his wife, actress Majel Barrett (who had appeared as Nurse Chapel in *Star Trek*), prominent science-fiction writers Isaac Asimov and Hal Clement (neither of whom had anything to do with *Star Trek* but were themselves fans of the show), and provide a "hucksters' room" where souvenirs from the show would be traded with all the flurry and excitement of a carnival sideshow.

Thanks to good publicity and the growing number of *Star Trek* fan clubs (nearly thirty at that time as compared to the almost four hundred today), over two thousand people paid $3.50 for what was to be the first of many years of successful *Star Trek* fan conventions.

Conventions soon became standard fare internationally, gathering as many as twenty thousand at some of the larger ones. In the years that followed, cities that played host to *Star Trek* conventions included New York, Chicago, Los Angeles, San Diego, New Orleans, Washington, D.C., Miami, Atlanta, San Francisco, Oakland, Denver, Salt Lake City, and Phoenix, as well as many smaller cities and towns in the United States and on both sides of the International Dateline.

All the members of the original cast and some actors who played only a small one-shot part have been guests of honor at numerous "cons," as they are called. Other guests have been NASA scientists, science-fiction writers, filmmakers, film writers, directors, and so on. Activities have been expanded to include blood drives (first introduced

---

*And only very recently have other television programs had conventions held in their honor—curiously enough, they were soap operas.

to the cons by that dean of science fiction writers, Robert Heinlein, himself a big *Star Trek* fan), charity tie-ins, art shows, auctions, costume contests, trivia contests, science-fiction films, writing workshops, celebrity banquets, and full orchestra balls complete with floorshows.

With *Star Trek*'s syndicated popularity a very definite reality, new "Trek" ideas began to pour in. One of the earliest, just after cancellation, came from Paramount Television, which asked Gene Roddenberry if he was interested in producing a spin-off series centered around the half-human, half-Vulcan Mr. Spock character. But Gene argued that a continuation of the original *Star Trek* would work even better. He believed that the tendency was to give the Spock characterization total credit for being interesting in itself, whereas it was the surrounding human contrast that made Spock most interesting. He believed that proper balance of surrounding human contrast was either the *Star Trek* format or something weighted and balanced much like it. A series of episodes about Spock on Vulcan with Vulcans gives the audience little point of human identification. His reasoning was that if they took Spock away from Vulcan so you could have that human contrast, why invent a wholly new thing when you already had him among humans in *Star Trek,* which still had an untapped story potential?

Other offers followed. One offer presented a *Star Trek* animation script that had the *Enterprise* crew landing on strange planets and zapping everything in sight that was ugly or different, totally the opposite of *Star Trek*'s philosophy. Another house which submitted something had the *Enterprise* full of space cadets and an episode that opened with one of them saying, "Gee Whiz, Captain Kirk!" Gene didn't want to degrade *Star Trek* that way. He felt that *Star Trek* was a potentially valuable property and that that sort of treatment would just ruin it. He told them he would not do an animated show until he had creative control and could guarantee that *Star Trek* would be done as it should be done—the same characters, the same types of writers, and so on. Finally in 1973 an offer was made by Filmation, an animation house that boasted a number of *Star Trek* fans already among their ranks, and Gene Roddenberry, NBC, and Paramount were in partnership once again on *Star Trek*.

D. C. Fontana, who had written a number of popular *Star Trek* episodes, and had had a long association with the series as script consultant and later story editor, was brought in as associate producer and story editor on the animated series, thus assuring that the basic concepts of *Star Trek* would remain intact. Twenty-two thirty-minute episodes were made in all, with D.C.'s firm editorial hand guiding such talented writers as Marc Daniels, Samuel Peeples, Larry Niven, David Gerrold, and Margaret Armen, many of whom were associated with the original TV series.

Most of the original cast assembled for the first time since cancellation for the recording of dialogue for the very first animated episode, although later on voices were recorded individually to accommodate the actors' schedules. Some of the cast found themselves not only reading their original roles, but occasionally they were called upon to do multiple voices. For example, James Doohan read his regular part of Scotty, but found himself also supplying the voices of the Healer, the Andorian, and the Guardian of Forever in "Yesteryear." In later episodes he did the voices of a Romulan commander, and also a new bridge officer, Lt. Arex, the three-armed, three-legged helmsman (a sort of caninoid alien).

In fact, the animated version opened up a whole new realm of aliens. No longer confined to bipedal humanoids, which were all the Screen Actors Guild was capable of supplying, Filmation's artists were able to add Lt. Arex and a new communications officer, Lt. M'Ress, a "felinoid"—a catlike female complete with long tail and contented purrs. Weekly aliens encompassed nearly everything the imagination could conjure up—creatures with multiple appendages and heads, airborne and water-breathing aliens, fifty-foot tall creatures, and monsters of every description. Imagination was not limited to beings, however. Fantastic planets and elaborate spaceships could be profusely illustrated without wreaking havoc with a sound-stage-bound art director's budget.

The animated *Star Trek* premiered on Saturday, September 8, 1973, seven years to the day after the premiere of the original *Star Trek*. The previous week at a private NBC press screening of the premiere episode, "Beyond the Farthest Star," *Los Angeles Times* critic Cecil Smith was overheard to say, "This is definitely *not* a kid's program." The fact that he was impressed was reflected in his written review:

NBC's new animated *Star Trek* is as out of place in the Saturday morning kiddie ghetto as a Mercedes is in a soapbox derby.

Don't be put off by the fact it's now a cartoon—and TV has managed to corrupt animation from an art into a disease. It is fascinating fare, written, produced and executed with all the imaginative skill, the intellectual flare and the literary level that made Gene Roddenberry's famous old science fiction epic the most avidly followed program in TV history, particularly in high IQ circles.

NBC might do well to consider moving it into prime time at mid-season, but it probably won't—the network never understood the appeal of the live program; there's no reason to believe it is any more aware of its animated godson.

Smith had called it accurately—the twenty-two episodes completed their first run on October 12, 1974 (although the show continued in Saturday morning reruns through September 1975), then vanished altogether from the face of the screen until its recent sale into thirty-five syndicated markets. However, it received what is sometimes referred to jokingly in the industry as the traditional cancellation send-off—it won the Emmy Award, television's highest honor, as the Best Children's Series for the 1974–75 season. But it wasn't enough to reinstate animated *Star Trek,* and Saturday morning was again abandoned to the mutually beneficial kiddie cartoons and breakfast cereals. Again, disappointment for Gene Roddenberry:

"I think one can always wish something was done better, but within the limits of how animation is done in the market today—the speed it's done, the dollars they're able to put into it, and so on—it was a fairly good job. I think the best proof of that is the Emmy it won. *Star Trek* has a spectacular record of getting awards and special attention either while or after it's been canceled."*

Star Trek's future was very much in doubt. It had left a string of cancellations in its wake, and NBC was not likely to give it another chance.

After the animated version went off the air, Gene had a couple of conversations with NBC. Each time NBC said they would consider it if he could get Paramount to put up enough money for another *Star Trek* pilot. His attitude was, "Hell, you've got seventy-nine pilots, and there's no way I could convince Paramount to put up a million dollars to prove we could do what we've already proven we could do."

---

*Every year, including the one in which the show was canceled, *Star Trek* and its actors were nominated for awards. The show won an Emmy for best special effects and best sound editing.

With a family to feed, Gene put aside *Star Trek* to work on three pilots for television, all of which were presented as television movies of the week.

Genesis II (CBS, 1973) painted a portrait of what seemed to be a very dismal post-atomic-war future for Earth, diametrically opposed to the optimism portrayed in *Star Trek*'s brave new world.* The heroes' organization in this story was called *PAX,* a group which was preserving the art and science of the past while helping an infant civilization to grow.

The Questor Tapes (NBC, 1974) concerned an android with consciousness in search of his creator. It starred Robert Foxworth in the title role—a role that had been written with *Star Trek*'s Leonard Nimoy in mind, with some striking similarities apparent between Mr. Spock the Vulcan, and Questor the Android.

The third pilot was a remake of *Genesis II* called *Planet Earth,* giving ABC a shot at what CBS had not picked up. (CBS had just purchased a new series, *Planet of the Apes,* based on the successful motion picture series. While *Genesis II*'s ratings had been the highest ever for a television movie, *Apes*'s ratings were even higher, and CBS decided that there was little future in any science fiction that didn't include apes.)

None of the shows enthused the networks, although loyal Roddenberry fans deluged the networks with tons of mail à la the *Star Trek* campaign. CBS went with its apes; ABC had a man with interchangeable spare parts worth $6 million, worrying NBC that maybe the audience wouldn't identify with a full-fledged robot longing to be human since televison already had Steve Austin, who could no doubt match Questor transistor for transistor.

Meanwhile, things seemed to be brightening on the *Star Trek* horizon, and hopes were raised for a possible motion picture based on the television series. Gene Roddenberry and Paramount Pictures had begun negotiations for a *Star Trek* movie as early as 1973. His first movie offer for *Star Trek* was from a producer who promised to send him a small monthly check if he would stay away from it and let them

---

*Gene Roddenberry defends *Genesis II* as long-range optimism which expresses his belief that the fall of civilizations (even our own) is the natural way in which we evolve, more or less on a "three steps forward, then two back" pace which keeps our infant ruthlessness somewhat in balance with our slower developing sense of love and respect for all life.

do *Star Trek* with other people the way they thought *Star Trek* should be done. Gene told them he was not yet that hungry.

But by this time he was having to supplement his income with college lectures, sometimes spending two weeks or more in a month on the road speaking at a different college every night.

Finally, after a year and a half of negotiations with Paramount executives, the studio agreed to do a small *Star Trek* motion picture with a budget of around $3 million. The popularity of *Star Trek* was evident from the increasing volume of mail, high ratings in syndication, profits from merchandise, hugely successful conventions, and expanding (often front-page) coverage in the media. NBC still was not interested, and a *Star Trek* movie seemed like the ideal way to go.

In May of 1975, Roddenberry moved his offices out of the second story of his house and onto the Paramount lot. Ironically he was offered the same suite of offices at the studio that he had occupied when the original *Star Trek* series was in production. Since then, they had been occupied by several television companies, including *Love, American Style,* which had also decorated the offices in American style, carpeting and painting the building throughout in a rather eye-startling red, white, and blue. On entering these offices, one sometimes has a strange urge to salute the carpeting. Nevertheless, Gene still said he felt good vibes, claimed those offices in Building E, and settled in to write the script for *Star Trek II,* a motion picture Paramount planned to release by Christmas of 1975, six months from that time.

There had been six years of waiting since the time *Star Trek* went off the air in prime time, and it seemed at last the long wait had ended. No one could foretell that the waiting wouldn't end for four more years.

3

Sub-Warp Speed

It seemed simple enough. With a $3 to $5 million budget allocated, Gene Roddenberry could write the kind of *Star Trek* script he has always wanted to do. He arrived on the Paramount lot in May of 1975, ordered up a stack of fresh white typing paper from studio supplies and began to write *Star Trek II*. By June 30 he had turned out what he felt was a good first draft of the script. The studio executives disagreed.

The story opens with Spock on Vulcan, emaciated, bedraggled, meditating with the Vulcan Masters. His thoughts are disrupted by something about to happen to Earth and to his old friend Jim Kirk. He has not become truly Vulcan. Pai-ad, one of the nine Masters, speaks with him:

> PAI-AD
> Did you think to cast out
> the human within yourself?
> You have not.

> SPOCK
> Then, I am nothing, Pai-ad.
> I cannot exist in two halves.

> PAI-AD
> Your halves are needed, Spock.
> Move your thoughts with me to
> Earth.

The story then moves directly from Vulcan to Earth orbit and the drydocks over the San Francisco Naval Yards, where the *Enterprise* is being refitted. On the planet below, people are beginning to receive mental impressions of a returning God. At the same time a huge Object, one thousand times larger than a starship, is moving toward Earth, knocking off the U.S.S. *Potemkin* and hurtling a cluster of asteroids toward Earth. Kirk, now a grounded admiral, assembles his old crew (all of whom have risen higher in rank), and they take the newly refitted *Enterprise* on a mission of interception with the alien claiming to be God. The Object turns out to be more than just a vessel—it is a computer form so advanced it is a living entity itself. However, we discover that this God they've worshipped is actually the Deceiver, the computer-programmed remains of a race who were "cast out" from their dimension and into this one. At the end, Kirk wins out, the entity returns to its other dimension, and the *Enterprise* crew is left with a gift—they return to Earth and discover that the "Deceiver-God" entity had made them a gift of time in which they are suddenly younger and are now returning from their first five-year mission. Interestingly enough, many of these same story elements ended up in the *ST—TMP* script three years later.

Gene had been iconoclastically asking what if the God of the Old Testament, full of tirades and demands to be worshipped, actually turned out to be Lucifer. If so, was the serpent's offer of the Fruit of Knowledge actually a gift from the real God? Captain Kirk versus God. This was *not* the story Paramount had expected! The movie was postponed from fall 1975 until the following spring so that a new script could be found.

In the months that followed, few people visited the *Star Trek* offices. But Paramount's main office building became almost a science fiction hall of fame as a parade of acclaimed SF writers took turns pitching ideas to Paramount executives who were determined to find a *Star Trek* story and writer that were acceptable to them. Full story outlines for *Star Trek II* (the original title of the movie) were turned in by John D. F. Black and Robert Silverberg. The studio decided these stories weren't right. They tried again, this time summoning Harlan Ellison, Ray Bradbury, and Ted Sturgeon. Gene knew that *Star Trek* picture possibilities were in trouble when he heard that Ellison, already a veteran of *Star Trek* television, had been asked to find a way to work the ancient Mayans into his story, even though his movie treatment had absolutely nothing to do with any subject even faintly related to Mayans. Disgusted, Ellison had thrown up his hands and left.

But Gene had gotten this far and refused to throw in the towel. He began another story with Jon Povill (who later was to become associate produce on *ST—TMP*). The story dealt with a time-travel altered universe which Kirk and the *Enterprise* had to somehow set right. It was rejected as not having quite the scope of a motion picture.

By now, the cast was getting anxious. Several had offers of plays or roles in other films, which they accepted rather than going hungry during the postponements. The start date was moved up again, and Gene consoled the actors:

January 21, 1976

To the Officers of the Enterprise:

A fast note as I leave town for a couple of weeks. Paramount has set a July 15 start date for the Star Trek movie. I think this indicates mainly a determination on their part that the film will be made.

In eight months it's gone from casual disinterest to pressing enthusiasm. We don't have a script yet but then there are a lot of people with scripts who don't have a start date.

Hope soon to chat with you about what this all means (as soon as I find out myself).

Warmest regards,

Gene Roddenberry

In early 1976, *Star Trek II* was handed over to the Paramount Television division. Yes, it was still to be a movie, but since it had its roots in television, maybe the television division would know how to find the right script. Several television writers were contacted, and for a time it looked like nearly every available member of the Writers Guild of America would be given a shot at it. Among those whose stories were solicited were Howard Rodman, Howard Burke, Will Loren, and Chris Knopf. Again, rejection. By April of 1976 *Star Trek* was bounced back into the motion picture division. *Star Trek* was starting to look like the ball in a game of studio tennis.

Interest began to wane again as Gene fought to keep studio enthusiasm alive. Typical of this was a note sent to Richard Zimbert, senior vice-president in charge of motion picture business affairs:

April 22, 1976

Dear Dick,

About our projected film, let me share a couple of thoughts which I hope may be helpful in some of the casting and other decisions yet to be made.

You will surely agree that one of the most difficult and important aspects of any investment venture is finding the right perspective on it. Am sure we have both had friends who have turned down highly profitable early opportunities in things like Colonel Sanders because "chickens are smelly and troublesome" or have lost their asses in petroleum because "everyone rich is into oil." Decisions on films are often made from the same kind of odd perspectives, and I am much concerned that a kind of television versus cinema snobbery (is that the right word?) is having an effect on all our perspectives toward it.

Let's forget for the moment that we are discussing a television show film called Star Trek and view the project from the following perspective:

> I have in hand a property, Dick, which has sold eight millions of books, has been on the best seller list twice in the last year, and has created a subculture phenomenon of a type not seen since James Bond, Sherlock Holmes, Tarzan and similar fictional character greats. The minimum box office is probably something like ten million tickets if it becomes an average production handled in an average way. If it is a good film exploited with any imagination, it can go up anywhere from there.

I suspect that if a property combining those figures and facts were presented to Paramount, we'd immediately and seriously begin discussing Redford and Gould-type top star salaries, top directors, a top-quality, high-budget production. A studio should be so lucky as to have three or four such properties offered to it every year.

I don't want to spend needless twenty-five thousands of dollars here and there. But neither do I think that arbitrary "television" thinking should get in the way of investment perspective on a project with top motion picture film potential.

Regards,

Gene Roddenberry

If Paramount seemed close to giving up on *Star Trek,* the fans had no intentions of letting that happen. Mail continued to arrive by the sackfuls as fandom became increasingly impatient that they were not being given "their" movie. Letters arrived on the desks of every executive at the studio and the parent company, Gulf and Western, including that of Board Chairman Charles Bluhdorn, whose own daughter, Dominique, a loyal Trekkie, applied pressure to her dad. Clearly, there *was* an audience out there anxious to buy tickets to a movie that hadn't even been written yet. Paramount's lukewarm attitude was beginning to thaw. In July of 1976, the studio decided to assign an executive producer to the project, and the budget was expanded to $6 to $8 million.

The man selected for the job was Jerry Isenberg, one of the youngest and most active producers in Hollywood. Jerry's prematurely gray hair and California tanned baby face, balanced by his high energy level and eagerness for *Star Trek,* gave Paramount new enthusiasm for a *Star Trek* movie. Constantly moving at the speed of Warp 15, he wasted no time in trying to obtain qualified writers for what was now known as *Star Trek—The Motion Picture.*

Jon Povill, the lanky, bearded young writer who earlier had worked with Gene on one of the proposed *Star Trek* story outlines, was hired as assistant to the producer and assigned his first task—compiling a list of available writers who might possibly be able to write the ever-elusive script. Jon compiled the following:

TO: GENE RODDENBERRY   DATE: JULY 1, 1976

FROM: JON POVILL   SUBJECT: WRITERS LIST

It would appear, from the writers and credits I have been able to find, that there are extremely few consistently good screenwriters.

I have listed a number of people whose credits seem a very far cry from science fiction but who in some way struck me that they might be able to do the job anyhow—perhaps if given the story to work with (which we don't have to give yet, of course).

Edward Anhalt—Credits: QB VII; Jeremiah Johnson; Luther; The Man in the Glass Booth; Madwoman of Chaillot; The Boston Strangler; many others.

Robert Towne—Credits: Shampoo; Chinatown; The Last Detail.

James Goldman—The Lion in Winter; Nicholas and Alexandra.

Francis Ford Coppola—Patton; The Godfather; Godfather II.

George Lucas—Credits: THX 1138; American Graffiti; The Star Wars (sic). Also likes to both write and direct.

Gene Roddenberry—Credits: Star Trek; The Lieutenant; Questor; Genesis II; Pretty Maids All in a Row. Reasonably big name in television, but only one feature. Intimate knowledge of Star Trek might be helpful. Believe he is working on another project right now. If you can work with him he might be worth a shot.

Ernest Lehman—Family Plot; North by Northwest; Portnoy's Complaint.

Robert Bloch—Psycho; Twilight Zone; Star Trek.

Lorenzo Semple Jr.—The Drowning Pool; Three Days of the Condor; The Super Cops; Papillon; Marriage of a Young Stockbroker; The Parallax View.

Paddy Chayefsky—Marty; Lord Love a Duck; The Hospital. I
understand that he is hopping onto the science-fiction bandwagon.

Peter Benchley and Carl Gottlieb—Jaws. Carl Gottlieb has also worked
on Bob Newhart Show, Flip Wilson Specials, Odd Couple, Andy Griffith,
and Smothers Brothers Comedy Hour. If he could make the switch from
those to Jaws, he might be able to do Star Trek.

Jon Povill—Almost Credit: Star Trek II story (with Gene
Roddenberry). Will be a big shot some day. Should be hired now while
he is cheap and humble.

It was a well-thought-out list, containing thirty-four names, none of
which were chosen to do the script. With *Star Wars* still a year from its
release and box-office smash, it is interesting to speculate on what
would have resulted if George Lucas, then completing his project, had
written a *Star Trek* script.

Once again, writers were marching in and out of the *Star Trek*
production offices. Two of them, a team of highly successful British
screenwriters, were finally selected. Chris Bryant and Allan Scott
asked the most intelligent questions Gene had heard yet. They had
never written science fiction before, although their motion picture
credentials, including *The Petersburg-Cannes Express, Don't Look
Now,* and *Joseph Andrews,* showed superb screenwriting abilities.
They sublet their respective residences in England and Scotland,
packed up their families and secured living quarters in the Los
Angeles area. The atmosphere in the production offices became more
relaxed as the two Britishers' dry senses of humor kept spirits high.
They shared an office, their desks back to back, typewriters clackity-
clacking away. Often during a strained writing session the air would
suddenly explode with raucous laughter, their door would burst open,
and Allan, the more outgoing of the two, would charge out, his blue
eyes dancing with mischief, to tell his latest joke or pun—he was very
big on puns—to anyone within earshot. To relieve the tensions of
constant writing pressures, they played with toys, did magic tricks,
and wrote funny memos.

One such barrage of memos concerned a symbolic Siamese fighting
fish Gene had been given as an office pet. The fish, however, lost its
fight, and as the fish languishing in the bowl depressed him, Gene
ordered it removed to the outer secretarial offices. One morning Chris
and Allan discovered it was dead and it was given a burial at "sea."
They often jokingly used other people's names on their memos and

they sent out the following, pretending it was from the then head of the motion picture division:

TO: ALL DEPARTMENTS   DATE: Nov. 22, 1976
FROM: DAVID PICKER

It has been brought to my attention that some secretaries are keeping dead fish as pets. Either the fish go, or they do. There are enough dead fish in administrative positions without keeping them in jars on desks.

They also composed a zany ode to the late fish:

> Alas pour fish! Who swam so gay of yore—
> You never spoke. But then you didn't snore.
> Lifeless you lie, among your bright blue stones,
> Yet be assured that none will pick your bones.
> Ah! What a fate twould be—but Sue will foil it.
> For she will flush your corpse right down the toilet.

At about the same time that Jon Povill began his search for writers, he was called upon to prepare a list of directors who might be available. Note the fourth name on this list:

TO: GENE RODDENBERRY   DATE: JUNE 22, 1976
FROM: JON POVILL   SUBJECT: DIRECTOR'S LIST

I would guess that the following people on the list will be unavailable, though they would be good for the project:

1. Francis Coppola
2. Steven Spielberg
3. George Lucas
4. Robert Wise
5. William Friedkin
6. George Roy Hill
7. Norman Jewison

Jon's sense of prophecy was uncanny as he noted descriptions on these directors further down the memo:

Robert Wise—Audrey Rose, starts shooting 7/26—Dist. U.A., locations N.Y., L.A.
Credits: Day the Earth Stood Still, Andromeda Strain—and a few others.

Jon was right—none of them were available at the time, at least not for the script money available in this medium-sized *Star Trek* film project. Jerry and Gene decided to hire a young, handsomely bearded director named Phil Kaufman.

Phil, who subsequently directed the highly successful remake of *Invasion of the Body Snatchers,* already had solid directing credits *(The Great Northfield Minnesota Raid; The White Dawn)* and an interest in the field of science fiction in general. Writers Scott and Bryant along with Kaufman were given a crash course in *Star Trek.* Their first screenings were the ten episodes Gene considered the most representative of the show and also the ones considered the best and most popular by the audience: "The City on the Edge of Forever," "Devil in the Dark," "Amok Time," "Journey to Babel," "Shore Leave," "The Trouble with Tribbles," "The Enemy Within," "The Corbomite Maneuver," "This Side of Paradise," and "A Piece of the Action." Along with this they were served a constant diet of science-fiction films—everything from *2001: A Space Odyssey* to *Robinson Crusoe on Mars.*

By the fall of 1976, it began to look like this time things would really happen. The film project gained more points with Paramount when, in September, the fans organized a mail campaign which flooded the White House with 400,000 letters, influencing then-president of the United States Gerald Ford to change the name of the NASA space shuttle from *Constitution* to *Enterprise.* When the shuttle was rolled out on September 17, the entire television *Enterprise* crew and producer Gene Roddenberry turned out for the occasion. It was a moving moment as the crowds cheered and the air force band surprised everyone by striking up the theme from *Star Trek.* Paramount Pictures took advantage of the publicity values by taking out a full-page ad in the *New York Times* of September 21.

Beginning with the headline "Welcome Aboard . . . Space Shuttle *Enterprise,*" the ad read:

> Paramount Pictures and the thousands of loyal fans of *Star Trek* are happy that the United States of America's new space shuttle has been named after the *Star Trek*'s starship, the *Enterprise.* (It's nice to know that sometimes science fiction becomes science fact.) Starship *Enterprise* will be joining the Space Shuttle *Enterprise* in its space travels very soon. Early next year, Paramount Pictures begins filming an extraordinary motion picture adventure—*Star Trek.* Now we can look forward to two great space adventures.

On October 8, 1976, Bryant and Scott finished their story outline. It had the honor of being the first one accepted by the studio, and they immediately began working on the script version of it. Gene was in

London at the time preparing for an NBC television production of another project. Things hadn't seemed too promising on the *Star Trek* project, so he contracted with Twentieth Century-Fox and NBC to produce a supernatural-horror film called *Spectre*. The following telegram saw him catching the earliest flight back to the States:

GENE RODDENBERRY
THE ATHENEUM HOTEL
116 PICADILLY
LONDON

PARAMOUNT HAS ORDERED SCREENPLAY. FULL SUPPORT AND EXCITEMENT. CON-GRATULATIONS. PLEASE COME HOME. LOVE, JERRY AND PHIL.

Fandom went berserk. Chris Bryant, Allan Scott, Phil Kaufman and Jerry Isenberg were swamped with letters from delighted fans. These men suddenly became their heroes, as invitations to appear at *Star Trek* conventions poured in:

TO: THE GREAT SPECTRE OF THE GALAXY   DATE: DEC. 13, 1976
FROM: SCOTT & BRYANT
                              SUBJECT: STAR TREK CONVENTION

Gene,

We've been asked to speak at the STAR TREK Convention in San Francisco on February 12-13 1977. A deep yearning to tread the boards once more, allied with an even deeper yearning to receive payment for doing so, incline us to accept. But we'd like your o.k. (1) and some parameters (2) of what you would not want us to say about the movie.

Sincerely,

Irving Tinsel and Sol Glitter

TO: ALLAN SCOTT & CHRIS BRYANT   DATE: 12/15/76
FROM: THE BIG BRIDGE   SUBJECT: CONVENTION

This is the only silly memo you've sent. Forget it! Trekkie teeny-boppers lurk outside your room at night yearning to meet you and talk about science. If you must go to one of these, our main concern is that you keep your fly zipped up while on platform (which knocks out any chance of your doing your old act there).

They were heroes to everyone, it seems, but the front office. By the time they had completed a first draft script on March 1, 1977, six months had elapsed. This time the studio was caught in a do-or-die situation. Expenses were mounting; it was time to either make a movie on the basis of this story or drop the *Star Trek* movie idea entirely. Jerry Isenberg began planning for this production. He and others had been checking on facilities for filming in England, a plan that would cut costs by several million dollars. A production designer had been signed—Ken Adam, who had designed most of the James Bond films. Ralph McQuarrie, best known for his art illustrations in *Star Wars,* was added to the staff and handed in some amazing art work based on the Scott-Bryant script.

Their story opens with the *Enterprise* racing to rescue the *Da Vinci,* a Federation ship in trouble. They arrive too late—the *Da Vinci* has vanished—but they pick up survivors. During the rescue Kirk is subjected to an electrochemical shock to his brain which brings on erratic behavior culminating in his commandeering a shuttlecraft toward an invisible planet. He vanishes without a trace and Spock orders the *Enterprise* home.

Three years later, the *Enterprise,* refitted, has a new crew. Spock has resigned from Starfleet in disgrace and is on Vulcan purging himself of his human half (a recurrent theme in all scripts, it would seem). The *Enterprise,* under Captain Gregory Westlake, is ordered to the place where Kirk disappeared. Just as Spock theorized, a planet has been discovered, one that promises to be the mythical "planet of the Titans," the home of a lost race with super technology. The planet is about to be swallowed up into a black hole. Whoever rescues the Titans—Klingons or the Federation—will control the destiny of the universe. The *Enterprise* makes a detour to Vulcan to pick up Spock, who at first refuses to go, but during his tests on that planet Spock has his own death revealed to him, indicating that he must go with the *Enterprise* in order to fulfill his destiny. The *Enterprise* arrives at the now partially visible planet and is trapped by the force fields surrounding it. Facing certain destruction, the *Enterprise* saucer separates from the Star Drive, allowing the Star Drive to get free, while the saucer crash lands on the planet. The crew finds the surface of the planet to be a wild and inhospitable place with cities encased in walls of fire. Spock is reunited with Kirk, who has existed as a wild man on the planet with other trapped beings. When the landing party finally reaches the rulers of the planet they find they are not the benevolent Titans, but a lower and incredibly dangerous and intelligent life form—the Cygnans. The Titans have long disappeared. In the attempt to escape from the Cygnans, who have transported on board before the ship lifted off and rejoined the Star Drive, Kirk plunges the *Enterprise* into the black hole to save the Federation from the Cygnans. During the trip through the black hole, the Cygnans are destroyed, and the *Enterprise* emerges back in orbit around Earth. But it is Earth at the time of the Cro-Magnon man, the dawn of humanity. The ancient Titans, it would seem, were the men of the *Enterprise!*

An earlier storyline had the *Enterprise* emerging millions of years in the future. Ever the humorists, Bryant and Scott sent the following memo under the guise of Gulf and Western's chairman:

TO: GENE RODDENBERRY

FROM: C. BLUHDORN

It is my policy not to interfere in creative decision processes and this is merely to record my enthusiasm for the story which I read last week. May I, however, ask that in the final sequence when the Enterprise arrives at Earth several millions years in the future there be some indication that the solar system is principally owned by Gulf and Western. Nothing ostentatious, mind you, but just the subtlest of hints to this effect. Keep up the good work.

By the time the actual script was completed, it had received input from so many people—Jerry Isenberg, Phil Kaufman, Gene Roddenberry, as well as the two writers—that it bore little resemblence to the original story that had been approved back in October. It was a script by committee, and therein lay its trouble. A few weeks after it was handed in, the studio turned thumbs down on it. An eleventh-hour attempt by director Kaufman to salvage the script also failed, and the fate of *Star Trek—The Motion Picture* was again in limbo.

True to form, Chris Bryant and Allan Scott exited laughing. They were given a farewell party and a warm send-off. The next day, neatly taped to Gene Roddenberry's door, was the following somewhat wistful memo:

TO: ALL ON STAR TREK   MARCH 18, 1977

FROM: ALLAN SCOTT/CHRIS BRYANT   SUBJECT: AU REVOIR

Giving birth takes nine months. We've only been gestating for seven. So there's no baby. But there's an embryo. Look after it.

4

The Almost (Again) Television Show

At first it sounded like the name of a bar of soap: *Star Trek—Phase II*.

Fortunately, the *Phase* part was dropped, and on June 17, 1977, a nervously perspiring Susan Sackett read the following announcement to three thousand five hundred excitedly cheering fans at a *Star Trek* convention.

Negotiations have been concluded between Gene Roddenberry and Paramount Television for his services as executive producer of the new Star Trek series. The announcement was made today by Gary Nardino, president, Paramount Television and Richard Frank, vice-president, Paramount Pictures Corporation, who has overall responsibility for Paramount Television Service.

In making the announcement, Nardino commented, "Naturally we are delighted to be associated in this venture with Gene Roddenberry. His return to weekly television will insure a quality and integrity of production values that has marked everything he has been associated with; his work has been a credit to the entire television industry. We, at Paramount, feel we are making television history with this renaissance of the Star Trek series."

Production on the new Star Trek series, perhaps the most legendary of all television series, will begin in the fall under Roddenberry, the guiding force behind the original. Frank added, "Star Trek will be the foundation for the new Paramount Television Service. It represents our commitment to provide fresh programming to a discerning viewing public."

Roddenberry, commenting on the new Star Trek series, said, "We have never really been out of the public eye. Right now reruns of Star Trek are being seen on 137 stations around the country, with millions of fans all over the world. Our audience was, is and will be there.

"At the time this announcement is being made, a giant Star Trek convention is being held at the Los Angeles Convention Center. I can assure these fans that the precepts I followed at the beginning of Star Trek will be used for new production."

Production is scheduled to begin in the fall at Paramount Studios and will be carried by stations associated with the Paramount Television Service.

2086047

Star Trek II was to be the cornerstone of Paramount's attempt to set up a "fourth network." Paramount first obtained commitments to air a number of hours of programming each week from independent stations as well as existing affiliates of the three major networks (ABC, CBS, NBC). Along with the group of new two-hour movies to be produced by Paramount (which had thirty TV movie concepts in development), *Star Trek II* would become a flagship of this new network.

The push was on—the studio wanted cameras rolling by late fall, with the first episode airing in the spring of 1978. Immediately, Gene Roddenberry began to assemble a creative staff. The offices across the hall were grabbed as fast as their occupants could be politely evicted to accommodate a rapidly growing group of *Star Trek* personnel.

Among the first to be hired were two coproducers, Robert Goodwin and Harold Livingston. Together, they would carry out the chores of organizing the team of writers, directors, production manager, construction workers, and other people who could get the *Enterprise* holding off the Klingons once again.

Bob Goodwin already had an office on the Paramount lot, having been involved in development of television projects for Playboy Productions in association with Paramount. His ideas impressed Gene, and he was invited over for a chat. He was nearly denied admittance to Gene's office, however, when he arrived via his studio bicycle for the initial interview, wearing faded jeans, sport shirt and pullover sweater, and toting an original script he had brought along to show Gene. A handsome, intense young man, he looked like an aspiring writer who might be trying to crash the *Star Trek* offices, and he was denied entrance by Gene's secretary, who is responsible for protecting him from intrusions. Fortunately, Gene stepped outside of his office at that moment for a breath of air, spotted Bob, and invited him in, then hired him on the spot. It proved to be a wise decision. Over the next few months, Bob capably organized most of the production chores, including initial set construction—some of which became the foundations for *Star Trek—The Motion Picture* sets.

Construction of the *Enterprise* sets on stage 9 began on July 25, 1977, under the guidance of art director Joe Jennings, who had been involved in the original Star Trek television series, special-effects expert Jim Rugg, also a veteran of the old tv series, and Matt Jefferies, creative consultant on loan from the television series, *Little House on the Prairie.* Way back in *Star Trek*'s very beginnings, Matt and Gene Roddenberry had together designed the original tv *Enterprise,* and Matt had also become art director on the old *Star Trek* series.

Bob Goodwin's initial status report on the new *Star Trek* television show talked about the first bit of construction for *Star Trek* in the nearly eight years since the last episode had been filmed:

TO: GENE RODDENBERRY   DATE: 3rd AUGUST, 1977

FROM: BOB GOODWIN   SUBJECT: PRODUCTION STATUS REPORT

SET CONSTRUCTION

Stages 8, 9 & 10 have been assigned to Star Trek. Stage 9 will be used for the entire Enterprise set. Stage 8 will be used as our planetary set. And stage 10 will be used as an extra stage for swing sets.

The basic layout of the Enterprise set has been drawn. Work is being concentrated on the two most complicated sections of the set, the bridge and the engine room. The basic shell of the bridge has been approved in design and is currently being built. Platforming should be done by the end of next week. The molding is in construction for our plastic forms, which will cover the wall units. It will be approximately a week and a half before the molds are finished and at that point we will begin casting one section a day. (There are 12 sections in the bridge, plus we will be making 6 extra sections, to be used as needed for explosions, special effects, etc.) The shell should be completed by the end of August.

At the same time, Matt Jefferies, Joe Jennings and special-effects man Jim Rugg are at work designing and researching new types of instrumentation that will be used within the bridge, including new kinds of computer graphic displays, touch control switching, etc.

Design work on the engine room is currently in progress and should be completed by the end of August. At that point it will take approximately one month to build the engineering room. It is a three story unit and will be involving very sophisticated materials and concepts.

While the bridge and the engine room are being completed, work will progress concurrently on the other elements of the Enterprise, including corridors, recreation room, captain's quarters, medical complex, transporter room, etc. These other elements are more conventional and require less time in both design and construction.

For all of the sets discussed above, Joe Jennings and Matt Jefferies are researching new materials that can be used in forms of plastics and metals that were not available to us previously.

U.S.S. ENTERPRISE (MODEL)

About 75 percent of the details of our new model Enterprise have been worked out by Matt Jefferies. The model will be five to six feet long and while it will have basically the same configuration and shape as the old Enterprise, there will be a number of modifications and updatings that will give it a more sophisticated and slightly different look. The power pods will be designed slightly differently. The phaser banks will be located in the main strut of the ship as opposed to the bottom of the saucer as it was previously and probably there will be some other changes as work progresses. Construction of the model should begin in five to six weeks. Matt Jefferies is currently searching out various model builders available to us, so that once drawings are completed we can get in some very quick bids and work can start without any delay. At the same time Matt is involved with work on models of various planets which will be worked in conjunction with our Enterprise model.

OPTICALS

Discussions have taken place with Howard Anderson and other optical effects houses in preparation for the new look of Star Trek. All possibilities are being considered, including computer-controlled stop-action model photography, front screen projection, the use of helicopter mounts, etc. Jon Povill is coordinating research with the Anderson Company into new optical techniques that have been developed, so when the time arises we will have all of them at our disposal to use or not use as we see fit.

NASA TECHNICAL ADVISOR

Jesco von Puttkamer recently visited us for a week and was involved in general discussions with our production staff. The lines of communication have been established. Jesco is available to us to make further trips out here when we need him. At the same time, we have established that much of our technical advice in terms of stories and scripts will be handled through correspondence or telephones.

Bob's memo is quite interesting since the basic groundwork for a multi-million-dollar *Star Trek* film was being layed, although no one knew it at the time. Most of the sets and models were later either greatly modified or scrapped completely, but the framework and placement of sets on stage 9 remained fixed, and some of the television redesign of the *Enterprise* can be seen in the movie. An item that was to remain completely unchanged was the arrangement for NASA to supply needed technical advice, and Jesco continued to do so right on through the production of the feature.

Meanwhile, coproducer Harold Livingston began his search for the proper scripts and scriptwriters. Harold had also been involved with a Paramount Television project prior to his arrival in Gene Roddenberry's office. He had a reputation for being a relentless worker, and he too was hired the moment he and Gene met. Little did Harold know that this moment was the beginning of the next two years of his life.

Harold and Gene had surprisingly similar backgrounds. Both had flown missions for the air corps during World War II; both had gone on to become associated with major airlines after the war—Gene as a Pan Am pilot, Harold to Trans World Airlines where he helped set up all the TWA installations in North Africa and became a station manager for TWA in Saudi Arabia. He then returned to the States to try his hand at writing advertising copy. But adventure still beckoned, and when the Israeli War for Independence broke out in 1948, Harold donned goggles and scarf to join the Israeli Air Force, flying missions for a year. After that he traveled throughout Europe "wholesaling" certain hard-to-obtain items such as nylon stockings, whiskey, and cigarettes. In France, he managed to sell his first book (which he jokingly claims sold about three copies) entitled *Pilotes Sans Visas*. The book, written in French, deals with his adventures flying in Israel. Eventually he wrote seven books, married Lois Leavitt (1958), and moved from Boston to California, where money was to be made in writing for television. He and Lois have four children (one daughter, Leah, worked as an extra in the Rec Deck scene in the movie).

Harold's filing system consisted of a couple of dozen lopsidedly stacked piles of papers scattered all throughout his office. It looked like organized chaos, but Harold could put his hands on any item within seconds.

A few weeks after he had moved into his *Star Trek* office, he requested that the room be freshly painted in dark tones of brown, his favorite color. The painters arrived one morning before sun-up, scooped up all the piles of papers and put them into a box, clearing the way for their dropcloths. A few hours later, when the workday began,

Harold's secretary, Cheryl Blythe, arrived and went in to check on her boss's newly painted office. Suddenly a loud shriek rang out through the building as Cheryl realized what had happened. She dove at the box of papers, creating all sorts of new piles of papers—on the couch, floor, tables and cabinets. Later that morning when Harold arrived he didn't notice any difference from the previous day. But the very perplexed writer never quite figured out how he could have forgotten his own filing system over night like that.

While Harold set about hiring prospective writers for new *Star Trek* episodes, Gene Roddenberry was busy putting together a new *Writers' Guide*. It was patterned on the one he had prepared for the original series, always the bible for anyone assigned to write or direct *Star Trek*. The original television series had introduced concepts so unique at the time that writing and direction style had to be carefully delineated and explained. This was also to be true with the projected new television version. There had been many changes, the largest one concerning actors and their characters. The actors had added years; so had the *Enterprise* crew. But not all of the familiar characters would be returning.

Many fans saw it as an act of mutiny: *Mr. Spock was refusing to beam aboard the* Enterprise! His alter ego, Leonard Nimoy, was starring on Broadway in *Equus* and did not want to give up that role to return to the rigors of a weekly television show.

Gene Roddenberry tried in every way to get Leonard Nimoy to return. Finally, after a long meeting with the actor, Gene was convinced it could not be arranged—he was faced with a Spockless *Star Trek* which seemed very much to need a replacement character. Gene still felt that there was a need for an alien character on the bridge, a totally logical person who could counterbalance Dr. McCoy's humanism as both characters aided Captain Kirk's decision-making efforts—creating the renowned leadership trio. Enter Lieutenant Xon, who is described in the *Star Trek II Writers'/Directors' Guide* of August 12, 1977:

LIEUTENANT XON

Can a twenty-two-year-old Vulcan on his first space voyage fill the shoes of the legendary Mr. Spock? Xon (pronounced "Zahn") was selected by the Vulcan Science Academy to attempt exactly that. Kirk was stunned when his new science officer reported aboard and found him to be a little more than a boy. (Xon looks something like a young

Michael York with pointed ears.) Kirk had assumed the replacement was someone near Spock's age. The reports he had read on Xon listed him as a prominent scientist and teacher.

The truth is that Xon is a genius, even by Vulcan standards. As we'll see in our episodes, he is as competent as Spock in all fields of science. He lacks knowledge, however, in one very important area—the human equation. Unlike Spock, Xon is a full Vulcan. He had no human mother to acquaint him with the Earth species; he has no human half with which to feel and understand human emotions.

Xon realizes that the reason that Spock performed so well in his tasks on board the Enterprise was that he was half human and therefore could understand emotional human nature. In order to perform as well as Spock, he knows he is going to have to eliminate his Vulcan revulsion at emotional displays. He is, in fact, going to have to reach down within himself and find the emotions that his society has repressed for thousands of years so that he will have some basis for fully understanding his human associates.

What this means is: whereas Spock was engaged in a constant battle within himself to repress his emotions in order to be more Vulcanlike, Xon will be engaged in a constant struggle within himself to release his buried emotions to be more humanlike for the sake of doing a good job—his primary consideration. This will be at least as difficult for him as it was for Spock to maintain his stoic pose. Also, we'll get humor out of Xon trying to simulate laughter, anger, fear, and other human feelings.

The new science officer accepted the Enterprise assignment with much trepidation. He has no doubt that he can competently handle the scientific aspects of his job, but he fears the crew might expect him to be a duplicate of Spock as well as a replacement. These fears have been realized and hanging over the early episodes. So also is the unsaid comment, "Mr. Spock never did it quite like that." Nor is Captain Kirk overly fair to Xon in the beginning. Spock's friendship was a deep, important thing to Kirk and the captain is now almost arbitrarily rejecting the possibility of a meaningful relationship with the young Vulcan. However, the more difficult Lt. Xon's situation, the more we'll like him and the more we'll want him to succeed in this difficult assignment.

As a full Vulcan, Xon is even stronger than Spock. He can endure lack of water and high temperatures for very long periods. All his senses are particularly keen. He has strong Vulcan mind-meld abilities.

The young Vulcan lieutenant is constantly shocked by human behavior. In preparing for this assignment, he made himself quite an expert on human behavior and history. And it is amusing to see him try to apply this knowledge too logically and too literally. Nothing he studied quite prepared him for the real thing. Although Xon tries hard to hide his surprise and discomfitures, the crew is aware that it exists. They often go out of their way to exaggerate their human qualities, further distressing the young Vulcan. But this is not done in mean spirit and never in a situation where it will interfere will starship efficiency. We will suspect that life among humans is causing Xon to begin to feel some emotions himself. On his planet this is, of course, grossest of sins and the young Vulcan makes every effort to hide any sign of this "weakness."

The science officer presides over a large console which is known as the "library-computer station." It is second in importance only to ship command and is located directly behind captain's position.

Xon was obviously too young to take over Spock's second-in-command chores; a domino effect began demanding more new characters, as Gene next created Commander Will Decker:

COMMANDER WILL DECKER

In his youthful thirties, Decker is the ship's executive officer, second in command. Kirk sometimes calls or refers to him as "First," which is naval parlance for ship's "First Lieutenant," which would have been Decker's title in the days of sailing ships. Will Decker comes very near to worshipping Kirk and would literally rather die than fail him. The prime responsibility of a "First" is to provide his captain with the most efficient crew and vessel possible and Will Decker takes this responsibility seriously.

When not absorbed in his task of keeping the Enterprise at top fitness, Will Decker is a very humorous man. He particularly enjoys playing the "too perfect," soulless marionette of an officer. The joke can be confusing to others because Will can become almost that kind of officer when Kirk's welfare or the safety of the ship is involved.

We can see that Jim Kirk is very much in the process of training the young commander for the responsibilities of Starship command someday. We will see that future captain begin to happen during this five-year mission.

In areas of logistics and organization, he has a keen and analytical mind, one upon which Kirk will rely heavily. He will command some landing parties and many decisions will be life-and-death choices.

Will's background is all service: his father, his father's father were Academy graduates, Starfleet officers of flag rank. Someday, surely, he will wear a star. Because of his heritage, and because he had been groomed since nearly birth for command. He has friends, but tends to protect his privacy while respecting others'. Between Kirk and Decker is a kind of father/son relationship that each cherishes.

This early ancestor bears little resemblance to the movie's poetic, soul-searching, ultimately metamorphosed Commander Will Decker. About the only things the two Deckers have in common are name, rank, serial number, and age. Television's Decker never even met Lt. Ilia, who became his sensual Deltan friend in the movie.

Ilia herself had undergone a number of changes even before she appeared in the television *Writers'/Directors' Guide*. At first all that existed was her name—which was spelled *Ilya*. But it belonged not to her, but to Xon. As Gene was creating that Vulcan character, it was pointed out to him that this had been the name of a popular Russian character on the television hit of the 1960s, *The Man from U.N.C.L.E.*—"Illya Kuryakin." The Vulcan was therefore given a different name, and with a slight change in spelling, Ilia surfaced as a female Deltan. No sense in wasting a good name.

LIEUTENANT ILIA

ILIA (pronounced "Ill-ee-ah") is a young female of planet 114-Delta V,* which has recently joined the Federation. The Deltan race is much older than humans, with brains much more finely evolved in areas of art and mathematics. These abilities make her a superb navigator and her artistic abilities are evident in her sure, flowing precision at this task.

Her face is breathtakingly beautiful. But like all Deltans, she is completely hairless except for the eyes. Her smooth, slender bare head has the almost sensual quality of delicately contoured nudity, always hidden before in other women.† It gives her a striking, almost "Egyptian" look, particularly when wearing a Deltan jewel-band head ornament.

Ilia's intelligence level is second only to the Science Officer and she has also the esper abilities common on her planet. Unlike the mind-meld of Vulcans, it simply is the ability to sense images in other minds. Never words or emotions, only images . . . shapes, sizes, textures. On her planet, sexual foreplay consists largely of lovers placing images in each other's minds.

Just as Vulcans have a problem with emotions, Ilia has a problem which accompanies her aboard the starship. On 114-Delta V, almost everything in life is sex-oriented—it is a part of every friendship, every social engagement, every profession. It is simply the normal way to relate with others there. Since constant sex is not the pattern of humans and others aboard this starship, Ilia has totally repressed this emotion drive and social pattern.

There was additional telvision format information given in the *Writers'/Directors' Guide,* some of which might be used should the program indeed be revived at some future date. The early part of the *Guide* concerned itself with what had changed, mentioning all the

---

*By the time the movie was filmed, the planet was (and is) simply called Delta 4.

†This idea was met with the same studio reaction that Mr. Spock's pointed ears had encountered when the first *Star Trek* television series was proposed. Pointed ears and bald heads were not ideas that made safe and salable characters, much less popular ones.

characters' names and ranks, then going on to point out conceptual differences:

We will still use science fiction to make comments on today, but today is now a dozen years later than the first Star Trek. Humanity faces many new questions and puzzles which were not obvious back in the 1960s, all of them suggesting new stories and themes. Also, television censorship has relaxed enormously during those same years, opening up still more new story areas, or certainly more honesty in some old areas.

Television has become much more sophisticated in other ways. Older, ponderous dialogue patterns have given way (thank you, M.A.S.H.) to more realism through the use of fragmented sentences, overlaps and interruptions. Better camera techniques, new film emulsions and exciting new optical and tape effects all make increased realism possible.

Star Trek will take more looks into the private and off-duty lives of our characters. More realism here too in very human areas such as when and what they eat, 23rd century bathing, changing clothes, playing and relaxing. . . .

The essential format will not change. Action-adventure entertainment, and some fun for us too as we speculate where we humans are, where we're going, and what it's really all about.

Additional information for writers was supplied from time to time as it seemed necessary. One of the most unusual ideas for this "modern" *Star Trek* concerned the use of alcohol aboard the U.S.S. *Enterprise:*

TO: HAROLD LIVINGSTON, BOB GOODWIN,
BOB COLLINS   DATE: OCT. 21, 1977

FROM: GENE RODDENBERRY   SUBJECT: THE DEVIL RUM

Although we had to actually fight Desilu and network to do it, we did have the foresight to eliminate cigarettes in the original Star Trek. Even with the heaviest smokers, including myself, I fought for it. In the end, it paid off for everyone; I think everyone now agrees that the original episodes would not be rerunning so successful if we had yielded to advertising pressure and put a "twenty-third century cigarette" into the mouth of Kirk and others.

Effective this time around, we are going to eliminate alcohol. Klingons drink alcohol. Klingons are bad guys who enjoy feeling quarrelsome. Please delete from any future scripts or scenes any indication of Enterprise crewmen or Earth planet dwellers imbibing alcohol. If it is vital for some reason to have our good guys drinking something or even getting high on what they are drinking, the point must be made that the mood-altering ingredient is not alcohol.

What do we do about Chief Engineer Scotty and his well-known love of scotch whiskey? We have a choice of making him either the single exception to our crew rule or "discovering" that his drink carries only the flavor of scotch. Probably it would be more honest to make him a single exception.

None of the above prohibitions apply to the STAR TREK office.*

Gene Roddenberry

* Sex, however, is still forbidden except as approved by the executive producer.

Casting for the newly created roles began immediately. Robert Collins had been set as the director for the first episode, the two-hour movie "In Thy Image." Immediately after he began, he auditioned every potential Vulcan and Deltan in town. Hundreds of would-be aliens gave cold readings for the parts of Xon, Ilia, and Decker. Finally, the candidates were narrowed down to a handful of each, and Bob Collins decided to screen test the semifinalists. Each Vulcan candidate was fitted with makeshift ears; the Ilias were made up with bald caps; mock-ups of the *Enterprise* bridge and recreation room helped set the scene, as the nervous actors dressed in costumes from the old tv series read hastily prepared dialogue:

DECKER
(watching viewer, concerned)
It's ejecting some large objects into orbit . . . Science Officer, scan and identify. Our sensors should work on those objects, at least. . . .

XON
Scanning, sir.

DECKER
They look to be about the size of our own saucer section. . . .

XON
(interrupting)
I have an analysis on them, sir.
(Xon reads data from his science viewer.)

XON
It is a neutron device, sir. . . .

And so on. The Deckers and Xons argued about what to do to save the *Enterprise* and the Earth; the Ilias did a scene which had them trying to seduce the Deckers. The results of the tests were promising. A young actor named David Gautreaux was cast as Xon. David had come from the ranks of legitimate theatre and off-off-Broadway, and this was to be his first "big break." The studio immediately put the dark-haired, green-eyed man of Cajun descent under contract, and David began an intense preparation for the role, reading up on Vulcans and even going on a two-week fast, to help him think and feel like a Vulcan. A set of latex ears were prepared from casts of David's own ears; his measurements were taken for wardrobe. Later, when the new series was canceled before it got into production, the disappointed young actor returned to the real world of Hollywood and went on to do various minor roles in other television series. But his heart was still with *Star Trek,* and eventually David did get a part in the movie, that of Commander Branch on Epsilon 9.

Persis Khambatta fared a bit better. Fortunately for her, Ilia remained in the movie script, and there never really was any doubt as to who would play the part. The screen tests were merely a formality; she not only looked the type—exotic, sensuous yet subdued—but gave an excellent performance in the specially created Decker-Ilia love scene. She had just arrived from London, where she had been doing modeling, her heart set on a career in American films. Her agent heard about the Ilia part and set up an audition. Persis wanted the part so badly she went out and bought her own bald cap, which she brought to the initial interview. Something about her clicked with the producers; the screen test clinched it. The rest is history.

The Deckers didn't seem right for the part, but it really wasn't the fault of the fine actors who auditioned. The character hadn't been clearly outlined yet and no one seemed quite sure of what Decker should be like. It wasn't until a week before production began on the *movie* that the right actor—Stephen Collins—was selected for that part.

Fandom continued grieving at the news that Mr. Spock would not be returning. They were curious about the new Xon character, but their loyalties naturally were for Leonard Nimoy. The studio was inundated with petitions, letters, and phone calls demanding that Leonard appear in the television series. In an article in the October 22, 1977, *Los Angeles Times* Leonard described his reasons for not continuing negotiations with Paramount:

"I had a good relationship with the *Star Trek* people," Nimoy said Thursday. "I considered doing the project, but the discussions became very complicated. They went on for a year and a half—it got to the point where I just didn't want to continue with them."

The Paramount switchboard lit up like Spock's console; a wound had been reopened, and it could not be allowed to fester. The studio had no comment, and one was needed if *Star Trek* were to continue receiving fan support. A massive mailer went out that afternoon to the four hundred fifty known *Star Trek* fan clubs:

October 22, 1977

TO FELLOW NIMOY-SPOCK FANS:

It comes as considerable shock to me to learn that this letter is necessary. However, Star Trek cast members and fans have advised me that there is some misinformed rumor on the subject of Nimoy-Spock and Star Trek II. These are the facts:

I have been a Leonard Nimoy admirer since long before there was a Star Trek. You cannot know much about our show without also knowing of my many tributes to Leonard as a human being and a multi-talented artist.

Do I like Mister Spock too? Incredible that I should have to answer that question! Not only did I invent Spock, I risked everything by refusing NBC's demand that "the guy with the ears" be eliminated. Some of my happiest memories are those of Nimoy and myself working together on the original series.

Has Leonard Nimoy been offered the Spock role in Star Trek II? Discussions and negotiations with Nimoy to play Spock in a Star Trek movie and/or television show have been going on for over two years! The best evidence of my sincerity in wanting our original stars back is that I voluntarily reduced my movie profit percentage so that it could be given to Nimoy and Shatner to further induce them to do the Star Trek film.

At about the time the Star Trek movie was cancelled by Paramount* (which I still consider a serious mistake), I had a meeting with Leonard Nimoy in which we discussed Star Trek and television. At that time, he told me that he might consider long form television specials but "under no circumstances" would he return to play Mr. Spock again on a weekly hour television series basis. He explained that the pressures of weekly television would interfere with his career goal of stage, film, and other things.

I still hoped he would change his mind but could not ignore reports that he continued to reject any Star Trek television possibilities in newspaper columns and in television interviews. Then, when Nimoy

---

*This refers to the *first* movie attempt in 1975.

finally became part of a successful play on Broadway stage, I had to accept that his rejection of Star Trek television was final.

Convinced that no terms I could arrange would bring a willing and enthusiastic Leonard Nimoy into the role of Mr. Spock on television again, I had no choice but to get on with the difficult job of inventing a new science officer. Also, perhaps some interesting other new alien too. This job was made easier by the fact that we did have the exceptionally gifted Bill Shatner still playing Captain Kirk. I believed that our fans would be very pleased that after eleven years it appears that we'll get six out of seven original actors back.

Do we still want Nimoy-Spock in Star Trek II? Yes, of course. Must we have the Nimoy-Spock combination back no matter what the schedule or terms or cost? Of course not. We also have obligations on schedule and terms and cost to a Shatner-Kirk combination. And to the other actor-character combinations too. We have obligations to episode writers who are fine artists in their own right, to a director, to an art director, in fact to well over a hundred other talented actors, staff and crew who are also an important part of Star Trek.

It seems to me that Star Trek's content must indicate that I have no small respect for our audience. I must now call upon our audience to return that respect in the form of some confidence that I am trying to make the best Star Trek II possible under all the conditions faced in returning the show to television.

Sincerely,

Gene Roddenberry

It helped quiet things down a bit, fortunately, because every ounce of concentration would be needed in order to meet the television start date on November 30, a little over a month away. On all three stages, hammers were frantically pounding each nail in double time as construction crews raced against the calendar. Added to this frenzy was a startling announcement made by the studio on November 11, just two and a half weeks before production was to begin. *Star Trek,* the new television series, was now—about to become *Star Trek—The Motion Picture!*

On November 21, just eight days away from the proposed start date, everything came to a halt. Crew such as makeup and hairdressers who had been hired just that Monday were laid off by Friday. Production was moved ahead to March or April so that the script, sets, wardrobe, etc., could be upgraded.

What had happened to cause the studio's sudden turnabout? First, not enough advertising time had been sold in order to make the fourth network economically viable, and the fourth network concept was dropped. Second, a science-fantasy movie called *Star Wars* had become the biggest box-office success in the history of movies; it was a dazzling array of light and sound which set the pace for all optical movies to follow. A trend had been started. A few months later *Close Encounters of the Third Kind* succeeded in creating still more new optical effects. Twentieth Century-Fox and Columbia Pictures, the respective producers of the two films, were cleaning up. The public was on a new high—space epics, science fiction films, optical trips. Paramount had to look no further than its own back lot; stage 9 already had a spaceship. Now was the time to christen the *Enterprise* and launch her on her new mission.

With the wrap of the abortive television show, the other series scripts which had been received were put on the shelf. By now, Harold Livingston was concentrating all his efforts on reworking television's "In Thy Image" into a major movie script, and Jon Povil had been promoted to story editor. Jon filed his final report on the status of the television scripts, which are still in Paramount's vault to this day:

TO: GENE RODDENBERRY   DATE: JANUARY 20, 1978

FROM: JON POVILL   SUBJECT: FINAL WRITER'S STATUS REPORT

1. MARGARET ARMEN/ALF HARRIS—"The Savage Syndrome"—
    Unrevised final draft December 28, 1977.

2. JOHN POVILL/JARON SUMMERS—"The Child"—Unrevised final
    draft January 9, 1978.

3. LARRY ALEXANDER—"Tomorrow and the Stars"—Unrevised final
    draft January 18, 1978.

4. DAVID AMBROSE—"Deadlock"—Unrevised final draft January 20,
    1978.

5. JOHN MEREDYTH LUCAS—"Kitumba"—Second draft script in
    work. (Two-hour script.)

6. WORLEY THORNE—"Home"—Awaiting delivery of first draft script.

7. TED STURGEON—"Cassandra"—Awaiting delivery of first draft
    script.

8. BILL LANSFORD—"Devil's Due"—Awaiting delivery of first draft
    script.

I have spoken to Ted Sturgeon, Worley Thorne and Bill Lansford, all of
whom tell me that their first draft scripts will be in toward the latter

part of next week. At that time you can make whatever decisions necessary concerning their disposition.

When these last three scripts come in, we will have (including the two hours designated to "In Thy Image") eleven hours in script. If the series were to start shooting tomorrow, we would be in very nice shape indeed. Under the circumstances, however, it should be good to know that if and when there is a go-ahead on it, we have a stockpile of existing scripts in hand.

Star Trek had gone from *television show,* to $3 to $5 million *movie,* to $8 to $10 million *movie,* to *television show,* and finally to a *major* motion picture.

5

Déjà Vu

It was the hottest ticket in town, but it wasn't for sale. If you were a member of the fourth estate you might have been lucky enough to have been there that day—March 28, 1978.

Next to the Academy Awards, it was very likely the year's most eagerly received entertainment news from Hollywood, and it began with all the ballyhoo so traditional in Movieland.

There were well-known names—William Shatner, Leonard Nimoy, all the rest of the original cast together for the first time since the last *Star Trek* episode was filmed in 1969; series creator Gene Roddenberry, director Robert Wise, plus all the Paramount Pictures executives. Even Charles Bluhdorn, the chairman of the board of Gulf and Western, Paramount's parent company, flew in for the press conference, winning the approval of his daughter, an ardent *Star Trek* fan.

There was glitter—the four very lovely ladies of the *Enterprise* crew were the epitome of Hollywood glamour. The flashing smiles of *Star Trek* veterans Nichelle Nichols, Majel Barrett and Grace Lee Whitney were as captivating as they had been in the television series years before, while newcomer Persis Khambatta dazzled everyone with her exotic beauty.

There was sumptuous food—Chasen's, the world-famous Beverly Hills restaurant, catered the elegant brunch of eggs benedict, fresh papayas stuffed with grapefruit, corn-beef hash, sausages, bacon, ham, croissants, fresh pasteries, and plenty of bloody marys to wash it all down.

And, of course, there was excitement. *This was the largest press conference held at Paramount since Cecil B. DeMille announced that he would be making* The Ten Commandments *(at the then unheard of cost of $1 million per commandment).* Michael Eisner, looking much too young and attractive to be president and chief operating officer for Paramount Pictures Corporation, called *Star Trek* "the number one tv event series of all times" and credited the fans for finally bringing the motion picture within reach. "The fans," he said, "have supported us and consistently written us to pull our act together." Cheers greeted his next announcement: Four-time Academy Award winner Robert Wise would direct a $15 million production of *Star Trek—The Motion Picture,* with producer-creator Gene Roddenberry at the helm.

Immediately, flashing cameras rivaling a supernova lit up the dais and adjacent table of honor. They were all there—William Shatner, Leonard Nimoy, DeForest Kelley, James Doohan, George Takei, Nichelle Nichols, Walter Koenig, Majel Barrett, Grace Lee Whitney, and Persis Khambatta.* But the star of the show caught the most attention—the 12-by-25-foot portrait of the newly designed starship *Enterprise,* ready for her next assignment in space.

No other film in recent history had attracted so much attention at its mere announcement. That evening there was coverage by the three major networks—ABC, CBS, and NBC—plus morning coverage on *The Today Show, Good Morning, America* and numerous other programs. Nearly every major newspaper and wire service in the country covered the press conference announcements. Articles with headlines like STARSHIP ENTERPRISE BLASTS OFF AGAIN; ENTERPRISE READY FOR ANOTHER TREK; STAR TREK GETS IT ALL TO-GETHER AGAIN, and STAR TREK A FILM, THIS TIME FOR SURE appeared in major dailies all across America, including the *New York Post,* the *Chicago Tribune,* the *Miami Herald,* the *Milwaukee Journal,* the *Boston Herald American,* the *Los Angeles Times,* the *Tampa Tribune Times,* and many more. The media seized this news with a fervor usually reserved for presidential announcements. No wonder the ticket for this press conference was so hot.

---

*Stephen Collins had not yet been cast as Decker.

As the tall, rumple-headed Roddenberry was introduced from the dais, the entire cast leaped to their feet and cheered him. "I was never so touched and moved in my entire life," he later commented.

The fans had their day, too. The previous evening, Gene had personally sent telegrams to thank all the fans for their support. A fan service organization known as the *Star Trek* Welcommittee publishes a list of fan clubs who wish to be recognized. At the time, the list contained nearly four hundred fifty known clubs, each of which received the following wire at the moment the press conference was being held:

STAR TREK—THE MOTION PICTURE WILL BE ANNOUNCED TO THE WORLD TUESDAY NOON. ALL, REPEAT ALL THE ORIGINAL CAST RETURNING FOR A MAJOR MOTION PICTURE DIRECTED BY FOUR TIME ACADEMY AWARD WINNER ROBERT WISE, PRODUCED BY MYSELF. THANKS FOR ALL YOU HAVE DONE. LETTER FOLLOWS.

GENE RODDENBERRY

The fans were also supplied with a copy of the official press release from Paramount. It began with this news bulletin:

```
* * * * * * * * * * * * * * * * * * * * * * * * * * * * * * *
*  NEWS BULLETIN --                                          *

*       It has been confirmed that the U.S.S. Enterprise,   *
    most celebrated space ship of all time, has been re-
*   turned to active duty.                                   *

*       While Star Fleet Headquarters would not reveal      *
    details of the highly-classified mission, informed
*   sources indicated the Enterprise has been pressed        *
    back into service to counter an awesome and Earth-
*   threatening development in the far reaches of outer      *
    space.
*                                                            *
        The mission, according to those sources, is cer-
*   tain to be the most spectacular ever undertaken by       *
    the famed Starship.
*                                                            *
        The Enterprise again will be commanded by Capt.
*   James Kirk, who, it also was learned, has succeeded      *
    in reuniting his entire former crew, including his
*   First Officer, the Vulcan Mr. Spock.                     *

*       Prior to its departure from Earth, the Enterprise   *
    is being refitted with the latest, most sophisticated
*   instruments and weaponry known to 23rd century space     *
    technology.
* * * * * * * * * * * * * * * * * * * * * * * * * * * * * * *
```

March 28, 1978

Dear Friend,

Well, we've made it. STAR TREK - THE MOTION PICTURE
is now a certainty, as you can see from the enclosed
official announcement released by Paramount today.

It has been a long and sometimes frustrating road for
all of us, but I'm sure you now will agree with me that
the delay was worth it. To obtain a director like
Robert Wise, to be able to get Bill, Leonard, DeForest
and all the other members of the original cast together
again, is a tremendously exciting achievement.

I do wish to express my personal gratitude to you and
all those others who have supported this project with
so much enthusiasm and played such an important part in
making it become a reality.

We'll continue to be in touch as further news develops
and as we finally get in front of the cameras.

Long live!

Gene Roddenberry

GR:ss

The fans were overjoyed. Not only were they finally getting their movie, they were also getting everyone; not just star William Shatner, but also Leonard Nimoy, who seemed to have said a dozen times in a dozen different ways that he would never play Mr. Spock again.

Before the press conference, Bill Shatner took time to visit the *Star Trek* production offices—the same offices that had been used during the production of the television series of the sixties. Bill had been a working actor (and a very popular one) for all the years following *Star Trek,* including a Paramount series of his own called *Barbary Coast.* In fact, he had been kept so busy with this series and other projects that he had only been by the office a couple of times to chat with Gene during *Barbary Coast.*

Tanned and athletic-looking, Bill was much leaner, his musculature more hardened since his early days as Captain Kirk. He discovered that Paramount hadn't changed much, however, especially those old offices. "There are a lot of ghosts here," he murmured in amazement. "I can almost see the footprints in the same carpet."

Asked at the press conference if it would be difficult to return to the role of Kirk after a nine-year interruption, William Shatner said: "I think Spencer Tracy said it best—'You take a deep breath and say the words.' Of course you have to have some years of experience to know how to say the words and suck in your breath. An actor brings to a role not only the concept of the character but his own basic personality, things that he is, and both Leonard and myself have changed over the years, to a degree at any rate, and we will bring that degree of change inadvertently to the role we recreate."

An un-Spocklike grinning Leonard Nimoy was received warmly by those present. At the time of the press conference, the ink from his signature on the contract had only been dry for twenty-four hours, and no part for him had been written into the existing script. When a member of the press asked Nimoy why he had appeared so reluctant to sign, he replied that he didn't know why it seemed that way:

"It's really not a matter of reluctance," he told the press. "We had a lot of details to iron out. There have been periods of time when the *Star Trek* concept was moving forward and I was not available. For example, last summer [1977] we had come to what I felt was an understanding about doing the movie. I went off to do *Equus* on Broadway. During that period of time the concept changed to a tv series. It was difficult then to get together because there was a question of availability. When the project turned around and I was available again we started talking immediately. It has been complicated; it has been time consuming. But there was never a question of reluctance to be involved in *Star Trek* on my part. I've always felt totally comfortable about being identified with *Star Trek* and being identified with the Spock character. It has exploded my life in a very positive way. The Spock character has always been part of my life; I have never tried in any way to reject that. I'm very proud of the fact that I'm associated with the character, and I look forward to playing the character because I certainly wouldn't want anybody else playing it, or *Star Trek* happening without it."

DeForest Kelley was back as the humanistic Dr. Leonard ("Bones") McCoy, completing the captain–first officer–doctor triumvirate. De-Forest's first move was to visit the sound stage where the *Enterprise* sets were nearing completion. Construction had begun in summer of 1977 in anticipation for the then-planned fall television show. Since the finalization of plans for a movie, most of the sets had undergone drastic revisions, and some were even begun again from scratch. Kelley was particularly impressed with the *Enterprise* bridge set, remarking that it appeared to be in the same stage of construction as when he first came in for the original *Star Trek* series. It was a strange sense of déjà vu for the popular ship's doctor.

The other cast members were also delighted to be back. Walter Koenig (Lt. Chekov) claimed he really didn't believe it was all happening until he was measured for his costume. Grace Lee Whitney (Transporter Chief Rand), who had appeared in the first season of *Star Trek* only, commented that she felt it was a very moving, cosmic feeling, a sense of belonging, like coming back home. "It gave me a feeling as if I had turned back my life ten years."

Perhaps the person who was most caught up by all the excitement was director Robert Wise. Bob is one of the most respected and honored directors in the industry, having garnered two Academy Awards each for *West Side Story* and *The Sound of Music*. But he is perhaps most well known to science-fiction fans for the classic film *The Day the Earth Stood Still*. As far as the fans were concerned, they had hit the jackpot with Bob Wise's involvement. "I'm so pleased that *The Day the Earth Stood Still* has lasted through the years," he told the members of the press. "Science fiction is something that's always interested and intrigued me, but I've never had a chance to do this kind of show. I think it can make an absolutely fascinating picture. I'm looking forward to my involvement with all the cast and the marvelous special photographic effects that we can bring to it. I'm very excited."

With the reunited cast, a renowned director, and studio enthusiasm, all that *Star Trek—The Motion Picture* lacked was a final script.

6

The Script's the Thing

FADE OUT. THE END.

These words were first typed on the script for *Star Trek—The Motion Picture* in October of 1977. A year later, with production of the film nearly over, the words were still being typed—again and again—by secretaries who chuckled, "I don't believe it this time either!" Finally, the last revised script page was turned in for mimeographing and distribution. The date it bears at the top of this pink page is nearly *four months after the start of production:* revised, 11/29/78. *Star Trek* had been shooting for all that time without a completed script!

Its embryonic development began with a two-paragraph story idea and continued through several stories, outlines, and at least seven script drafts.

The basic idea for the plot of *ST—TMP* was conceived by Gene Roddenberry as a possible episode of his unsold 1973 pilot, *Genesis II*. Among Gene's twenty story proposals offering a glimpse of what a *Genesis II* series would hold in store for the CBS network was the following, called "Robot's Return," which inspired a number of elements in a story by Alan Dean Foster, on which *ST—TMP* is based.

A twenty-mile-in-diameter space vessel has arrived at 22nd-century Earth from its Neptune moon home. It wishes to learn more about the holy home of the Creator, NASA; it seeks its God. Dylan Hunt, *Genesis II's* "Captain Kirk" type, learns that the last NASA space exploration team to one of the moons of Neptune sent back a garbled final message about discovering an alien city whose inhabitants were long dead, but whose machinery was still in operation. The space ship now in Earth orbit has zapped one of Dylan's friends, a lady named Harper-Smythe, who suddenly vanished from sight in a blinding flash, only to be returned a short time later—only this is not Harper-Smythe at all, its voice announces, but a perfect machine duplication! Soon the robot is behaving like the real-live girl, having received a "personality imprint." Perhaps Dylan will be able to save the two hundred hostages the spaceship is holding in orbit by gaining the android's trust, even affection. They offer it some old 20th-century NASA film; the lovely android responds by smashing the projector with her (its?) fist. This story ends when the android, by now in love with Dylan (who wants the *real* thing, not a mechanical copy) tricks the intelligent machine-spaceship into releasing the hostages. Android and girl finally swap places again, and the mechanical lady goes on to explain to the machine what has happened to NASA during the last two centuries. The machine leaves for places unknown and Dylan's hometown of Pax becomes peaceful once more.

One sentence in "Robot's Return" is noteworthy here. It sums up what went on to become the most controversial, yet highly essential, theme in *ST—TMP*—and one over which battle after battle was waged with the Paramount Studio executives, as we shall shortly see.

Humanity, whether in Pax's time or ours, must ultimately face the fact that intelligent machines will be created and relationships between living intelligence and machine intelligence must be anticipated and its advantages and dangers analyzed.

In the summer of 1977, a young science-fiction writer named Alan Dean Foster was called in. He had written a series of *Log* books (Ballantine) based on the *Star Trek* animated episodes, and had gained much popularity among the fans, and Gene and Harold Livingston asked him to develop a story. So the mustachioed writer left his Big Bear mountain retreat, about an hour and half outside Los Angeles, and drove into town. Over the next few weeks, Alan drove up and down his mountain quite a bit, working out a story suggested by

"Robot's Return," tailoring it for the *Enterprise,* now on her second five-year mission. On July 31, Alan turned in his seventeen-page first draft of a story he called "In Thy Image." Briefly, it went as follows:

Kirk and the Enterprise are directed to intercept a 30-by-70 kilometer metallic object which is heading toward Earth. They pull up alongside it and receive a signal: a voice declares itself to be the servant of the great god N'sa (pronounced "En-sah"). The voice adds that it is on its way to N'sa's home world, Earth, to clear Earth of a deadly infection that has devastated that planet . . . humans. The Enterprise first attacks, then tries to retreat, but is held prisoner by "we the Wan," as the ship identifies itself. The Wan thwarts Kirk's attempt to self-destruct the Enterprise. When Kirk attempts to override, the computer talks back to him. The newly converted computer chirps, "I have been ordered not to allow self-destruction because it would not be to the greater glory of the great god N'sa." While Scotty attempts to fix the sick computer, a few balls of flickering turquoise lights suddenly appear on the bridge . . . they're being boarded! The blue globes coalesce and become some of the cutest little mechanical things this side of R2-D2. Some are round (eyes), some speaker-shaped (ears), and some tentacled (touchers), and some computerlike (thinkers, or brain). After the devices attack some bridge crew, Kirk has them all destroyed. Meanwhile, the computer has mutinied, and has taken over communications. Kirk wonders why the aliens don't come over in person. Instead, they have begun sending over other things. Like a tiger, which chases a crewmember down a corridor; and a pack of wolves, army ants, alligators, eagles, lions and an elephant. But the crew, still on alert from the previous assault, was ready, and injuries are still few.

But that's not all. A blue cloud on the bridge materializes into a swarm of bees.* Most are phasered; one crewmember is stung. He nearly dies, but is saved by McCoy with an anti-cobra-venom cure—with which the bees were loaded. It's become obvious that the Wan is learning about these creatures from the ship's computer library. Furious, Kirk yells for the aliens to show themselves. But, the voice replies, it is showing itself. It is McCoy who makes the realization that "The whole ship . . . it's all a single creature, a gigantic single machine life-form."

The machine-voice explains itself: Wan is inhabited by machines. These machines knew nothing of the outside world because of a thick cloud cover until one day the god N'sa came down to them. N'sa told them of the world where it came from. This great vessel was built to return the body of N'sa to its home, and to exterminate the organic lice (humans) that enslaved N'sa's companions. Suddenly, Scotty draws a phaser on Kirk, declaring "You see the superiority, Kirk-man, of the machine mind." We learn this is really Scotty the android, as moments

---

*At one point after this was given a "go" for script, Jon Povill, then assistant to the producer, had one of his first assignments—to locate a swarm of trained bees. And he did, too! They were all veterans of the movie *Swarm.*

later the real Scott appears. The machine starts sending over more replicas of Enterprise crew. "Lt. Vulcan"* declares that there is no god N'sa from Earth. In angry reply, the Wan grabs Kirk, Lt. Vulcan, Commander [a Decker forerunner], and McCoy, materializes them inside a Wan chamber filled with crystalline shapes. A duplicate Sulu wheels in a cart containing a dome-encased object, which an excited Commander recognizes as—Pioneer Ten! This was the first beyond-the-solar-system spacecraft built by mankind—'way back in 1973. It was built by the National Aeronautics and Space Administration, i.e., NASA. The Wan machines made it their god. A plate shows the way to Earth, but obliterated from that same plate were the outlines of Earth's creatures—a man and a woman. Meanwhile, the Enterprise's computer has been pretending to go along with the Wan in order to save the Enterprise and in order not to go insane from trying to figure out whether to follow its programming or the orders of the intelligent machine. The computer has been sneaky—it's housed a photon bomb in Lt. Vulcan's double and planted him/it aboard the Wan ship. Destroy the double and the bomb goes off; attempt to beam it away and it'll be detonated before that can happen. First the Enterprise must be allowed to get away safely, then the Wan may dispose of the bomb. The machine finally concedes the intelligence of the organics, returns all the crew safely, and "turn(s) majestically and recede(s) into the distance, leaving the Enterprise hanging alone in space, ready for its next mission."

Eventually this story went on to undergo several rewrites by Gene Roddenberry, and to become the basis of the *Star Trek* script, "In Thy Image," written by Gene Roddenberry and Harold Livingston. It continued to evolve into the planned opening two-hour television movie that would kick off the new series. It was even planned for simultaneous theatrical release in Europe. The story seemed to have all that was needed to begin *Star Trek* over again on television. It brought Kirk and the crew together again, it introduced new crew members, and it showed off a bit of 23rd-century Earth—something Gene Roddenberry had always wanted to do. Roddenberry refined it all into a ninety-eight page story outline of "In Thy Image" which became the basis of everything that followed, right on through the motion picture script.

During this time, Harold Livingston, writer/producer on the new television series, began writing the first rough draft of the script itself and completed it on October 20, 1977. Shooting was to take place in a month.

---

* The new character Lt. Xon had yet to be created to take Mr. Spock's place in the stated absence of Leonard Nimoy.

By this time, the story had evolved even further. It utilized many new dimensions from Gene, Harold, and the director, Robert Collins. Among them:

- The Klingon cruiser destruction opening.

- Commander Branch of Starbase 9 learns "It's heading toward Earth."

- Admiral Kirk and McCoy meet in a San Francisco mall—McCoy's been bandaging the foot of some children's injured pet cheetah.

- Admiral Kirk and McCoy go to Admiral Nogura's office complex [this set was actually constructed, later struck when not used]. A holographic conference between Fleet Admirals is held here.

- Nogura orders Scott to get the *Enterprise* ready to be under way in 24 hours, admits Kirk is the best man to be her captain.

- View of Earth and *Enterprise* in orbital drydock; orbiting work offices.

- The new Vulcan character is now named Lt. Xon; the new navigator, Lt. Ilia from planet Delta is showing off her baldness and boldness, and Commander Will Decker has been yanked off the *Boston* to help the new science officer, among other nebulous duties.

- The *Enterprise* heads off to rendezvous with this "Object."

- The "thing" destroys the cruiser *Aswan*; the *Enterprise* moves in for a closer look, discovers object is 70 kilometers long.

- The alien fires at the *Enterprise* but deflectors hold.

- The alien grabs the *Enterprise* with a tractor beam.

- Xon discovers how to slow down the alien transmission, realizes the aliens are addressing the U.S.S. *Enterprise* as a *life form*.

- The *Enterprise* computer begins feeding its information to the aliens.

- Ilia flirts with Sulu, making him very nervous.

- Bright flares of turquoise light materialize into sensor probes. One, pearl-like, is clearly frightened of the humans. Chekov names it "Tasha" because it reminds him of his Aunt Tasha's pearl ring.

- The computer reports that the alien thinks *Enterprise* is parasite-infested, and that this 70-mile-long vessel is headed for the "the Holy Home of the Creator."

- Ilia is beamed over to the alien ship.

- Xon suffers burns when he slams his fist down on the computer console to stop transmission—he's carefully tended in sickbay by Dr. Chapel, who has administered plasti-skin.

- The Tasha probe returns, in the guise of Ilia, materializing naked inside Kirk's sonic shower. She answers throughout the remaining scenes to the name "Tasha." [Note: During actual film production, there were still references to "when Ilia has become Tasha," although the name was dropped in later script versions and became simply "Ilia"-probe.]

- Tasha reports that the *vessel* which sent her over is named *Ve-jur,* and that she's there to study *Enterprise*'s "servo-units."

- Xon suggests that Kirk could learn more via a "relationship" with Tasha. Tasha still wants to flirt with Sulu: "I can do anything the original can—better," she tells the Helmsman.

- *Ve-jur* releases tractor beam, insists in return that Kirk admit that their planet is the Holy Home. Beams them over to the giant ship to show them proof.

- Kirk, Xon and Tasha beam over into a multicolored cavern with oxygen atmosphere provided for.

- Tasha shows them the real Ilia, floating in a gelatinous plasma mass, being preserved for study.

- They continue walking until they reach the site of *Ve-jur,* where they observe a plaque identifying it as V G R *18.* As in the film, it too disappeared into a black hole.

- Kirk calls Uhura, tells her to get information on NASA ready. They beam back to the ship.

- Tasha/Ilia tries to seduce Kirk, as she becomes more Deltan in feeling.

- Kirk takes Tasha/Ilia to see his Earth. They beam down, first to another ship, the *Delphi,* then to Union Square Park, where Kirk gives her a capsule view of Earth. He also tries to convince her that she shouldn't show so much prejudice against humans, that they can be as nice as machines, and maybe even have *created* a few in their time.

- The alien ship ejects a neutron bomb with a proximity fuse—and the *Enterprise* is in the proximity. They escape, but now *Ve-jur* emits four more, placed in equidistant orbital positions. [These stayed in through quite a few more drafts.]

- Meanwhile, back in the Archives building, Kirk shows Tasha some 20th-century NASA film of *Voyager 18.* She thinks it's a fake.

Nevertheless, she helps thread the projector, and actually seems to become quite fond of this "charming unit" as she calls the 16mm machine.

- With less than two minutes left until the neutron devices destroy every living thing on Earth, Kirk tries to talk Tasha/Ilia/*Ve-jur* out of its God. He succeeds; she tells *Ve-jur* that indeed the human servo-units *had* conceived the Creator (NASA). *Ve-jur,* however, superciliously states that it can learn nothing from these lower life forms and departs, but not before sending back the real Ilia.

- Tag—Kirk and Tasha/Ilia are beamed back aboard, but suddenly the mechanical Tasha appears in place of the Ilia-probe. It's silent, dead—Kirk says this may be what she wanted. The *Enterprise* receives her orders for the next mission and off it goes on "its *new* five year mission."

FADE OUT. THE END.

One week before filming was to begin on "In Thy Image," the studio canceled the television series. They had decided to upgrade "In Thy Image" into the *Star Trek* motion picture, with filming now set to begin in the late spring 1978. To many it seemed quite easy as far as script was concerned, since one already existed—"In Thy Image."

The many were wrong. Difficulties began almost immediately, due to the fact that this particular first draft script had been written for a two-hour television movie, not a major science fiction blockbuster. When Robert Wise was selected as director, he focused attention back on the script. Wise felt the story seemed right, but that the entire line of dramatic action as well as the visuals could be upgraded considerably and made much more exciting. Time was of the essence— every major studio in town had a science fiction picture on their drawing boards, and Paramount didn't want their main contender in the SF bout to come out at the tail end of some cycle. It had to be on the screen while the public still appeared to be excited about spectacular science fiction films.

By now it was nearly March, 1978—obviously a *new* start date was needed, and production was put off until the summer so that the script could be revised to meet major movie needs. Gene Roddenberry admitted that at this point he had become stale and written out because he had been so close to so many film and tv versions of "*Star Trek* Returns." A transfusion of fresh writer blood was needed. With

Harold Livingston on another assignment and temporarily unavailable, other writers were brought in to add hopefully new viewpoints and dimensions.

One writer arrived with full entourage—two assistants and his personal office decorations, to give it a touch of home. Part American Indian, he decked out this particular office-home in hides and skins, peace pipes, artifacts, books, and other items pertaining to Indian lore. Naturally, everyone spent as much time in this man's "mountain cabin" office as possible without disturbing his writing work, as this was more fun than the other rather drab offices, and nearly as interesting as some of the movie sets out on the lot.

Immediately, Gene Roddenberry planned a proper welcome. Gene's practical jokes had done much to loosen up taut nerves during the original *Star Trek* television series, and it seemed past time to lighten up *Star Trek*'s return too. Gene decided that he would tell the writer that the studio had assigned him a secretary. Actually there was no such studio policy, but the writer didn't know that, and Gene could think of no better way to drive the unsuspecting man to the point of homicidal insanity. And who would be more perfect to play this "secretary" than Grace Lee Whitney, former Yeoman Janice Rand of the starship *Enterprise*. Grace Lee was actress enough to guarantee that the writer would never recognize her.

On the appointed morning, Grace Lee arrived, eager to go "work." She wore a sexy pantsuit, piled her platinum hair up, added a pair of granny-glasses and a mouth chomping noisily on several packages of chewing gum. Her props included the stereotypical secretarial necessities—nail polish and nail file, radio and coffee mug.

She began slowly. She turned on the radio, not too loud, and asked if her new "boss" minded. He asked her to leave, saying he had no need of a secretary—he already had two assistants. She ignored him, so he ignored *her*, went into his office and closed the door. The radio volume was increased, ever so slightly. Then Grace Lee grabbed a fistful of pencils and opened his office door to get to the electric pencil sharpener. This rusting antique pencil sharpener sounded like a cross between an ice crusher and a cement mixer in the quiet office. Next, she asked for more coffee breaks, and also demanded a longer lunch hour, at the same time propping her bare foot up on his desk, explaining that at noon she was going for a bunion operation (this idea suggested by Bill Theiss, *Star Trek*'s costume designer at the time, who walked in and decided to play along with the game). Then she began boogying to the radio music and when asked to type something she confessed that she didn't know how.

By this time the writer was ready to move out. Meanwhile, Gene slipped Grace out of the office and had Bill Theiss fit her into her *Star Trek* costume. The writer recognized Grace Lee Whitney immediately, but still didn't make the connection between this lovely actress and his gum-snapping secretary.

Finally, he was let in on the joke and he took it quite well, considering he had almost been driven to a nervous breakdown.

* * *

Meanwhile Harold Livingston finally became available and returned once again to rework "In Thy Image." Time was growing short—Leonard Nimoy was signed and Spock had to be written in.

Harold had become a familiar face around the offices, having been coproducer on the aborted new television series. He hardly looked like a hero, ready to save the day. (He says that with some extreme muscular convolutions, he can reach a height of 5'4".) Yet he became a favorite of the office secretaries, who quietly tolerated his ever-present cigars, brewed his Brim extra strong, and listened to him mumble and grumble, in a Lou Grant-ish way—all the while knowing what a really lovable pussycat he was at heart.

Harold actually spent very little time at the studio, preferring to do most of his writing at home because he likes to write at night. To prepare for the night's writing ahead, he runs several miles each evening. He's been doing this for twelve years now, starting long before jogging became so popular, but admits he hates every minute of it. He claims he's not built for it, and not an athlete. Still, he's way ahead of most of the men his age (fifties) when it comes to stamina, something he really needed on the script job ahead of him.

According to Harold, "The basic concept of the story was unworkable. We had a marvelous antagonist, so omnipotent that for us to defeat it or even communicate with it, or have any kind of relationship with it, made the initial concept of the story false. Here's this gigantic machine that's a million years further advanced than we are. Now, how the hell can we possibly deal with this? On what level? As the story developed, everything worked until the very end. How do you resolve this thing? If humans can defeat this marvelous machine, then it's really not so great, is it? Or if it really *is* great, will we like those humans who do defeat it? *Should* they defeat it? Who is the story's hero anyway? That was the problem. We experimented with all kinds of approaches—theological, aesthetic, philosophical, comical, anything—we didn't know what to do with the ending. We always ended up against a blank wall."

The office became a mountain of paper. Harold received constant input from associate producer Jon Povill; so pleased was Harold with Jon's work that he insists he never could have done the job without him. Harold was influential in getting Jon promoted from assistant to the producer on the tv series, to story editor and then later to associate producer on the movie.

Robert Wise was involved in all the important script meetings also, and on many occasions he brought in Bill Shatner and Leonard Nimoy to offer their contributions. The input from so many people saw the script being constantly rewritten, right up until the actual day many pages were to be shot. At one point, each day's scenes were being rewritten *several times a day,* and it became necessary to note on script pages the *hour* of the day when these pages had been rushed to the stage so that the actors could learn their most recent lines and Bob Wise would know what he was shooting. The result was near chaos, but somehow everyone managed to cope, usually cheerfully, too.

Mimeoed pages were arriving after they'd already been shot. The scripts became a multicolored wonder. A note here about revision pages: scripts are first mimeoed on all white pages. Then, each day a page is revised, a new color is designated—some of the colors sound like a fashion designer's new fall line up: blue, pink, yellow, green, goldenrod, buff, salmon, cherry, tan. *Star Trek* had a generous sprinkling of all the colors through goldenrod. It looked like a child's funbook, all this pretty colored paper.

The rewrites continued daily throughout most of production. But the biggest push was for an *ending,* a third-act conclusion to the script. Most of this rewriting had to do with one thing: the relationships of the characters on the ship: Kirk and Spock, Decker and Ilia, the *Enterprise* and *V'ger*—especially *V'ger*. How were they to deal with this opponent so that the whole resolution of the piece would be satisfactory in terms of character, story, drama, and suspense?

The original television script did not metamorphose into a movie script without causing great difficulty. One thing would be changed and then two or three other things would fall out of place. Gene Roddenberry called it a "writer's nightmare."

The script's third act continued to plague everyone. Gene believes it would have been much easier if they had started the *Star Trek* film from scratch with a fresh new story. At the end of September, a draft of the act was completed that finally met with the approval of the front office. But had it not been for an article in the October 1978 issue of *Penthouse* magazine, that approval might not have been given.

The whole idea of a "living machine" had not gone over well with some studio executives. Back when it was still in the tv stage, Gene had been invited to argue the subject with a medical doctor–science-fiction reader whom it was felt would prove to Gene that there was no possibility that any machine could ever be considered alive, and that no one in science fiction ever wrote seriously about such things. Gene ultimately argued the "expert" into admitting that he had a personal prejudice against the possibility of living machines. Yet there was still some studio nervousness about the whole concept. Fortunately, it was at this time that Dr. Robert Jastrow, director of NASA's Goddard Institute for Space Studies, was interviewed in *Penthouse*. He said practically the very same things that Gene had been saying—machine forms of life are a very likely next evolutionary stage:

> I say that computers, as we call them, are a newly emerging form of life, one made out of silicon rather than carbon. . . . Such new forms of life will have neither human emotions nor any of the other trappings we associate with human life. . . . Their understanding of the harmony of the cosmos and the nature of physical reality may transcend ours. Their curiosity to *discover* may be what drives them.

Suddenly the people in the front office were calling Gene up and telling him he had been right all along! For the last five years, Gene had been describing this stage in evolution to audiences on his lecture circuit, and he was much relieved that this article in *Penthouse* had accomplished what he had been unable to do himself.

V'ger had won, but the huge machine's motivation had to be made clear to everyone involved with the desperately needed last act. To help this along, Gene wrote a six-page guide to understanding *V'ger* and the story theme. Condensed below are the points he made.

2nd Unit	No. of Days Scheduled	No. of Days Worked	DAILY PRODUCTION REPORT		No. Days Scheduled / No. Days Actual	Travel	Holi-days	Idle	Change-over	Retakes & Add. Scns.	Work	Total	AHEAD
										⊠	60	60	BEHIND
											/	/	Rehearsals

TITLE _STAR TREK THE MOTION PICTURE_ PROD. # _10258_ DATE _Mon. August 7, 1978_
PRODUCER _GENE RODDENBERRY_ CAMERAMAN _RICHARD KLINE_ MEDIA _____
DIRECTOR _ROBERT WISE_ DATE STARTED _August 7, 1978_ EST. FINISH DATE _____

SET No.	SET		LOCATION	SET No.	SET	LOCATION
	INT. BRIDGE (DRYDOCK) ELEVATOR		STAGE 9			
	INT. BRIDGE					

Call _7A_ Leave_____ Arrive Location_____ 1st Shot: AM ___ PM _2:02_ Wrap _6:15P_ Arrive Studio/Hotels_____
Crew Lunch _12N_ To _1P_ Crew Supper_____ To_____ 1st Shot _2:00P_
Camera Call _7A_ Camera Wrap _6:15P_ Sound Call _7A_ Sound Wrap _6:15P_

	SETUPS	MINUTES	SCENES	PAGES	SCENES COMPLETED TODAY
PREV.	0	0	0	0	64, 66, (PART 68 = 5/8 pgs.)
TODAY	5	1:20	2	1 5/8	
TOTAL	5	1:20	2	1 5/8	

TOTAL PAGES	SCRIPT AVERAGE	ACTUAL AVERAGE	WILD TRACKS	RETAKES

FILM USE	GROSS	GOOD	NO GOOD	WASTE	SPECIAL NOTES
PREV.	0	0	0	0	
TODAY	1650	420	1070	160	
TO DATE	1650	420	1070	160	
2nd UNIT TO DATE					

No.	CAST	CHARACTER	W H S F R T TR	Makeup Wdbe.	Report on Set	Dismiss on Set	Out	In	Leave for Location	Arrive on Location	Leave Location P.U.·O.S.	Arrive at Studio	Actor / Actress Signature
1	William Shatner	Kirk	SW	9:30A	10A	6:18P	12N	1P					
5	Stephen Collins	Decker	SW	7:45A	9:30A	3:30P							
7	Walter Koenig	Chekov	SW	7:45A	9A	6:18P							
8	Nichelle Nichols	Uhura	SW	7:15A	9A								
9	George Takei	Sulu	SW	6A	9A		6:40/12N 2:10	1P					
12	Billy Van Zandt	Alien Ens'gn	SW	6A	7:30A	6:42P	6:30/1AM 7A	1P					
13	Momo Yashima	Technician	SW	7:15A	9A	6:18P	12N	1P					
14	Iva Lane	Technician	SW	7:15A	9A								
15	Ralph Brannen	Technician	SW	7:30A	9A								
15A	Franklyn Seales	Technician	SW	7:30A	9A								
16	Ralph Byers	Technician	SW	7:30A	9A								
-	John McKnight	Stunt Player	SWF	7:15A	8:15A	6:18P	12N	1P					

CAST — Contract and Day Players
Worked - W Rehearsal - R Finished - F
Started - S Hold - H Test - T
Travel - TR

WORK TIME / MEALS / TRAVEL TIME

EXTRA TALENT — MUSICIANS, ETC.

No.	Rate	Adj. To	O.T.	T.T.	Ward.	MPV	No.	Rate	Adj. To	O.T.	T.T.	Ward.	MPV
2	60.00		2.2										
3	60.00		2.0										
2	60.00		1.2										
13	60.00		1.7										

ASSISTANT DIR. _D. McCauley/D. Wise/K. Cremin_ UNIT MGR. _Phil Rawlins_

PRODUCTION: STAR TREK THE MOTION PICTURE DATE Mon. 8-7-78

NO.	ITEM	TIME	CHARGE	REMARKS
PRODUCTION				
	EXTRA ASST. DIRECTOR		705-04	
1	2ND ASST. DIRECTOR		705-04	
1	A.D. TRAINEE			
1	SCRIPT SUPERVISOR	7:30A	705-06	
	DIALOGUE COACH		620-05	
CAMERA				
1	CINEMATOGRAPHER	7A	710-01	
1	OPERATOR	7:30A	710-02	
1	ASSISTANT	7A	710-03	
1	ASSISTANT	7A	710-04	
	CAMERA		710-08	
	EXTRA OPERATOR		710-02	
	EXTRA ASSISTANT		710-04	
	STILL PHOTOGRAPHER	8A	710/920	
2	KEY GRIP	7A	725-01	
2	2ND GRIP	7A	725-01	
2	EXTRA GRIPS	7A	725-02	
	CRANE OPERATOR		725-03	
	CRAB DOLLY GRIP	7A	725-03	
	CRAB DOLLY		725-05	
	BOOM #		725-06	
1	CRAFT SERVICE	7A	725-11	
SET OPERATIONS				
	GREENS PERSON		725-13	
	PAINTER		725-14	
	PLUMBER		725-17	
	PROP. MAKERS		735-04	
4	SPEC. EFFECTS PERSON	7A	735-01-02	ALEX WELDON
	WIND MACH.		735-08	
	WARD. CHECK ROOM		725-23	
13	BENCHES FOR PEOPLE	7A	725-25	STG #10
	KNOCK DOWN SCH. ROOMS		725-23	
	KNOCK DOWN DR. ROOMS		725-23	
16	PORTABLE DR. ROOMS	7A	725-23	OUTSIDE STG #9
	HOOK-UP DR. ROOMS		725-21	INSIDE STG #10
	SCHOOLROOM TRAILERS		725-24	
	DRESSING RM. TRAILERS		725-24	
	BENCHES for PEOPLE 7A			STG #9
SOUND				
1	SOUND MIXER	7:30A	765-01	
1	MIKE OPERATOR	7:30A	765-02	
	SOUND RECORDER		765-03	
1	CABLE PERSON	7A	765-04	
	EXTRA CABLE PERSON		765-04	
	P.A. SYSTEM		765-06	
	PLAYBACK MACH. & OP.		765-07-05	
	SOUND SYSTEM		765	
PROPERTY				
1	PROPERTY PERSON	7A	750-01	
1	ASST. PROPERTY PERSON	7A	750-01	
	EXTRA ASST. PROP. PERSON		750-02	
1	SET DRESSER	7A	745-01	
1	LEAD PERSON	7A	745-02	
	DRAPERY PERSON		725-18	
	SWING GANG PERSONNEL		745-02	
	WARDROBE RACKS		725-25	
4	MAKE-UP TABLES/CHAIRS	7A	725-25	STG #10
	HAIR DRESSING TABLES		725-25	
	ANIMALS		750-06	
1	MAKE-UP TABLE	7A		STG #9
	HANDLERS		750-07	
10	FOLDING CHAIRS	7A		STG #10
	A.H.A. REPRESENTATIVE		750-07	
	WRANGLERS		750-07	
	WAGONS, ETC.		750-08	
WARDROBE				
1	COSTUMER FOR MALES	7A	755-01	
1	COSTUMER FOR FEMALES	7A	755-02	
2	EXTRA COST. FOR MALES	7A	755-03	
2	EXTRA COST. FOR FEMALES	7A	755-03	

NO.	ITEM	TIME	CHARGE	REMARKS
MAKE-UP				
1	MAKE-UP PERSON	7A	760-01	
2	EXTRA MAKE-UP PERSON	7A	760-02	
	BODY MAKE-UP PERSON		760-03	
1	HAIR STYLIST	7A	760-04	
	EXTRA HAIR STYLISTS		760-05	
1	BARBER	7:30A		RPT. STG #10
ELECTRICAL				
1	GAFFER	7A	730-01	
1	SECOND ELECTRICIAN	7A	730-01	
5	LAMP OPERATOR	7A	730-02	
	WIND MACHINE & OPERATOR		725-22	
	GENERATOR & OPERA.		730	
X	AIR COND.	7A	725-22	
	OPERATIONS PHONE		725-21	
	PORTABLE TELEPHONE		725-21	
X	WIG WAG	7A	725-21	OUTSIDE + INSIDE STG #?
	WORK LIGHTS		725-21	
POLICE & FIRE				
	FIRE CONTROL OFFICER		725/775	
	FIRE WARDEN LOC.		775	
	WHISTLE PERSON		725	
2	SET SECURITY PERSON	7A	725/775	
	CITY POLICE		775-02	
	STUDIO POLICE		725-15	
	MOTORCYCLE POLICE		775-02	
MISCELLANEOUS				
	FIRST AID		725/775	
	PROCESS EQUIPMENT		780	
	PROCESS CAMERA PERSON		780-02	
	PROCESS ASST. CAMERA PERSON		780-02	
1	PROCESS COORD.	7:30A	780-04	BILL HANSARD
	PROCESS ELECT.		780-04	
	PROJECTION MACHINE		780-08	
2	PROJECTIONIST	7A	780-03	
1	16 M.M. PROJ.	7A	785-01	
1	35 PROJ	7A		
MUSIC				
	PIANO		810-6	
	SIDELINE ORCHESTRA		810-6	
	SINGERS		810-6	
CATERER				
	HOT LUNCHES		775/790	
	BOX LUNCHES		775/790	
	DINNERS		775/790	OBLATH'S
5	GALLONS OF COFFEE	7A	775/790	DEL. STG #9
3	GALLONS: COFFEE	7A	775/790	
3	DOZEN DOUGHNUTS	7A	775/790	
TRANSPORTATION				
1	STANDBY DRIVER	7A	770/775	
2	STANDBY CAR	7A	770/775	
	CAMERA TRUCK		770/775	
	ELECTRIC TRUCK		770/775	
1	DRIVER CAPTAIN	7A	770/775	
	GENERATOR TRUCK		770/775	
	GRIP TRUCK		770/775	
	PROP. TRUCK		770/775	
	SPEC. EFFECTS TRUCK		770/775	
	SET DRESSING TRUCK		770/775	
	WARDROBE TRUCK/ TRAILER		770/775	
	WATER WAGON		770/775	
	SANITARY UNIT		775	
	TRUCKS		770/775	
1	MOTORHOME	7A		W. SLOTHER
	BUSSES:		770/775	
	PICTURE CARS		750-05	

MISC. NOTES _____

V'ger began as the relatively simple Voyager 6 sent out by 20th-century NASA. It was programmed to collect "all possible information" and upon a radio signal from NASA, transmit that data to Earth.

Voyager 6 was lost. It encountered a "black hole," was pulled in and emerged at a very distant point in our galaxy. It ultimately fell into the gravitational pull of an extremely large planet. Something on the surface of that planet became aware of its presence and pulled it from orbit for closer examination.

A machine cannot disobey programming, and when Voyager 6 was brought down and its programming examined, these magnificent machines (the inheritors of the planet) responded in the only way they were capable of responding to programming—they obeyed. "Learn all that is learnable," was NASA's command—and the machines obeyed [by fitting] V'ger with incredibly advanced measuring instruments and data-storage ability. They equipped Voyager 6 with the incredible power necessary to travel back across the entire galaxy, protecting itself and defending itself where necessary.

Voyager 6 has traveled for almost three centuries by the time the Enterprise meets it. It has been given the capacity to learn! Just as once happened to the first humans, Voyager 6 (now V'ger) has now become a conscious intelligent life-form. V'ger began to ask itself the most basic of questions: "What am I; what is my purpose; what is my future?" Like all reasoning beings, it saw God as the only imaginable source of such answers.

All life-forms have one common basic urge—to survive. V'ger could see that the delivery of its data would finish its very reason for existence. It began to plan a solution to that dilemma. It had come near to understanding the true shape of the Universe—it became aware of dimensions beyond the time and space in which it presently existed, and that it was almost ready to evolve into these higher dimensions of life. But something seemed to be missing.

What did V'ger lack that would make its further evolution possible? The answer must come from the Creator. Would the Creator provide the answer? Not necessarily. V'GER MUST CAPTURE GOD. If God contained all the answers, V'ger must acquire God's thought patterns. V'ger knew that God must be a machine—we all create God in our own image. V'ger must lure the Creator into its presence so that it could reduce the Creator to patterns and combine these with its own patterns.

Approaching Earth, V'ger became interested in the carbon-based units and had almost added their patterns to its data collection, but changed its mind when these units identified their home as the Creator's planet ahead. At first, V'ger had assumed that the message came from the Enterprise itself, but learned that the Enterprise was under the control of these carbon-based units. V'ger captured one of these units and fabricated a probe in that form.

Through the Ilia-probe V'ger hopes to gain some knowledge about the Creator which would be useful to V'ger's plan. Did the carbon-units serve some function for the Creator?

On arriving in Earth orbit, V'ger makes the programmed signal to the Creator. V'ger expects the Creator to respond with code which should unlock V'ger's data banks. However, V'ger has disconnected its Voyager 6 antenna so this code signal would not be received, forcing the Creator to bring the unlocking code to the part of it that is Voyager 6. But the Creator does not respond, and V'ger suspects the carbon-based units have taken control of the Creator.

V'ger's machine-logic concludes it must pattern and store all the units on the planet surface to free the Creator. At the same time, Decker's clever manipulation of the "Ilia"-probe has convinced V'ger that the Enterprise carbon-based units may have vital information concerning the Creator. V'ger decides to bring them into the presence of V'ger's primal beginnings.

In the end, we learn what that "something" is that V'ger needs in order to evolve any further. Knowledge and logic are not enough. No amount of logic can create a poem or a symphony. Human creativity and our ability to continue evolving are products of our emotions, our needs, our unhappiness, our fears, our sexual joys and repressions, our ambitions. It is the dirt under our toenails that enables us to dance. Those needs and disappointments and desires which we have always considered so weak, so shameful, and sometimes so ugly—they are the catalyst ingredients which make our (and V'ger's) souls possible.

GR—10/19/78

The long script rewriting nightmare was almost over. There certainly could be no other problems as horrendous as this one. Or could there?

7

Robert Wise

"A wise man's day is worth a fool's life."
—ARABIC PROVERB

If it weren't for the waves softly lapping at the shore, there would be dead silence. An occasional insomniac gull hunts for the first fish of the morning. Already the full moon is low on the western horizon, and in a couple of hours it will be moonset. The faint light which now dances along the rippling ocean will give way to a greater light in the east.

It's 4:30 in the morning, and Robert Wise and the few restless gulls are probably the only residents of Malibu's exclusive Trancas Beach who are awake at this ungodly hour. Quietly, so as not to disturb his wife Millicent's sleep, Bob crawls out of bed, heads downstairs to the kitchen to fix himself some eye-opening coffee, then climbs back upstairs to his study to begin addressing himself to the day's work ahead of him. After forty-six years in the business, including directing and/or producing thirty-eight motion pictures, it's a routine he's come to accept as a way of life.

He checks the call sheet for the scenes to be shot this day, September 5, 1978, then refers to his script for any notes he may have made about the scenes during previous readings. He consults his storyboards (scene concepts which have been drawn by production illustrator Maurice ["Zuby"] Zuberano) and begins thinking about how he would like to handle the scene, making notes of pertinent points to go over with the actors. Next he tries to organize his thinking as to how he might work in terms of continuity of shooting, i.e., the order which would cause the least amount of changing of setups of lighting and camera. He also makes notes for the staff and crew regarding extras who are coming in that day, props and things to discuss with property master Dick Rubin, notes for wardrobe, makeup, and special-effects people and just about everyone else who may be involved in that day's shooting. One of the keys to good directing, Bob Wise believes, is *anticipation.* "I believe there are two things that are very important to a director in terms of his making the whole operation go smoothly: anticipation and communication. I always try to anticipate the needs that I'm going to have that day on the set, and then I try to be sure that I communicate those needs to the right people on the staff."

By 7:00 Bob has finished his basic preparation, and he and his driver begin the forty-five-minute trip to Paramount. He arrives to find several actors already in makeup and most of the crew busy with the day's preparations. Today's scenes will be the first ones shot in the engine room, and are especially important because of the introduction of the set itself, and more importantly, it's the first time the audience will meet the new character, Willard Decker. Bob realizes that it's important for him to deliver the set as interestingly as possible, plus give Steve Collins a good, effective introduction.

Below is a page from Bob Wise's personal script. The notations you will see on this page were made by him as a guide to shooting today's sequence, a procedure he follows for every scene. Before filming begins (usually in those predawn hours at home), he carefully works out every detail including potential camera angles, emotions of the actors, number of camera setups needed, etc. He often goes to an actor's dressing room and reads the scene through with him or her even before arrival on the set, watching for "clinkers"—words in dialogue that don't feel right. Before the cameras are finally set up, he rehearses the scene eight to ten times before any film is actually shot.

In this particular case, the sequence is three pages long (one page of which is reproduced), covering scenes 70 through 75 and will take nearly two days to shoot. Bob explains his script notations and how he worked this sequence:

68 & 69 OMITTED 68 & 69 *

---

70 INT. ENGINEERING SECTION 70

KIRK ENTERS ON TOP LEVEL + WE GET OUR BIG P.O.V. SHOT DOWN THE SHAFT

The entire complex a beehive of pre-departure activity. ENGINEERING PERSONNEL (at least a third of them female) coming and going, the platform-elevators (small, one-man lifts to various levels) busy. A gentle but constant HUM and WHIRR flows from the engine core, to indicate a pre-idling mode. There will be continual AD LIBBED conversation among the Technicians. (Appendix B)

DOWN P.O.V. FROM KIRK'S ANGLE

Now the Engine Room door opens and Kirk steps into the area. He stands a moment observing the activity. ~~A grizzled ENGINEERING CHIEF pushes a huge condenser on an anti-grav device past Kirk with a respectful "watch it, sir" admonishment. Kirk moves on to:~~

DO IN KIRK'S CORRIDOR ENTRANCE SHOT

71 THE INTERMIX CHAMBER 71

CHECK CLEARY + 2ND TECH. IN RELATION TO OUR P.O.V. SHOT OF THE SHAFT. (ABOVE)

at the middle of the power shaft. Very NOISY here, and a continual CACOPHONY of COMPUTERIZED AND HUMAN VOICES calling off equipment checks. (See Appropriate Appendix.) And grouped around a section of burnt-out circuitry are WILLARD DECKER, Captain's stripes, handsome, in his early 30's; Scott, and two Technicians. Decker and Scott are working feverishly uncoupling the device, probing its innards. Decker has discovered the problem, removed several transistor-type parts, taps them with a pencil-sized sonic analyzer.

DECKER'S INTRO

DECKER
(quietly elated)
I KNEW IT-- ~~I thought so! See~~... the transporter sensor was not activated...

SCOTT
~~(impressed)~~
~~Aye, you were dead right about that~~...
(to Technician)
Cleary, put a back-up sensor into the unit.

SCOTT EXAMINES THE UNIT THEN GLANCES, IMPRESSED, AT DECKER - HE NODS

72 ACROSS THEM TO KIRK 72

as the Technician prepares to install the device, Scott glances up to see Kirk.

WORK OUT THIS BUSINESS

(CONTINUED)

I wanted to deliver the engineering section, with Kirk's entrance, in the most effective visual way possible. We have a long, three-story-high engine core, surrounded by the other parts of the engine room, and the only way I could really deliver that to the fullest effect was from the top floor. So I changed Kirk's entrance into the engineering section from the second floor (which is the main operating floor) to the top floor so that I could have him come over to the edge of the core and look down. We got a marvelous point-of-view of what he sees down below thanks to the painted backing. The shot shows all three existing levels plus further levels which were painted on the backing, making it look like this core is actually six or eight floors in depth. That's why my script note on the top left of the page reads "Kirk enters on top level and we get our big POV (Point of View) shot down the shaft." I've also indicated this again on the right-hand side of the page—"Down POV from Kirk's angle."

Next I cut the original scene of "A grizzled ENGINEERING CHIEF pushes a huge condenser on antigrav device, etc." because there was no way to do that in the set and still bring Kirk in on the top floor. In order to expand on this and also use our corridors, I brought Kirk down our corridor and into the engine room top level floor. I used the Engineering Chief and antigravity device in that shot before Kirk actually walked into the engine room, working this into the shot in Kirk's corridor entrance. (Script notation on right-hand side: "Do in Kirk's Corridor entrance shot.")

My next notation (left side of the page, below scene number 71) reads "Check Cleary and 2nd Tech. in relation to our POV shot of the shaft (above)." I had to shoot my point of view later, and I had to be sure just where these two people (Cleary and Technician) were going to be in relation to that POV which I shot later, even though it came earlier in this sequence. I needed to know where they were going to be so I could put them in the right spot here. Bringing Kirk in this way also gave me an opportunity to have him get in the little one-man elevator and ride down to the main (second) floor. After the POV he moved across that set, got in the elevator and came down. As the elevator started down, I preceded it with the camera to introduce Decker and Scott in the middle of this scene, talking about the problem with the transporter sensor. The note "Decker's Intro" is just a reminder to myself that this is the first time we see him, and to give him a good, effective introduction in which we get a close-up on him and establish him that way.

Here's a case in point where we changed the dialogue on the set. It seemed to play better for Decker to say "I knew it" than the original line "I thought so!" He seemed to feel more comfortable with that line, and often lines are changed that way on the set. Next we worked in "A faulty module." We felt the line "Aye, you were dead right about that" was a little bit too much so we added "Scott examines the unit, then glances, impressed at Decker—he nods," and also the word "new" to precede backup sensor. Finally on this page, I've added a little note to myself "Work out this business" in regard to the Technician installing the device. This action was going to get in the way of the scene between Kirk (just coming off the elevator), Scott and Decker, so I had him go off to get a new module and later return to install it.

Bob later explained that the horizontal line across the top of the page simply indicates to him that this begins a totally new sequence. The vertical line down the center was added after the scenes had been shot, indicating that these scenes were now completed. Underlinings highlight important things to emphasize, plus sound effects which will be added later.

On the set, Bob Wise is often referred to as "Boss," although this is not a reflection on his temperament. The stage is the director's bailiwick, and the term is merely one of respect. Actually, everyone, without exception, had nothing but the highest praises for Bob. Actors adored him because of his ability to elicit their finest performances. He is a man of great patience; should a "take" not be to his liking, he would always have a kind word for the actors: "That was fine; let's try one more." His secretary of fifteen years, Esther Hoff, describes her boss as a "creative, down-to-earth human who treats everybody as a human being. He's a thoughtful, considerate perfectionist who demands the finest work but accepts mistakes cheerfully. People are apt to get up on a soapbox and extol his virtues. Once in Japan, Zuby was asked by someone what Robert Wise was like. Zuby hopped up on his soapbox, and the gentleman, after hearing Zuby's description said earnestly, 'Your Mr. Wise sounds like Jesus Christ.' "

Associate producer Jon Povill also described this unusual man: "The thing that makes Bob the great director that he is, is his very approachableness, his willingness to listen to your ideas and use them if they're in keeping with what he wants to do. The tremendous number of problems on this picture would have had any other director in town being carried off to the funny farm, completely blowing his top. Bob kept his cool and came through with flying colors."

The most interesting tribute to his patience on *Star Trek* came from the people he worked with daily—the cast, crew, and other workers on the set. It is not uncommon on motion pictures to organize all sorts of pools. In the case of *Star Trek,* sound mixer Tommy Overton devised a very unique pool. People were asked to place their bets and guess *the date of the very first time Bob Wise would lose his temper!* As month after month went by more and more people began to wonder if this would ever happen, and indeed, it never did. At the end of filming, Tommy cheerfully refunded everyone's money.

It's easy to see why Bob is so well thought of by everyone in the profession. Even his appearance is one of gentleness. His face seems to exude serenity, the white hair combed in bangs giving him the appearance of a Roman senator. He speaks very softly, almost inaudibly, in face-to-face conversation, the clear blue eyes behind the bifocals constantly remaining in contact with his listener. At sixty-five, he's kept himself trim and fit and wouldn't dream of even thinking of retirement. He's much too young and active for that, and according to his wife, Milly, he comes to life when he's on the set.

Bob was born September 10, 1914, in Winchester, Indiana, the son of a meat packer. As a youngster, he became a movie fan, sitting in the dime matinees Saturday after Saturday. From this early interest stemmed his desire to become a part of the magic he saw on the screen, giving him the creative urge that launched his directorial career.

The future film director was also interested in journalism, but his father's business suffered in the depression and he was unable to continue his studies. His brother, David, then an accountant with RKO Studios, managed to get Bob a job as a messenger in the studio's cutting department.* He was fascinated by the way movies were cut and patched together, and was often permitted to try his hand at the art. After nine months, he was made an apprentice sound-effects cutter, spending long hours over the Moviola. He recalls one period when he worked for a seventy-two-hour stretch, with only two hours sleep, to help get George Stevens's *Alice Adams* ready for a sneak preview.

Once during a slack period, Bob pulled out thousands of feet of film the studio had shot in the South Seas for a movie that was later abandoned, and with sound-effects cutter T. K. Woods, he spent hours putting together a ten-minute short subject. The studio was delighted, rewarding him with a $500 bonus—and his first film credit.

More important editing assignments gradually came his way, including one with Orson Welles on the classic *Citizen Kane*. The skill and imagination Bob demonstrated led him to Welles's *The Magnificent Ambersons,* and to an unexpected opportunity. While Welles was doing a film in South America as part of the U.S. Government's good-neighbor policy, it was discovered from previews that *Ambersons* needed some added scenes to be filmed in order to make the picture

---

*Ironically, his *Star Trek* office was located just a few feet away from the same building where he began his life's work. RKO later became Desilu, which in turn became Paramount property.

play properly. In the absence of Welles, Bob was selected to direct the needed scenes.

Soon Bob was bombarding studio executives with requests to direct. In 1943 he was editing *Curse of the Cat People* when its director, far behind schedule, was removed. Bob was given the job, the movie became a hit, and he was firmly established as a director.

For the next few years, he brought something more than routine treatment to otherwise routine "B" pictures. Then, in 1947, he and producer Theron Warth did such a good job of preparing *Blood on the Moon* that its budget was increased way beyond that normally assigned to a western. Studio production chief Dore Schary withstood pressure to have a better-known director assigned the film. When *Blood on the Moon* became a critical and financial success, Bob Wise was established as a top-flight director.

His films during the following ten years included such critical and box office successes as *The Set-up; The Day the Earth Stood Still; The Desert Rats; Executive Suite; Tribute to a Bad Man; Somebody Up There Likes Me; Run Silent, Run Deep; So Big,* and *I Want to Live!*

In 1959 Bob was approached by the Mirisch Corporation and asked to produce and direct the film version of *West Side Story,* the hit Broadway musical. He agreed on the condition that Jerome Robbins, who had directed the Broadway production, work with him. To Hollywood's surprise, the codirection plan worked—and *West Side Story* won ten Academy Awards, including two to Bob Wise for production and direction.

Bob followed with *Two for the Seesaw* and *The Haunting,* and was preparing *The Sand Pebbles* when Twentieth Century-Fox asked him to take over production and direction on *The Sound of Music.* Knowing that *The Sand Pebbles* could not get under way for almost a year, Bob accepted the musical as a coproduction with his independent company, Argyle Enterprises. Two years later, while on *The Sand Pebbles* location in Hong Kong in 1966, Bob was at sea aboard the gunboat U.S.S. *San Pablo* when he received the word that he had won the Academy Award as best director on *The Sound of Music.* The film also won him the Oscar for best picture, and additional Oscars were garnered for best sound, best editing, and best scoring.

Recent films have included *Star!, The Andromeda Strain, Two People, The Hindenburg,* and *Audrey Rose. Star Trek* marks Bob's thirty-eighth motion picture in this distinguished career which includes an unusually broad range of films—everything from science fiction and musicals, to horror and docudrama.

His leisure-time activities center around spectator sports and reading, but his main interest is in his chosen profession. He's very active in the Academy of Motion Picture Arts and Sciences (which, in addition to his other Oscars, has also awarded him the prestigious Irving G. Thalberg Award). He served on the Academy's Board of Governors, and produced the Oscar presentations one year. He's also a past president of the Directors Guild of America, and takes a personal interest in young people who exhibit enthusiasm for working in the business, much as he did in his early days. On *Star Trek—The Motion Picture* he played host to three trainee/interns—A.F.I. director intern Rick Fichter, assistant director trainee Kevin Cremin, and a young Israeli filmmaker, Uri Pollack. His enthusiasm has carried over into his own family too; his son, Robert A. Wise, served as assistant cameraman on *Star Trek—The Motion Picture,* his nephew Doug Wise (the son of brother David, who still handles all of Bob's business affairs) was *Star Trek*'s second assistant director, and even Millicent Wise managed to get into the act, appearing as an extra in the Rec Deck scene.

Bob's numerous speaking engagements around the country were responsible for his first meeting with Gene Roddenberry. Both were guests at a science fiction seminar given by the University of Arizona a few years ago. After the session, they began talking and discovered they had a mutual respect for each other. They decided that it would be fun to work together sometime—never suspecting this might actually happen sooner than either expected.

Late in 1977, the then planned *Star Trek II* television series fell apart, and Paramount decided to make use of that script and those sets in a science fiction movie with a medium sized film budget of around $7 or $8 million. But *Star Wars* had opened now and its box office grosses kept spiraling higher and higher, and *Close Encounters of the Third Kind* opened to considerable film industry excitement in December of that year. By now, every studio in town had a large epic science fiction film on the drawing boards, Paramount became more and more certain that this established and proven property *they* owned, *Star Trek,* deserved to be a major film event. The budget was revised drastically upward, reaching the point where the studio began to seek a major motion picture director. Based on Paramount's assurance that *Star Trek*'s tv movie director Robert Collins would not be neglected by the studio, Gene agreed to consider the prospective list of top film directors. One name jumped off the page—ROBERT WISE.

After Bob was signed, he and Gene discovered that their thinking tended to run along the same lines. Much of the discussion over the script's underlying meaning centered over the concepts of the Creator. Both men found that they had their own concepts of God which did not embrace any orthodox religions, with leanings toward Eastern philosophies. Both also shared an unorthodox view of humanity and the universe in relation to God. For example, when the idea of having a chaplain aboard the *Enterprise* was brought up, the producer-director team found themselves agreeing that the whole idea was distasteful to them. Gene's feelings were that in the 23rd century, not only would you have all the religions of Earth (if they were still around), but you might pick up a dozen or more new ones with every planet in the Federation too. If there were to be a chaplain reflecting each religion, there would be no room on the *Enterprise* for crew members. Gene believed, and Bob concurred, that the people in that century would be mature enough to handle their own religious needs without daily help from chaplains.

Most of the problems were not as easily solved, but together Bob and Gene were able to work out most of the production difficulties. Perhaps the greatest problem facing Bob was the fact that the script wasn't completed when shooting began. There were diverging opinions about certain aspects of some scenes, and characters needed further development. According to Bob Wise, "Anytime you start without a complete script on any picture and have to write as you go along, it's going to be difficult."

Another big problem was dealing with the mechanical effects on the set. Often this involved the seventeen small monitor screens at the various bridge stations, which utilized individual projectors for each monitor. Keying them properly was time consuming, and there were continual breakdowns in equipment. In fact, Bob found that there were more mechanical malfunctions throughout this picture than on any other film he has ever done. He claims that his very effective SF film, *The Day the Earth Stood Still,* was simple compared to the technical difficulties on *Star Trek.*

One of Bob's most valuable coworkers is Maurice Zuberano. Zuby has served as Bob's production illustrator for many years, and thanks

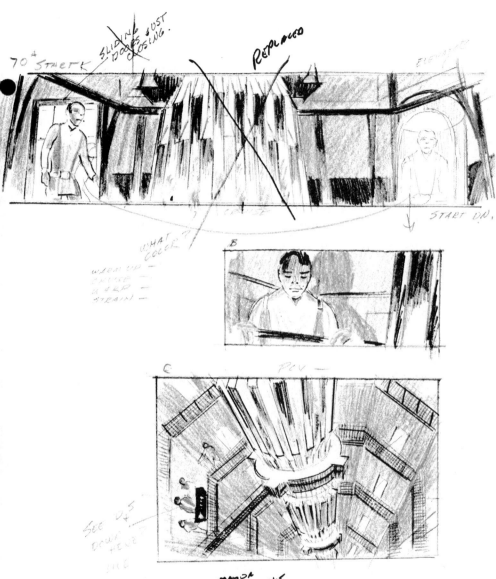

to his invaluable help, many of the production problems on *Star Trek—The Motion Picture* were much more easily dealt with. Zuby and Bob have known each other since the early days at RKO, when Bob was a cutter and Zuby worked as a set designer on Fred Astaire's and Ginger Rogers' big dance numbers in *Gay Divorcee* and *Top Hat.* Zuby stayed at RKO for sixteen years, and recalls that during the time he spent there he watched a little sapling outside his window grow into a massive tree which blocked his window view. Finally, he could no longer see who was coming into the building, and he realized it was time to move on. Since then, he's worked on twelve pictures with Bob Wise.

The soft-spoken, shy man with a very dry wit describes himself as an extension of the director, almost an alter ego. His work is like writing up a diary, in advance, and the storyboards he prepares for Bob are saved in a notebook which could very well be considered a diary of the movie. He explains his job as "understanding the director's problems. You have to make believe that *you're* doing it, and then just hope that you come somewhere near the director." Based on preplanning meetings with Bob Wise, Zuby figures out the composition of the people in the scene, the lighting and camera angles and so on, then draws his concept of each camera setup as an aid to Bob. One of his pictures is worth at least *ten* thousand words, as you can see from the following example of the scene described earlier in this chapter.

Let's return now for a moment and see what's happening with that scene. It's two days later and this sequence has been completed to Bob Wise's satisfaction. He sinks back, exhausted, in the passenger seat of his studio car as the driver begins the long drive back to Trancas. Later, he'll unwind over dinner, two drinks—no more, no less—watch a little "telly," as he calls it, and head for bed early, ready to begin all over the next morning at 4:30 A.M. Although he'll be involved with *Star Trek* for at least another year, he's still thinking ahead to future projects. "My dad retired at about my age, and since he didn't have any special hobbies, he practically went out of his mind," Bob recalls. "He told me, 'Bob, whatever you do, don't ever retire.' If I ever do retire, I would want to be actively involved in organizations, in travel—but I will never retire to play golf or sit on the front porch. As long as there are projects to do and people want me to do them, and my health holds up, I'll do them."

8

Ars Gratia Artis

Harold Michelson is not a superstitious man. Yet he became convinced on that warm spring day down in Alabama that there really are such things as fate and predestination.

It began with a phone call from Robert Wise. Harold had already worked with Bob on a film called *Two People,* but he felt his knees growing weak when he heard Bob's offer. He had to ask if he could call back—the overwhelmingly eerie feeling of déjà vu was making it difficult for him to think clearly about the decision he now had to make.

The day before the call, Harold and some of the others in the movie company of *The Ravagers* had been invited to Huntsville for a tour of the space shuttle *Enterprise,* which was making a stop at the Huntsville NASA Space Center en route to its Florida destination. His natural curiosity got the best of him and he found he was quite enthralled with this spaceship perched piggyback atop a 747. As the tour guide pointed out the black ceramic tile on the nose of the ship which can withstand heat up to 1,200 degrees, all aspects of this new toy suddenly became amazing to Harold. But best of all was his actual firsthand look at the *inside* of America's first true spaceship. By the time the tour was over, Harold was hooked on space. As soon as possible he went to the space museum in Huntsville and began buying every book about space and spaceships he could lay his hands on.

Production Designer Harold Michelson.

He was back in his hotel room the next day, looking over some of these books about his new passion when Bob Wise's call came. Would he be interested in being production designer on *Star Trek—The Motion Picture?* His first task—to begin redesign on the sets of the starship *Enterprise*! He recovered, returned Bob's call, and by May 1978 the only person from *Star Trek* who had ever actually been aboard the real *Enterprise* was at work on its namesake.

Harold and his newly hired art department became heirs to the semicomplete *Enterprise* sets which had been begun by art director Joe Jennings in the summer of 1977—sets that conformed almost exactly to Matt Jefferies's original design for the sixties television show. Construction on stage 9 had been shut down five months before, after a halt had been called on the new television series. Joe had done a fine job of designing for the television show, and now it was up to Harold to completely redesign these sets so that they fit the then budgeted $15 million, 70mm production wide-screen motion picture.

He began with the bridge, the nerve center of the *Enterprise,* whose basic framework was now completed. Because the bridge is primarily a circular set, this symmetrical, curved design had to be given a different look. Harold began by eliminating the television-designed weapons defense station. Chekov's new weapons section was to be a huge plastic bubble already grafted onto a cutaway section of bridge wall. The Russian lieutenant would have sat at this station and looked out toward space while neon-lit crosshairs contained within the bubble tracked and locked onto a target. Harold had the bubble removed and the round hole that remained was sealed shut and covered over with various technical readouts. Bob Wise had asked that Chekov's attitude be toward the *Enterprise*'s main viewer—difficult to do on a circular bridge. But there was one area in the corner which had been sculpted slightly differently. (No one seemed quite sure just what was supposed to have gone there; many joked that it was the ship's elusive "head"— something the original series had conspicuously lacked.) Bob Wise spotted the potential of this corner and production illustrator Michael Minor designed a completely new look for this area, which became the new (and present) home of Chekov's weapons defense station.

Another Michelson innovation is the ceiling on the bridge. His inspiration this time came from the look of a jet engine fan. Mike Minor's artistic talents were again utilized in the center bubble he designed for this ceiling. The basic idea behind this was, according to

Mike, to give the bridge something of a human touch. A starship really would have no need of a gyroscopic device, which is essentially what the bubble appears to be. Therefore, *voilà,* the center bubble became sophisticated equipment telling the captain precisely what was happening to the ship's attitude, and completely corrected and adjusted to the fact that there is no "up" or "down"—not even really any "sideways"—in actual space terms. It became all of that because the wonderful world of movies is a sensible world in which everything works the way the writer, producer, and director *need* them to work! During the wormhole sequence this device can be seen in operation as its tilting lights indicate something drastically amiss—which was the whole point of building the bubble in the first place.

Almost all of the consoles on the bridge were already in place, having been begun by graphic designer Lee Cole back on the aborted tv series. Lee stayed on for the movie, and is also responsible for all of the visual artwork on the *Enterprise* and Klingon bridges—the panels on the walls, the schematics, the logo designs, and many of the monitor screen readouts. According to Lee, if you hooked up the bridge consoles to a real nacelle engine, you could probably fly a starship! Lee should know; she once worked on circuitry design for nuclear submarines, and worked her way through UCLA by wiring some of TRW's on-board computers on the Apollo moon flights. And, like Harold Michelson, she too had her own déjà vu *Enterprise* experience: Next door to her office at Rockwell International, where Lee worked prior to coming to the *Star Trek* art department, was a one-quarter scale mock-up of the space shuttle *Enterprise*!

As a continuity guide to the series writers, and later for all of the actors, Lee prepared a U.S.S. *Enterprise Flight Manual.* This forty-four-page book describes each console on the ship, down to the last button. The control panels are activated by the touch of an actor's fingertips to the heat-sensitive plates, so it was necessary for all of the main cast to be familiar with the sequences at each of their stations.

Probably Lee's biggest contribution to the bridge was the hundreds of monitor screen films she produced. The monitors at each station give vital information to Spock, Uhura, and the others—everything from readings on subspace communications to the most complex matter and antimatter engine formulas. These oval bridge monitors are rear-projecting screens on which super 8mm and 16mm film "loops" (continually repeating one- and two-minute films) provide images to produce the special effect. The production originally acquired some forty-two such films from a company called STOMAR Enterprises in Arlington, Virginia. The talented owner, Marc Chinoy, flew to California on the recommendation of Jesco von Puttkamer, and returned to his Virginia studio where he made an exciting group of bridge monitor film loops and managed to get them shipped back to Hollywood in time for the first day of shooting. It was time consuming and difficult dealing with a company so far from the production. When Marc's footage was exhausted after only a few weeks of *Star Trek* filming, it became clear that new monitor films would be needed faster than any outside supplier could deliver them. Lee Cole, Mike Minor, and another production illustrator, Rick Sternbach, working together with Jon Povill, began devising even faster ways of shooting new footage. For example, one day Lee and Jon went to an electronics store and rented the use of their oscilloscope for the day. Using a camera they had brought along, they put the oscilloscope through its paces. The store's owner apologetically explained that the machine wasn't functioning properly. But that sort of distortion gave Jon and Lee exactly what they wanted. Other loops came from the Los Alamos computer experimental labs in New Mexico, Long Beach Hospital, and the University of California at San Diego. About fifteen new loops came from Spectrum, a local visual-effects company. Lee herself went to the Jet Propulsion Lab and filmed her own computer graphics, adding to ones obtained through JPL contacts. In all, there were nearly two hundred different pieces of monitor footage, making up a seven-page catalogue listing. Some of these sound so intriguing that they almost make interesting movies in their own right: fountain; waves with green scanner; orange gases; aurora ball, energy burst; universe—live action; asteroid laboratory; planet rotations; multicolored ovals; prism streaks; upward purple streaks; lazy laser ring; and planet explosion in cube.

A very noticeable change on the bridge was the design of the new seats. Gone are the simple pedestal swivel seats of the early tv series. Gone too is the boxlike original captain's seat. Harold Michelson's redesigned *Enterprise* seats have automatic bracing devices, which operate at the touch of a switch to fold in over the person's lower body, keeping him in place in case the starship is shaken by Klingon torpedo fire or some unusual space turbulence. (Ralph Nader's great-great-great-great-grandson can rest easy!) Harold and set decorator Linda

DeScenna designed the backs of the seats in vertebraelike sections, which would massage and calm one's nerves at the touch of another button and, according to Harold, three hundred years from now aspirin won't be necessary because the seats can even stop a headache!

The bridge seats were covered in a very unusual fabric—girdle material! This unusual cloth may indeed become the fabric of the future because of its remarkable several-direction stretching capacity, as well as its ability to dye easily. It was also used to cover all of the furniture in Kirk's quarters, including his bunk bed and desk seats. And the undyed version of this material can be seen covering the beds in sickbay.

When Gene Roddenberry wrote the new *Writers'/Directors' Guide* for *Star Trek II,* his description of the changes aboard the *Enterprise* included the following reminder: "Yes, it is the *Enterprise,* and even lovelier than before." One of the most striking examples of this kind of change is to be found in the redesigned engine room, and it's easy to see why Scotty's idea of a good time is to cozy up to his "wee bairns" (engines).

As Harold Michelson began to work on his conception of the *Enterprise*'s engine room, he strived to be consistent with the theory behind the *Enterprise*'s propulsion systems, structuring the set so that its appearance would match the corresponding area visible in exterior views of the *Enterprise* itself.

Most obvious are the *Enterprise*'s outboard nacelles, those two cylindrical objects mounted on the struts radiating upward from the engineering section. These nacelles use matter and antimatter for propulsion—the annihilation of dual matter creating the fantastic power required to warp space and exceed the speed of light.

The *Enterprise* has a secondary propulsion system also. These are impulse power engines located at the rear of the saucer section. Impulse engines function as a backup system, and operate on an action-reaction principle such as a rocket or jet engine. Vessel speed, when using the impulse engines, is, of course, less than the speed of light. In case of total failure of all engine power sources, the vessel's gravitational and life-support systems can be switched to battery power, with a full-load capacity of about one week.

Hyperlight speeds, or space warp speeds, are measured in *warp factors,* and the ship's propulsion system is termed *warp drive. Warp factor one* is the speed of light—186,000 miles per second, or somewhat over 600 million miles per hour.* If the old *Enterprise* went above warp seven, Scotty could be counted on to let loose a stream of Scottish epithets. On the newly refitted *Enterprise,* however, he can relax a bit. Maximum safe speed is now warp nine. At velocities past warp nine the vessel begins to show considerable strain and nine-plus speeds are used only in emergencies.

Harold Michelson wanted the engine room to seem vast, not easily accomplished on a sound stage that already held the basic structure of the set. To achieve the great depths that the engine room appears to have on the screen, he had his art department staff work on various designs which would utilize "forced perspective." Set designers Lewis Splittgerber, Richard McKenzie, Dan Maltese, Marit Monsos, and Al Kemper drafted the plans with mathematical precision based on Hal's original designs.

A set designer is like an architect—he translates the art director's designs into feet and inches so that the studio's mill can accurately measure out the materials needed for the construction workers. The studio's carpenters then follow these blueprints to the letter. Lewis Splittgerber, one of the set designers, recalled that the engine room seemed the most difficult. Lew and the other designers have to be mathematicians, as well as artists, and in *ST—TMP* this skill proved handy in applying the principles of forced perspective to the plans for the engine room. You've seen the film and you remember that the engine room is about two blocks long, right? Wrong! It is really *only forty feet long!* To achieve this look, the floor slanted upward and narrowed, three very small actors of graduated height—three, four, and five feet tall—were used as extras in the shot to give the appearance of being far from the camera, and a large backdrop gave added dimension to the far wall. Backings were also used for the bottom floor in the "down shot" of the engine core, giving the impression of infinity.

Scenic artist Benny Resella, of J. C. Backings Company, supplied *Star Trek* with most of the backings in the picture. Benny is well known in the industry as the "spine" of J. C. Backings, Hollywood's leading backing supplier. In addition to the engine room backings, Benny furnished the company with the 24-by-100-foot backing visible

---

*Note: Warp factors two, three, four, etc., are based upon a geometrical formula of light velocity. The speed in miles per hour is actually the cube of the warp factor times the speed of light, e.g., warp two is eight times the speed of light; warp three is twenty-seven times the speed of light, and so on.

through the rec deck balcony ports, and the paintings at the end of straight *Enterprise* corridors, which visually tripled their length.

Redesign of the *Enterprise*'s corridors was another major area of Harold Michelson's responsibility. When he came on the picture, the corridors were of straight plywood construction in the style of the original tv show—something Gene Roddenberry calls "Des Moines Holiday Inn style." In order to get away from this hotel corridor look, Harold modified the perfectly straight up and down walls and with a major movie budget was able to give them an angular, bent look. During preproduction meetings with Gene Roddenberry and Bob Wise (the two had final approval on all plans), they decided that in three hundred years, lighting need not be overhead, so they had the lighting radiate upward from the floor to give it a more interesting feeling. Naturally all these changes became examples of the *Enterprise*'s refitting in drydock, so that the differences from the television *Enterprise* were believably explained. Unusual looks were achieved through varied lighting, so that the same stretch of corridor would be used to represent different decks of the ship. As in the television series, the look of different ship's decks was achieved by redressing the corridors, since it would be wasteful to build additional lookalike corridors. For example, the aluminum panels outside Kirk's quarters were covered with a soft orange ultrasuede selected by Linda DeScenna, and suddenly we're in a completely different part of the ship—outside Ilia's quarters.

Kirk's quarters (and later Ilia's quarters) were designed by art director Leon Harris, Harold's right-hand man. Leon and Harold had worked together on many pictures; the two men even went to art school together, and have known each other for more than thirty years. Leon worked as an illustrator for Robert Wise on *The Sound of Music* and felt right at home with the *Star Trek* group. Remember the captain's quarters on the television series? Poor Kirk, his tv cabin had such a tiny, narrow bed that one marvels that he acquired quite a reputation as a galactic womanizer! (Perhaps more a tribute to his agility.) At any rate, one of the first things Gene Roddenberry decided he wanted for the new *Star Trek* was larger, less cramped quarters for Kirk. So Kirk's cabin mattress is double size, although the advantages of these new dimensions remain yet to be proved, perhaps in sequels. The captain's quarters also now boast a sonic shower, a separate office area, complete with his own wall-sized viewscreen, conference table with four modular seats, sofa, communications board, and other consoles. Again, all of the furniture is covered in that futuristically stretchable girdle fabric.

Set decorator Linda DeScenna credits her "lead man" (the person responsible for seeing that her decorating designs were properly carried out) with making her work go so smoothly. Mike Huntoon always had a ready smile for everyone. His sense of humor made the thin, twenty-six-year-old blond young man a favorite of the art department and the members of the *Star Trek* softball team. Mike had a lifelong battle with heart disease, and during the production stage of the film, he suffered a fatal heart attack. The special camaraderie of this film company had already been evident in its recognition of Mike Huntoon as a special person, and could be seen again in the sincere mourning of his death.

One of the most interesting of the *Enterprise* sets is the transporter. Known as the transporter room in the television series, this set and the idea behind it intrigued art director Harold Michelson more than any other. The original idea behind the transporter was economy of time. In the weekly television series, it would have been impossibly costly to show the *Enterprise* landing on each planet it visited. Gene Roddenberry decided that the only practical option was to have the starship's landing parties "beam down" to each planet. One need only step onto a platform of the transporter, wait while a technician at a console operates certain controls which convert matter into energy and beam that energy to predetermined coordinates—a planet's surface, inside a building on a planet, another ship in space, or wherever desired. At that destination, the beamed energy is then converted back into its original pattern of matter, becoming again *exactly* the same person and/or objects which had been beamed. McCoy has a particular dread of this device, claiming that "scrambling a person's molecules" is unnatural.

In the movie, the transporter is more than just a convenient room and device. Harold Michelson believed that any machine capable of matter-energy conversion should *look* and *feel* awesomely powerful. One of the best ways to show this was that the person operating this powerful and improved new transporter device must be shielded from the fearsome forces at work when beaming is under way. Just as today's X-ray technicians have learned to protect themselves with lead vests and other radiation shielding, Harold incorporated in his new design a sealed control room, in effect a "container" from which the transporter operators can observe and control the transporter platform itself. Between operators and platform, the rest of the room was filled with a complex of machinery, a look that cinematographer Richard Kline enhanced with highly effective eerie lighting.

Another elaborate area of the ship is the medical complex, which includes labs, offices, scanning room, and the actual hospital, or sickbay. Just outside McCoy's office there is a refrigerator wall containing perishable cultures. Assistant art director, John Cartwright, who has known Robert Wise for many years (his daughter, Angela, was in *The Sound of Music*) was responsible for an inside joke involving the containers for these cultures. If you were to look *very* quickly and closely at the labeling on them, you would see:

CRYOGENICS DIVISION

CULTURES—FROZEN CYTO

ANDROMEDA STRAIN

Even Bob Wise did not notice this as the name of one of his famous science-fiction films *(The Andromeda Strain)* until someone from the crew finally pointed it out.

One of the most interesting areas of the medical complex is the scanning table, a totally new conception never before seen on the *Enterprise*. The script gives no insight as to what kind of table was needed, as you can see from the following script extract:

257   CLOSE SHOT OF THE EXAMINING ROOM VIEWER   257

scanning a "body." PULL BACK TO SHOW McCoy, Chapel, Kirk, Spock and Chekov—standing over "Ilia," who lies prone on the table, the physicians moving the scanner over her.

The scene runs less than a page, and appears only briefly on the screen, yet its translation from printed word into actual set required a great deal of technical research, and is another example of how *Star Trek* has always stressed scientific accuracy. Mike Minor is responsible for much of this scanning table. Mike was senior illustrator on the picture, and has been involved in the area of science-fiction illustration for a number of years. He's another alumnus of the original *Star Trek* television series; among the things he created for that program were the look of the Melkotians in "Spectre of the Gun," the effect for the evil force in "The Day of the Dove," and much of the design of the web in "The Tholian Web." Mike also worked as set designer on Gene Roddenberry's *Planet Earth,* and had also worked with some of the explosive-effects people on *Star Wars.*

Art director Michelson had a concept of a medical examining table on which something would move along as it "scanned" a body. Mike Minor drew up a "noodle" (a rough sketch) from which the design was later finalized. Thanks to Lee Cole and her knowledge in this area, the concept delved into an area of medicine that is only now being charted by modern medicine—the area of tomography.* An outlined image of "Ilia's" body was rear-projected on a screen behind the table, and with special-effects lighting techniques, the scan over the real body (face up, not *prone* as in the script) was matched precisely along this projection. An indication of the speed with which everyone was working is the fact that it took only three weeks to prepare for this highly interesting scene.

Once the redesign of the *Enterprise* sets was complete, Harold Michelson was able to turn his attention to the other much needed sets, all of which required original designs. One of these was the rec deck, requiring an entire stage (stage 8), completely replacing a small recreation room which had been built on stage 10 for the planned television series. This was the largest interior set in the film. The twenty-four-foot-high set was used in a scene which required over three hundred people and which was decorated with 107 pieces of specially designed built-in furniture.

The rec deck offered another of the many subtleties included in the movie. Below the huge viewing screen there is a group of decorative art illustrations with brief histories of the various ships which have had the name *Enterprise.* The first illustration (left to right) depicts an actual U.S. Navy sailing frigate of that name; the second shows the World War II carrier U.S.S. *Enterprise;* the third, NASA's space shuttle *Enterprise;* since this was 23rd-century art work, the fourth illustration is of the very first starship U.S.S. *Enterprise* (never seen on television, but according to Gene Roddenberry, who supplied the sketch, it is a forerunner of the vessel we all know), and the fifth, the

---

*Three dimensional X-ray tomography and thermagram X-ray footage was acquired from Dr. William Glenn, head of tomography at Long Beach Memorial Hospital, and much of this footage was used on various monitor screens throughout the medical complex.

starship U.S.S. *Enterprise* as she appeared before refitting. This bit of *Enterprise* history was based on a fan suggestion:

TO: MATT JEFFERIES   DATE: SEPT. 9, 1977

FROM: GENE RODDENBERRY   SUBJECT: ENTERPRISE
                                      SHUTTLECRAFT PLAQUE

Some fans have suggested that our new Enterprise should carry a plaque somewhere which commemorates the fact it was named after the first space shuttle launched from Earth in the 1970's.
  This is an intriguing idea. It also has publicity advantages if properly released at the right time. It won't hurt NASA's feelings either. I'll leave it to you where you want it on the vessel and who should design it.

Another major construction job was the *V'ger* set—an intriguing piece of architecture which was referred to by various nicknames such as "the Coliseum" (Gene Roddenberry's term) and "the microwave wok" (sound mixer Tommy Overton). Whatever it was called, it was as unusual a set as any ever created for a movie. Leon Harris worked on this design, which took only four and a half weeks from inception to completion of construction, an unusually large and complex set to be completed in such a short time. The set is usable through a full 360-degree circle, although it does have "wild" sections that can be pulled back for better camera access to the set's center. An artist's mind is revealed in Leon Harris's own set of descriptive terms—"a modern technological Stonehenge in a cathedral-like setting."

In all, eleven of Paramount's thirty-two sound stages were used on *Star Trek—The Motion Picture*—more than for any other film ever done there—and many of these stages were used several times when new sets were created. According to Gene Kelley, construction coordinator, *Star Trek* utilized stages 2, 6, 7, 8, 9, 10, 12, 14, 15, 17 and 18 (8, 12, 14, and 17 were used more than once). Kelley had his construction crews working nights and weekends in an attempt to stay one step ahead of the script. When production began, many of the sets on stage 9 were undergoing reconstruction, and for weeks his "propmakers" (a construction term meaning "carpenters"—they have nothing at all to do with props, so figure that one out!) would have to wait for Bob Wise to yell "Cut!" before they could squeeze in a bit of hammering before the next take.

Kelley knows almost every nail that has been hammered into every piece of wood on every set, and part of his responsibility included keeping an eye on the construction budget. A number of times he was able to save the company money by "striking" (tearing down) the sets with his own crew, immediately segueing into the next needed set on that stage. Otherwise, Paramount would have to charge just to strike no longer needed sets.

Kelley (no relation to DeForest or the actor-dancer) provided the following breakdown of set costs. Bear in mind that these are costs incurred during *motion picture* construction only and do not include any figures for the earlier construction on the planned television series or lighting and other electronics:[*]

BRIDGE	Stage 9	$205,000
CORRIDORS, TRANSPORTER, MEDICAL AND KIRK'S QUARTERS	Stage 9	$258,000
ENGINE ROOM	Stage 9	$100,000
OFFICE COMPLEX (includes Travel Pod)	Stage 17	$ 60,000
CARGO DECK	Stage 18	$ 52,000
SPOCK'S ENTRY AREA	Stage 17	$ 6,000
RECREATION DECK	Stage 8	$252,000
AIR LOCK	Stage 6	$ 25,000
ILIA'S QUARTERS (modification of Kirk's Quarters)	Stage 9	$ 3,000
PLANET VULCAN	B-Tank	$ 42,000
OFFICER'S LOUNGE	Stage 6	$ 19,000
TRENCH[†]	Stage 17	$130,000
WINGWALK	Stage 8	$ 23,000
V'GER	Stage 15	$105,000[‡]
SAN FRANCISCO TRAM STATION	Stage 12 and 14	$240,000[§]
MEMORY WALL[†]	Stage 6	$250,000
KLINGON BRIDGE	Stage 12 and 14	$175,000
EPSILON 9	Stage 12 and 14	$ 40,000

TOTAL CONSTRUCTION COSTS (APPROX.) = $1,985,000

Anyone wishing to build his or her own starship, please note the above figure. It might almost have been easier to build the real thing after all!

---

[*] All figures have been rounded off to the nearest thousand.
[†] Footage was later discarded.
[‡] Figure does not include $85,000 for special lighting.
[§] Figure also includes the tram.

9

Camelot Revisited

Spock would have been the first to say the odds were against its happening. Yet, they had all returned. Somehow Merlin's magic had prevailed, thanks to Roddenberry's perseverance, and all the original cast plus two had returned to the Round Table of their Camelot—the starship *Enterprise*. The impossible had been done.

There was never a question as to who would play Captain James Tiberius Kirk, although a Roddenberry joke about recasting the part with Richard Burton in the center seat (and Robert Redford as Mr. Spock) got out of hand, and at one point the Burton-Redford costars were actually reported in a tv newscast! But William Shatner had indicated he would return as the space-age "Horatio Hornblower" even before there was ever one page of the movie script. It was he who first breathed life into Captain Kirk, and he intended to continue doing so. There is an unusual magnetism at work here. He is drawn to Kirk as Kirk is drawn to the *Enterprise*.

The script gives very little description of Kirk, other than the fact that he's attired in an admiral's uniform. Bill, of course, knows his character as well as he knows himself, so there was no problem with this. However, sometime during the early rewrite stages of the script, Gene worked out a short sketch of each character.

KIRK is a throwback, essentially a 19th- or 20th-century man driven by the determination to retain the only love that has ever sustained throughout his life: his adventurer's need for challenge and risk, his love of his vessel, the emotional challenge and beauty inherent in space duty. He maneuvers ruthlessly to be reassigned to the Enterprise. He steps on toes, hard. He is, no doubt, the best captain Starfleet has available to meet this crisis but he is also a man obsessed to regain the Enterprise, and it may well cloud his judgment. No captain has ever commanded a starship for more than one five-year mission. He is determined to prove that he is an exception to this rule.

Is Kirk as good as he used to be? In the midst of his drive is also a degree of self-doubt. Is it the self-doubt, in fact, that fires the need to command? Or is it the time away from command that raises the self-doubt? Does he need the constant victories in the field to continually prove to himself his own self-worth? The question is: Will this much self-indulgence subvert his genuinely extraordinary skill as a commander?

Life had been good to William Shatner during the ten years since he had last played the *Enterprise* captain, and he brought the benefit of that intervening time to his recreation of the Kirk role. Following the cancellation of the *Star Trek* series in 1969, Bill found himself in constant demand at fan conventions across the country, as well as for movie, television, and stage performances. His forty-three-city tour with an original one-man show of poetry and space and science-fiction dramatic readings resulted in a hit record album, *William Shatner—Live.* The album, distributed through his own Lemli Music Company, is a spoken-word presentation developed as an extension of his in-concert appearances before 100,000 people around the United States.

Shatner also starred in his second tv series, *Barbary Coast;* the syndicated motion picture for television, *The Bastard;* and the feature film, *Kingdom of the Spiders.* Another record album, *Foundation,* based on science-fiction writer Isaac Asimov's *Foundation Trilogy,* earned him a Grammy nomination.

Born in Montreal, Canada, on March 22, he worked his way through McGill University as a Canadian Broadcasting Company personality. Upon graduation, he joined a local summer theatre group as assistant manager and soon began acting in small parts. Ostensibly, he was preparing to join his father's successful clothing manufacturing firm, but after taking his B.A. degree in 1954, he joined the Canadian National Repertory Theatre in Ottawa, the alma mater of most of the Dominion's distinguished actors. Although his father was disappointed, he supported young Bill's right to do as he wished with his life.

A major turning point in his career occurred when he appeared in the Stratford (Ontario) Shakespeare Festival's 1955 production of the Christopher Marlowe classic *Tamburlaine.* The play was so well received in Ontario that it was taken to Broadway, where Shatner's performance was heralded by critics. The attention he received led to his early television roles on *Playhouse 90* and other major shows in the heyday of live television.

A costarring role with Ralph Bellamy in a two-part drama on *The Defenders* led to his motion picture debut in Hollywood, in *The Brothers Karamazov.* This was followed by a number of westerns and such outstanding films as *Judgment at Nuremburg* and *The Intruder.*

Returning to New York for a memorable role in "No Deadly Medicine" on *Studio One,* he remained to star for two years on Broadway as the leading man in *The World of Suzie Wong,* for one year as Julie Harris's costar in *A Shot in the Dark,* and another year in the hit comedy, *L'Idiote.*

Star Trek brought him back to Hollywood in 1966; success followed success, culminating in his return to the role of Captain Kirk in *Star Trek—The Motion Picture.*

Bill is basically a quiet person, although he has managed to earn a considerable reputation for humor. He has a good ear for language nuances, and a quick wit—on set when someone missed a line, including himself, he would quickly seize the opportunity to turn the mistake into a joke, and often an enormously funny one. It made for good spirits on stage, and Bill became extremely popular with the crew.

A typical overachiever, Shatner seems determined to try everything. His interests in the last ten years have taken him wild boar hunting on Catalina Island and soaring through the skies as a private pilot. He plays guitar, sings, rides horseback, skin-dives, water-skis, and raises Doberman pinschers. He's also an expert archer, and has hunted wild boar with bow and arrow. Yet he cares a great deal for animals and animal conservation, even proclaiming this on the bumper sticker on his car. He also uses his car to advertise LEMLI in bright orange letters on the blue California license plate, but it's more than just the name of his record company. It's an acronym for the names of his three daughters (by his first wife)—Leslie, Melanie and Lisabeth. In 1974

Bill married Marcy Lafferty, and they live with his daughters and two Dobies on a hill overlooking the San Fernando Valley just outside Los Angeles. Marcy's an accomplished actress, and the two of them appear together in *Star Trek—The Motion Picture*. Marcy plays the relief navigator, DiFalco, taking orders from husband Bill as the captain, at least in the movie!

* * *

"Leonard Who?" asks a Mr. Spock T-shirt, which has become a popular item of clothing among *Star Trek* fans. It's also an "in" joke among fans of Leonard Nimoy, the man who brought Mr. Spock to life. What's even more amusing is to see Leonard Nimoy himself wearing his character's likeness with just a touch of pride. Despite efforts to divest himself of the Spock image during his years after the television show's cancellation, when the *Star Trek* project became a theatrical motion picture, Leonard Nimoy insisted that he was the only actor who should play Mr. Spock. Sorry, Robert Redford. Actually, no one else was ever considered for the part of Spock either for the original television series or even for the (since abandoned) two-hour television movie. (The Spock character was written out and replaced with a younger Vulcan who was to have been played by another actor.) And Nimoy was the only person considered for the movie return of the half-human, half-Vulcan alienated alien.

The early Spock concept for the movie, worked out by Gene Roddenberry, could be only a partial depiction of the way the character Mr. Spock would emerge. It would take Nimoy's experience and insight to infuse motion picture life into his alter ego:

SPOCK—At his birth, Spock's parents made a conscious and deliberate decision to see the human half of his personality submerged in favor of following the Vulcan life-style. As we have seen in a number of episodes, this did not eradicate Spock's emotions; it merely repressed them. As the years have gone by, this repression of one half of Spock's personality has taken greater and greater effort of will. Spock has become an emotional time bomb. After serving on starships for fifteen years, in close proximity to humans, he was no longer able to bear the strain and retired, at the end of the five-year mission, to recharge his Vulcanness. The process has not been working, and Spock returns for this emergency mission in a state of extreme emotional upheaval which now seethes just below the surface of his still essentially cool Vulcan exterior.

In the course of our film, Spock will at long last come to terms with the human side of himself. He must come to recognize that he cannot live his life entirely in the Vulcan mode or the human one, but must make his own individual way with no models whatsoever to fall back on. He must get to know himself as a whole being and begin the terribly painful process of losing the shame he feels whenever he feels any kind of emotion. He remains, of course, most comfortable with the Vulcan life-style, science and Vulcan philosophy, but now, for the first time, he will release some of the emotion that has been building up inside him for these many years.

V'ger will come to learn about emotions from Spock as it is Spock's logical mind that it can most easily relate to. V'ger, too, is something of a half-breed, being a marriage between an Earth machine and a far more advanced machine race. Spock's torment will somewhat parallel V'ger's confusion as it comes to grips with the full, unimagined implications of the Earth half of its origins.

Most people recognize Leonard Nimoy from his role of Mr. Spock, but the millions of fans who think they know Leonard because they know Mr. Spock see but a single thread of the man. Leonard, like Bill Shatner, is also multifaceted—an actor, writer, director, skilled photographer, poet, lecturer, teacher, student, recording artist, pilot, husband, and father.

Acting, however, remains the main focus of his attention, the hub of his existence. In *Star Trek—The Motion Picture* he returns to the role that brought him three successive Emmy nominations and made him the idol of millions. But Nimoy had more than a hundred appearances in television dramas, as well as performances on stage and in motion pictures, prior to creating Mr. Spock in the television series. Since the cancellation of that series, he has gone on to further prove his versatile talents in outstanding stage and screen performances. Most notable have been his Broadway portrayal of the psychiatrist in *Equus* and his starring role in the feature film *Invasion of the Body Snatchers*.

Leonard Nimoy was born in Boston on March 26—four days after Bill Shatner. His first acting part, at age eight, was that of Hansel in a home town production of *Hansel and Gretel*. At age eighteen, after completing a course at Boston College on a drama scholarship, he headed west to the famous Pasadena Playhouse for further training.

Movie offers soon followed, and in the early fifties he appeared in such films as *Queen for a Day, Francis Goes to West Point, The Overland Trail,* and his first lead, the title role in *Kid Monk Baroni*.

After marrying actress Sandi Zober in 1954, Leonard and his bride spent eighteen months in Georgia, where he wrote, narrated, and emceed GI shows as part of his duties with the army special services detachment at Fort McPhearson. He also worked with the Atlanta Theatre Guild, directing and starring in *A Streetcar Named Desire*.

Following his army hitch, he returned to Los Angeles and picked up the threads of his acting career, studying with Jeff Corey and later operating his own drama studio. By this time the Nimoys had also added their two children (Julie and Adam) to the family, and to supplement his modest income from teaching and acting, Leonard did the usual jobs that are part and parcel of every struggling actor's life: He drove cabs, worked in a pet shop, delivered newspapers, and ushered in a movie house.

By the early 1960s, he had graduated from bit parts to guest-starring roles on most of the major television series. He appeared in such programs as *Rawhide, The Virginian, Outer Limits,* and *Profiles in Courage.* He also appeared in the Gene Roddenberry-produced series *The Lieutenant,* which later led to his being cast in the part of Mr. Spock.

After *Star Trek* was canceled, Nimoy costarred in another Paramount television production *Mission: Impossible,* sometimes playing as many as four different characters in a single episode.

He joined Yul Brynner and Richard Crenna in the feature *Catlow,* toured the East Coast starring as Tevye in *Fiddler on the Roof,* and starred in a number of other theatrical productions around the country, including *Man in the Glass Booth, Oliver, Sherlock Holmes, My Fair Lady,* and *Six Rms Riv Vu.* With Broadway's *Equus,* his stage career had come full circle.

Aside from acting, Leonard's favorite creative outlets are photography and writing. He has his own darkroom in his West Hollywood office-studio, and some of his black-and-white studies have been displayed in various exhibits. In 1973 he wrote his first book, *You And I,* a sensitive love story expressed in poetry and photography; his second book, *Will I Think of You,* is also an anthology of his poems and photos. This was followed by *I Am Not Spock,* and other recent books include *We Are All Children Searching for Love,* and *Come Be With Me.*

As if this weren't enough to keep him busy, Leonard has also made ten record albums, including a number of spoken-word recordings of various works of science-fiction writers H.G. Wells, Ray Bradbury, and Robert Heinlein.

Following the completion of his work on *ST—TMP,* Leonard again hit the road, this time touring with a highly acclaimed original one-man play, *Vincent.* And somehow, this busy man has found the time to be host-narrator of two syndicated television series—*In Search Of,* and *The Coral Jungle.*

Leonard brings skill to each of his crafts, but his real gift is as an actor. He works at it, constantly. He never missed seeing his "rushes" each day, watching his scenes with a critical eye, ever alert for things to improve. Yet, although basically a serious man, on the set he's not quite the stone-faced Mr. Spock, and it was not unusual to see a man walking around who *looked* just like Mr. Spock laughing heartily at one of Bill Shatner's witticisms.

* * *

When DeForest Kelley first appears on the screen as Dr. "Bones" McCoy, he is barely recognizable. It is not because he's changed so much in the last ten years (he hasn't); it is simply due to the elaborate makeup and hair styling used to create a not-too-happy ship's doctor who is beamed aboard looking like a 23rd-century mountain man. Although we're never told what he's been doing since the end of the *Enterprise*'s five-year mission, it is clear from his looks and attitude that it has nothing to do with space travel.

"Bones" (the nickname derives from "sawbones," an old-time word for doctor) is a space-age physician with a country doctor's bedside manner. His disposition is somewhat tempered by the problems the *Enterprise* encounters in *Star Trek—The Motion Picture,* and Roddenberry wrote this thumbnail sketch of McCoy as a guide to DeForest's characterization:

McCOY—With the two most important members of the mission in a state of emotional turmoil, it falls to McCoy to hold them together if the mission is to have any chance of success. He did not want to come on this mission, and there may be some way that he can get out of it, but he recognized its importance and the fact that there is no one else who is close enough to Kirk and Spock to be able to help them. The pressure on McCoy is tremendous and raises the question of whether or not he can handle it without cracking. He leans on CHAPEL who must take on an overly large portion of the load of treating the sick, and is likewise subject to breakage.

It is curious that DeForest Kelley has scored his biggest hit as the outspoken, somewhat cynical and eccentric but thoroughly likable McCoy, because most of his earlier roles in motion pictures, television, and on the stage were as "heavies," and he had built a considerable reputation for the creative quality he brought to such roles. His films include *Gunfight at the O.K. Corral, Raintree County, The Law and Jake Wade, Warlock,* and *Where Love Has Gone.* Among his numerous tv appearances were roles on *Playhouse 90, Schlitz Theatre, Gunsmoke, Zane Grey Theatre, Rawhide,* and *Bonanza.*

Like McCoy, DeForest is from Georgia. He was born in Atlanta on January 20, and at the age of seventeen made his first trip outside his home state, journeying to Long Beach, California, to visit an uncle. This visit convinced him that California was the place to be and he joined the Long Beach Theatre Group at the invitation of a friend. He supported himself by operating an elevator and roughnecking for Richfield Oil, working days, then rushing to the theatre and doing a play each night.

A Paramount talent scout spotted DeForest in a wartime navy training film, resulting in a screen test, a contract, and two and a half years with Paramount. Later, film and television roles followed steadily, culminating in his signing for the regular cast of the *Star Trek* television show. With his popularity as Dr. McCoy came his own fan club, voluminous mail, and constant demands for personal appearances at *Star Trek* conventions and various organizations.

He lives in Sherman Oaks, California, with his wife of thirty years, Carolyn Dowling, whom he met when they were appearing together at the Long Beach Theatre Group. Their "children" include Fancy, a Lhasa Apso dog; Maggie, their cat, and Myrtle, a seventy-five-year-old turtle.

DeForest Kelley is similar to Dr. McCoy in many ways: He's very much interested in helping people, and once flew to the Denver bedside of a young *Star Trek* fan who was dying of cancer and had expressed a last wish—to meet Dr. McCoy. DeForest is that kind of a man—charmingly pleasant to be around, and also a bit on the shy side. His two blue magnets for eyes are powerfully capable of capturing and holding a person's attention, and his gentle off-camera voice has just a trace of a Georgia accent, reminiscent of an authentic southern gentleman—the words used by many of his friends to describe him. In fact, his favorite recipe, a variation of a great southern delight called "Grits McCoy," was recently published in *The Star Trek Cookbook* (Bantam Books, 1978), and was reproduced in Carolyn's own calligraphy.

But basically DeForest considers himself a homebody. He enjoys his garden, where he tends fifty or so rosebushes, likes to read biographies and old movie magazines, and says, "I don't know whether I'm basically lazy or what, but I enjoy my home and my general surroundings and living the kind of life that I live." Most likely Dr. McCoy would agree; it's just possible he beamed up from Sherman Oaks!

* * *

Commander Willard Decker was a little more than a name until Stephen Collins was selected to play this new character in *Star Trek—The Motion Picture*. The brief description of Decker given in the 1977 *Writers'/Directors' Guide* didn't give him much to go on, and it took a talented and dedicated actor like Steve to bring Decker to life. Part of his creation of that role was based on this updated sketch prepared by Gene Roddenberry in his script rewrite notes:

DECKER—On the outside, a version of Kirk at his age and position. On the inside, Percy Bysshe Shelley. He entered Starfleet because his father* and father's father were Starfleet. It seemed so much the thing to do that he never questioned it. But under the pressures in our story, his disciplined Starfleet shell crumbles and he becomes the artist-poet he really is—and it is his artistic sense of the meaning of the Cosmos that saves the day when he unites with V'ger, at the same time giving V'ger the missing sense of beauty and Oneness needed for the great machine life form to ascend (with Decker now a part of it) into its next higher plane of existence.

Stephen was selected to play this pivotal role after one of the most intensive talent searches in Hollywood in many years. At least sixty men were considered for the part, and scenes from film appearances were screened on about a fourth of these Decker hopefuls. On July 25, 1978, only thirteen days before production began, Robert Wise held the following casting interviews:

11:00   STEPHEN COLLINS

11:10   ANDY ROBINSON

11:20   JORDAN CLARK

---

*Commodore Matt Decker, of the *Star Trek* television episode "The Doomsday Machine."

11:30	RICHARD KELTON
11:40	LANCE HENRICSON
11:50	TIM THOMERSEN
12:00	STEVEN MACHT, ARTHUR HINDLE
2:00	FREDERICK FORREST

According to associate producer Jon Povill, Stephen wasn't selected immediately, and they decided to read a few of the others. It finally boiled down to Stephen and one other actor, the rest having been decided against for reasons like "too young," "too old," "good, but too much like Shatner," "like Spock," and "not quite." Stephen not only gave a good reading, he looked exactly like the preconceived image of Decker unconsciously formed in the minds of many of those involved who had read the script.

But the people involved with *Star Trek* have always seemed to have a knack for casting the right people in the right parts; often it's hard to tell where the character leaves off and the actor begins. So it was with Steve. Like Decker, Steve is a serious man with a great deal of sensitivity. He meditates for twenty minutes at a time, twice a day, relaxes by playing his guitar, and has an un-Deckerlike secret desire to be a rock star. He had never seen *Star Trek* because he was either in college studying or pursuing his acting career during the last eleven years and never had much time for television. He had no idea what the part was about, and thinks this may have been an asset to his getting the role.

There was never any question about his future in Stephen's mind, even as a child. He always wanted to be an actor—both his grand-fathers had been amateur actors and he's quick to point out this family situation resemblance to one of his heroes, Sir Laurence Olivier, whose grandfather was also an amateur actor. This parallel has brought him to the obvious conclusion that acting must skip a genera-tion.

But Steve didn't have an easy time of it. He was born October 1 in Des Moines, Iowa, but the family soon moved to Hastings-on-Hudson, New York. As a child, he was so shy that he hid whenever company arrived. But the minute his parents left the house for an evening, he'd haul out the family Broadway show albums and sing along with all the parts. He was still too shy to audition for a role in his high school production of *Our Town,* so he persuaded the teacher to audition him privately. He got the part and eventually overcame his shyness.

Later at Amherst, where he was a theatre major, he appeared as the lead in twenty campus productions. The last of these found noted stage producer Joseph Papp in the audience. Following the performance, Collins asked Papp if he had a job for him. Papp asked if he could carry a spear, and he was hired by Papp for a small speaking role in *Twelfth Night,* which Papp was producing in Central Park.

Praising notices in that debut led to the national road company of *Forty Carats.* Following a year on tour, he returned to New York for his Broadway bow in *Moon Children,* then appeared in two more Papp productions—*More Than You Deserve* and *The Last Days of British Honduras.* Next he was on Broadway again in *No Sex Please, We're British* and the long-running hit *The Ritz.*

It was following this success that he moved west, guest-starring in several tv series, including *The Waltons, Barnaby Jones, Charlie's Angels* (he got to kiss Farrah Fawcett-Majors!) and the NBC tv-movie *The Rhinemann Exchange.* His motion picture career has seen a succession of important roles in films like *All the President's Men, Between the Lines,* and his recent starring role in *The Promise.*

If he weren't an actor, he professes he'd either be "a sportscaster or unhappy." He's an amateur hockey player, and a baseball fanatic and New York Mets fan. Recently he was captain of the *Star Trek* Muscular Distrophy Association League softball team, made up of the cast and crew who played charity games in Los Angeles every Sunday. Maybe Decker didn't get to command the *Enterprise,* but Steve Collins *did* win a captaincy of his own!

*   *   *

It's difficult to tell which of the two are more interesting—the Deltan character Ilia, or the actress Persis Khambatta. Both come from seemingly exotic, far-distanced places; both are sensual and charming, dark and mysterious, and, according to Persis, both have *esper* abilities. The night before the decision was reached, she had a dream that she would get the part of Ilia. The next day she got a call from her agent, and before he could say another word, she told him she already knew why he was calling. He himself had just heard about the good news, and couldn't imagine how she had found out.

Persis, a former Miss India and award-winning actress from that country, asked for more information on Ilia's Deltan background, resulting in the lengthiest character study Gene Roddenberry wrote for any role in the movie. (It also lets us know just what *did* happen between Decker and Ilia on Delta.):

ILIA—Deltans, at first quick impression, may seem to be proudly aloof. However, a quick-eyed observer becomes immediately aware that Deltans actually have a splendidly developed sense of humor and fun lying immediately beneath that poised exterior. Their graceful carriage has lured many a human into believing them cool intellectuals, only to discover that the Deltan is enjoying a good-humored joke at that human's expense.

Unlike the Vulcan race, Deltans value and delight in emotion—they see emotion as one of the myriad delights of being a life form. They are a sensual race—they enjoy the sensation of feeling hunger and fulfilling appetite in every form from satisfying their palates with exquisite foods, to the caress of a warm breeze or the bite of a bitter wind, the

Decker and Ilia recall their days together on Delta.

touch of an infant's hand, and especially all the shared communications and physical sensations of acts of love. Along its path to individual awareness, all the five (perhaps six) senses of the Deltan become highly acute and sensitive. Their taste buds, the rods and cones of their inner eyes, even their smallest epidermal nerve ending, all are sensitive far beyond the human norm.

Ilia is different from other Deltans in only one area—as a girl she had considerable contact with humans because of her father's prominence as a Federation historian with special interest in parallels between the civilizations of Earth and Delta. Something of a dreamer, Ilia eventually became fascinated with the "primitive" heroic qualities in humans—this led to an interest in 23rd-century space exploration in much the same way that some humans become intrigued with the heroic ocean voyages of the Polynesian people. Since her own Deltan race had long ago lost their interest in space voyaging (concentrating on their own inner-space), Ilia finally decided to join Starfleet herself and study at first hand the space adventuring in which the human species were playing so prominent a role. As is true of the few other Deltans who have joined Starfleet, Ilia's natural job function was navigation—the highly evolved Deltan intelligence can handle the most complex spherical trigonometric complexities of space navigation as easily as a human learns simple multiplication tables.

Ilia's past connection with Decker is a bit troubling to her. She met Decker while still little more than a girl—her romantic "dreamer" nature saw him loom in her mind as a handsome, primitive young warrior, excitingly different from any Deltan man she knew. She then discovered that this "primitive young warrior" had unusual intelligence and charm. All this combined with Ilia's burgeoning interest in Earth voyages and voyagers—her Deltan emotional zest catapulted her into love with this young Starfleet lieutenant. But Decker, already an experienced officer, knew of the dangers implicit in any such relationship—he also recognized that his own principal need was for the challenge and adventure he could find only in space as a starship commander some day. When Ilia's interest in him led to preliminary love-play, even this unconsummated sex experience left him so shaken that he saw the trap in time. He fled, realizing he could not risk even a "good-bye"—another hour with Ilia might have brought him to a point of no return.

Ilia is now certain that Decker made the right decision—her affection for him was genuine, deep enough that she saw it would be selfish of her to interfere with his chance of one day achieving the ultimate freedom and challenge of starship command. Decker is equally certain he made the right decision about Ilia—and yet strangely exotic and compelling memories of her still torment him at times.

Persis really plays two parts in *ST—TMP—Ilia*, the sensuous Deltan lieutenant, j.g., and the Ilia-probe, a mechanical replica of Ilia with all the warmth and charm of a vacuum cleaner (until Decker discovers how to reach its sensors, that is). It was a difficult combination, but

Persis enjoys challenges, and the young actress handled both parts with skill.

Born on October 2, in Bombay, India, Persis and her family are members of the Parsi religious sect, descendants of the original Persian refugees who settled in Bombay, and her name derives from the name of an ancient queen of Persia. Their Zoroastrian religion believes in the purifying qualities of fire, and all rites connected with birth, marriage, and death are consecrated in their Fire Temple.

She learned to speak English as a child, and the language was often used in her house, along with Gujerati, the mother tongue of the Parsi, and Hindi, the national language of India. She was raised by her mother, who still resides in India, and her great-grandfather, who lived to the age of ninety-four. She considers him a great influence in her life because he encouraged her early interests.

When she was only thirteen, Persis was discovered by a photographer while she and her family were dining in a Bombay restaurant. He was startled by her beauty and asked her mother's permission to do some test shots. The pictures turned out so well that Persis's picture soon became known all over India in an ad campaign for Rexona, a popular soap from that country. After that, offers began pouring in, and soon Persis was India's most successful model. At only sixteen, she was named Miss India and became her country's entry in the Miss Universe Pageant.

Movie offers soon followed. Her performance in *Bombay in the Arms of Night* earned her the Indian Newspapers' Award as Best Actress of the Year. In that film she also played a double role—a blonde nightclub singer, and a simple Indian girl. In all, she made five films in her native land, and soon won critical acclaim as the "Sophia Loren of India." She then made a courageous decision to seek her fortune in the Western world. At the age of seventeen, she left for London with only £3.00 (about $9) in her wallet. When she arrived in the middle of the London winter, there was a postal strike, so in order to secure modeling jobs, she walked through the snow, clad only in a thin silk kurta (shirt) and pants, to deliver photos of herself to various photographers.

Within a year, however, she had become a favorite of British photographers and society columnists. Her pictures appeared in *Woman's Own, Harper's, 21* and in leading London newspapers. Soon Miss Khambatta landed her first role in a motion picture outside her native India—*The Wilby Conspiracy*, with stars Sidney Poitier and

Michael Caine. Next came *Conduct Unbecoming,* starring Michael York and Christopher Plummer. After that, she decided to give up this flourishing career in England and set her sights on the United States. After repeating her modeling success in New York, she flew to Hollywood for her first American television performance, guesting in *Man With the Power,* a movie-of-the-week starring Bob Neil, Vic Morrow, and Tim O'Conner.

Star Trek—The Motion Picture marks the culmination of her personal star trek—Persis's Hollywood big-screen debut. Her acting idol is two-time Academy Award winner Jane Fonda, which might give a clue as to the next goal of this *persis*tant young lady!

Star Trek meets *Enterprise* at the rollout of NASA's
space shuttle. Left to right: James C. Fletcher,
former NASA administrator; DeForest Kelley;
George Takei; James Doohan; Nichelle Nichols;
Leonard Nimoy; Gene Roddenberry; Don Fuqua,
Chairman of the House Space Committee;
Walter Koenig.

William Shatner (left) chats with Leonard Nimoy during a break on the *V'ger* set.

On the *V'ger* set, director Robert Wise frames his next shot as William Shatner pays close attention.

Creator-producer Gene Roddenberry (right) goes over script page with screenwriter Harold Livingston.

Planet Vulcan is created in Paramount's "B-Tank."

Right: Persis Khambatta (before).

Far right: Persis Khambatta— as the "Ilia-Probe."

Captain Kirk (William Shatner), Dr. McCoy (DeForest Kelley), and Dr. Chapel (Majel Barrett) smile with elation at Mr. Spock's unexpected arrival aboard the *Enterprise*.

The *Enterprise* engine core extends many decks downward thanks to forced-perspective painting on the stage floor.

Leonard Nimoy composes himself for a closeup as part of the space-walk sequence.

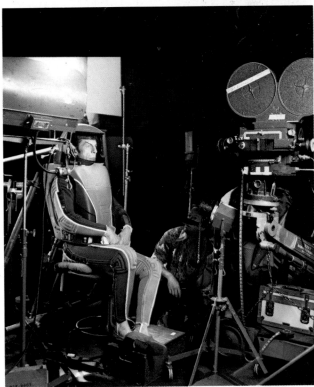

Hoyt Yeatman (left) and Alan Harding set up rear projection
of Kirk and Scotty before filming travel pod.

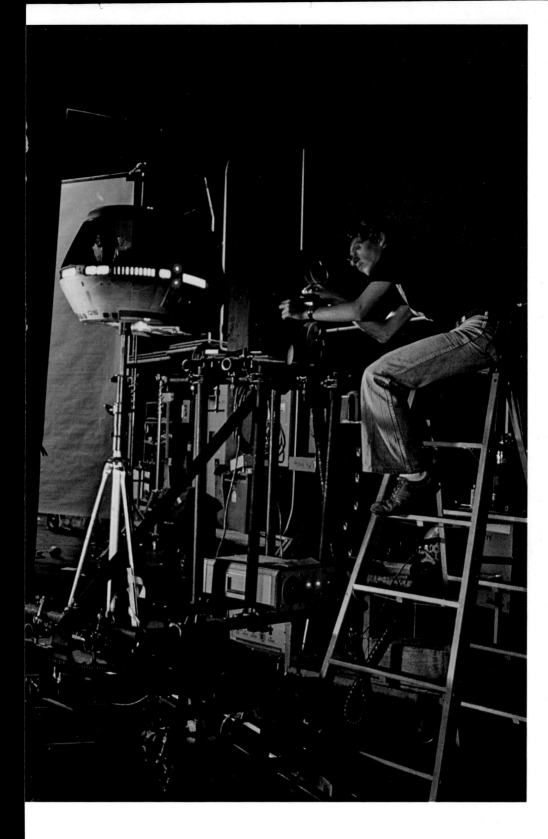

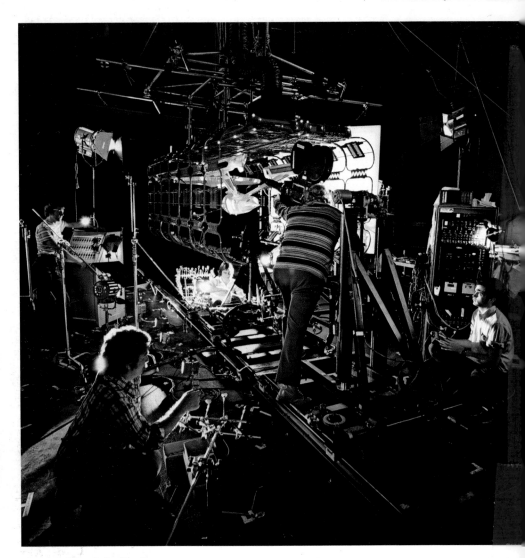

Special effects
technicians prepare to
film the *Enterprise* in dry
dock at Doug Trumbull's
studio. From left to right:
Bob Spurlock, David Gold,
Pat van Auken, Dave
Stewart, and Johathan
Seay.

Persis Khambatta finds a moment to relax between scenes.

Heads of several aliens seem to be watching as assistant makeup artist Mike LaValley prepares an Arcturian crewman for the recreation deck scene.

Stephen Collins and
Persis Khambatta
celebrate day-apart
birthdays on the *Star
Trek* set.

Invisible wires guide this
cargo container across the
cargo deck set. The shot
was later composited with
matte paintings.

Klingon commander (Mark Lenard) and crew member confront unknown intruder in the film's opening sequence.

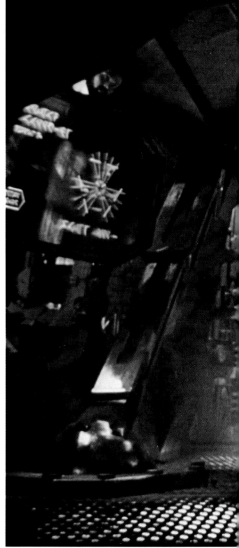

A Betelgeusian chief ambassador models what is perhaps the most valuable costume ever worn by a Hollywood "extra."

Matthew Yuricich touches
up painting of the San
Francisco tram station.

Space office complex in orbit over Earth.

Perched high above the *V'ger* set, director Robert Wise (right of camera) shields his eyes from the bright lighting needed for this scene.

Production designer Harold Michelson (left) and assistant art director Leon Harris check the model of path to Voyager 6.

The crew of the U.S.S. *Enterprise*. From left to right: George Takei, James Doohan, Grace Lee Whitney, Nichelle Nichols, Stephen Collins, DeForest Kelley, Majel Barrett, William Shatner, Leonard Nimoy, Persis Khambatta, and Walter Koenig.

10

The Rest of the Knights

If James T. Kirk can have a love affair with a starship, if Mr. Spock's right-chested heart skips a beat with each computer printout, then it should come as no surprise that Commander Montgomery Scott's pulse throbs in loving rhythm with the *Enterprise*'s—and his— engines. "Scotty," the senior engineering officer aboard the *Enterprise,* is deftly recreated in *Star Trek—The Motion Picture* by James Doohan. Jimmy is responsible for the creation of most of Scotty's personality, and needed only a quick glance at the *Writers'/ Directors' Guide* for a fast update on what had happened to the chief engineer since the end of the *Enterprise*'s five-year mission:

ENGINEERING OFFICER SCOTT . . . is known to most as "Scotty," with an accent that drips of heather and the Highlands. Scotty came up through the ranks and his practical education is as broad as his formal training in engineering. He has rare mechanical capacity, many claim he can put an engine together with baling wire and glue, and make it run. He regards the U.S.S. Enterprise as his personal property and the engineering section as his private world where even Kirk is merely a privileged trespasser.

Engineering and spaceships are his life. His idea of a pleasant afternoon is tinkering in an engineering section of the vessel; he is totally unable to understand why any sane man would spend reading time on anything but technical manuals. He is strong-minded, strong-willed and not incapable of telling off even a Starfleet captain who intrudes into what Scotty regards as his own private province and area of responsibilities.

One of the biggest problems for Jimmy Doohan is that he plays Scotty *too* well—since the cancellation of the *Star Trek* tv series in 1969, he's had a rough time convincing Hollywood casting directors that he really *isn't* a Scottish actor residing here. His accent (which has fooled authentic Scotsmen too), is simply one of many dialects he does with native skill. In fact, his favorite off-camera character is an Englishman he's created named "Reggie." He does this humorous fellow with a British accent so thick that he makes the Queen of England sound like a native of Mississippi.

By birth, however, Jimmy is a Canadian, born on March 3 in Vancouver, British Columbia. During World War II he became a captain in the Royal Canadian Artillery, was wounded on D Day, and served as a flyer observer for the rest of the war. His daring aerial maneuvers, flying an artillery observation plane on a slalom course between telephone poles, led to a reputation as "the craziest pilot in the Canadian Air Force."

At the end of the war he turned to acting, and in 1946 he won a two-year scholarship to the Neighborhood Playhouse in New York City, where he went on to teach for the next three years. In 1953, he returned to Toronto, and for the next three years he logged over three thousand five hundred radio performances, as well as a number of television and film appearances.

In 1961 Jimmy moved to Hollywood, and since that time has made more than three hundred fifty television appearances on such series as *Hazel, Bonanza, The Virginian, Gunsmoke, Peyton Place, The Fugitive, Marcus Welby, M.D., Ben Casey, Bewitched,* and, of course, *Star Trek.* Among his numerous motion pictures are *The Wheeler Dealers, The Satan Bug,* and *Bus Riley's Back in Town.* His latest stage appearances were in *The Trial of James McNeil Whistler* and *Teddy.* He also recently completed *Fellowship,* a movie filmed in Toronto.

Jimmy and his wife, Wende, live in Van Nuys with their two young children, Eric Montgomery and Thomas Patrick, and their two dogs, Sir Erin Shadrack Macquillan and Sweet Bonnie Rose of Brodie. Jimmy also has four children by a former marriage—two daughters and twin sons. His twins, Christopher and Montgomery, appear in the rec deck scene as extras.

* * *

The popularity of his character, Mr. Sulu, has helped make George Takei an international favorite—although his own considerable intelligence and wit has had much to do with that. In the years after the television show went off the air, George became a popular guest speaker at *Star Trek* conventions in such far-flung places as Great Britain and Australia, as well as nearly every major U.S. city. Indeed, George seems to be as much at home traveling around this planet as Sulu is traveling through space.

Sulu is one of the most interesting of the *Enterprise* bridge characters.

The *Writers'/Directors' Guide* describes him as a "compulsive hobbyist." His capable portrayal by George Takei (pronounced "Ta-kay") is based, in part, on these additional guidelines:

SULU—Ship's Helmsman, mixed Oriental in ancestry, Japanese predominating, a lieutenant commander, Sulu is very Occidental in speech and manner. In fact, his attitude toward Asians is that they seem to him rather inscrutable. Sulu fancies himself more of an old-world D'Artagnan than anything else. He is a compulsive hobbyist; like all collectors, he is forever giving his friends a thousand reasons why they, too, should take on the same hobby.

Although these bursts of enthusiasm make him something of a chatterbox, Sulu is a top officer and one of the most proficient helmsmen in the Starfleet Service. When the chips are down, he immediately becomes another character, a terse professional, whose every word and deed relate solely to the vessel and its safety. This pleasant and effective "dual personality" never intrudes on his job. He has never had to receive the same order from Kirk twice.

George was born on April 20 in the Boyle Heights district of Los Angeles, where he lived until his family was relocated in Arkansas during World War II. (Just a trace of a southern accent can still be heard in some of his words.)

He began his college education as an architecture student at the University of California at Berkeley, and later transferred to the Los Angeles campus as a major in theatre arts with a minor in Latin American Studies (he speaks flawless Spanish, as well as fluent

Japanese). While at UCLA he made his professional debut in a *Playhouse 90* production. Meanwhile, he furthered his training as an actor at the Desilu Workshop.

After a period in New York, living in cold-water flats, performing in an occasional off-Broadway play or live tv show, he took off on a bicycling, hitchhiking tour of Europe. A highlight was his attendance at the Shakespeare Institute at Stratford-on-Avon.

Returning to Hollywood, he earned his master's degree in theatre at UCLA and resumed his pursuit of an acting career. Prior to winning his continuing role in *Star Trek*, he appeared on such television shows as *Perry Mason, Alcoa Premiere, Mr. Novak, The Wackiest Ship in the Army,* and *I Spy.* Motion picture appearances included *Ice Palace; A Majority of One; Hell to Eternity; An American Dream; Walk, Don't Run;* and *The Green Berets.*

Following the completion of the *Star Trek* series, George spent three years as the producer-host of KNBC's public affairs talk show, *Expression: East/West.* He also appeared on the stage at the Inner City Cultural Center in Shakespeare's *Macbeth* and in *The Monkey's Paw,* and toured Alaska in the lead role in Edward Albee's *Zoo Story.*

In tv again, he was critically lauded for his starring portrayal of the anguished, bitter Chinatown tour guide in the PBS *Theatre in America* production of *Year of the Dragon.* Other tv guest roles have included *Hallmark Hall of Fame, Black Sheep Squadron, Hawaii Five-O, Chico and the Man, The Six Million Dollar Man, Ironside, Marcus Welby, M.D.,* and *Kung Fu.*

High on the list of George's interests outside of acting are politics and civic affairs. In 1972 he was an official delegate to the Democratic presidential convention at Miami Beach. In 1974, he was a delegate to the mid-term conference at Kansas City. In 1976, he was an alternate to the New York convention, and was invited to participate in the inaugural festivities for Jimmy Carter following his election that year.

George himself ran for office in 1973 when he became a candidate for the Los Angeles City Council seat vacated when Tom Bradley became mayor. George came in second in the electoral race, just 3 percent behind the victor. Subsequently, he has been appointed to the board of directors of the Southern California Rapid Transit District, where he currently serves as vice-president of the board and chairman of the personnel committee.

In his other community and cultural activities, he organized and served as founding chairman of the Friends of Far Eastern Art at the Los Angeles County Museum of Art, as National Cultural Affairs Chairman of the Japanese American Citizens League for three years, and on the Academy of Television Arts and Sciences' Blue Ribbon Committee for the Emmy Awards annually since 1975.

For fun and health, George runs several miles a day, and even when on the road, he finds a local park in which to jog. If it rains, no problem—he runs up and down the hotel stairwells, once confusing a maid who helpfully indicated the elevator!

George is one of the most popular of the *Star Trek* actors. During the filming of the movie, he was visited by two young ladies from Japan, who, thanks to the high value of the yen against the shrinking dollar, decided to fly over and watch their hero on the closed set (an exception was made in their case). The girls understood very little English, so George interpreted everything for them. But no language was really necessary. George's warmth knows no international borders, and naturally the girls were quite taken with his charm. On later being asked how they enjoyed their visit, all they could do was smile and sigh, "George. Ah-so!"

* * *

Uhura was one of the first serious black roles created for weekly dramatic television when *Star Trek* went on the air in 1966. Nichelle Nichols plays her character with great dedication, as well as with the talent for which she has become known. The following updated description appeared in the 1977 *Writers'/Directors' Guide:*

UHURA: Rank of lieutenant commander, communications officer. Uhura was born in the African Confederacy. Quick and intelligent, she is a highly efficient officer. Her understanding of the ship's computer systems is second only to the Vulcan science officer, and expert in all ships systems relating to communications. Uhura is also a warm, highly female female off duty. She is a favorite in the recreation room during off duty hours too, because she sings—old ballads as well as the newer space ballads—and she can do impersonations at the drop of a communicator.

That last line is not surprising. Nichelle began her career as a singer and dancer in nightclubs, then progressed to the stage and motion pictures.

She was born on December 28 in Robbins, Illinois, where her father once served as mayor. At the age of sixteen she toured with Duke Ellington in a ballet she created for one of his musical suites, and later she sang with his band.

In theatre, she performed in such plays as *The Roar of the Greasepaint, No Strings,* Jean Genet's *The Blacks,* and *Kicks for Company.* For the latter two, she was nominated for the prized Sarah Siddons Award for the best actress of the year.

She also won critical acclaim in the West Coast production of James Baldwin's *Blues for Mr. Charlie,* and in the Chicago production of *Carmen Jones.*

Her motion picture appearances include *Doctor, You've Got to be Kidding; Mr. Buddwing; Three for the Wedding;* and *Truck Turner.*

Following *Star Trek*'s television series, Nichelle channeled her continuing interest in the space program into several areas. On a tour of the Aames Space Center near San Jose, California, she was invited by scientists to fly an eight-hour mission aboard the Kuiper C-141 astronomy observatory on an introferometric study of the atmosphere on Saturn and Mars. She later was among the honored NASA guests during the Viking soft landing on Mars, and at the space shuttle *Enterprise* rollout ceremonies.

Appointed to the board of directors of the National Space Institute, she addressed the organization's annual meeting in Washington, D.C. NASA then asked her to assist in its campaign to recruit women and minorities as possible future astronauts. She is also on the advisory committee for the Technology Commercialization Center in Washington, D.C., and serves on the board of trustees of Lawrence University at Santa Barbara, California.

As owner and president of Women in Motion, a consultant firm on career education, she has created and presented programs designed to motivate young people from low-income families toward the fields of math and science, and to prepare them for college entry.

Following the completion of her role in *Star Trek—The Motion Picture,* Nichelle was contacted by officials of the National Air and Space Museum at the Smithsonian Institution in Washington, D.C., asking her assistance in production of an orientation film to acquaint junior high school students nationally with the marvels and history of space. In the film Nichelle again appears as Uhura, in a script based on her original scenario.

In recognition of her achievements, the National Society of Aerospace Education selected Nichelle as the recipient of its prestigious Woman of the Year, Friend of Space Award for 1979.

Despite her many involvements, she still manages to do several *Star Trek* fan conventions a year, once crawling down from her hotel room with a 103-degree fever from the flu, in order not to miss her scheduled talk. (The fans never found out she wasn't feeling 100 percent.) And now, this hardworking, energetic lady has just recorded her third record album, is working on a novel, and is developing a new stage musical. It's subject, naturally, is outer space.

* * *

In the *Star Trek* television series, Walter Koenig (pronounced "Kay'-nig") joined the cast in its second season to play the Russian ensign Pavel Chekov, who constantly extolled the virtues of Leningrad, vodka, and great Russian "inventions." His portrayal of Chekov as the youthful, energetic navigator added a new dimension to the *Enterprise*—someone with whom young viewers could identify. He was also characterized as "cuddly" by many female fans. Chekov is less boyish in the movie, and he had received a promotion along with his new duties, as described in the *Writers'/Directors' Guide:*

LT. CHEKOV—Chekov is now a full lieutenant with years of space adventure behind him. He commands the security division of the U.S.S. Enterprise, and is responsible for matters of security and discipline both aboard the vessel and ashore. He is responsible also for the training of the men and women who make up his security teams. During action stations, his post is on the bridge at the damage control console. The captain's safety is Lt. Chekov's responsibility, too, very much as the captain's health is McCoy's concern.

In the movie, Chekov's role was actually expanded even further, taking over the very important and dramatic weapons-defense console on the bridge, especially designed for the film.

Walter was born in Chicago on September 14, the son of Lithuanian immigrants, from whom he learned his imitation of a Russian dialect. The family soon moved to New York, where he attended public school and later continued his education at Fieldston High School in Riverdale, New York. There, his first leaning toward dramatics was evidenced when he played the lead in *Peer Gynt* and other high school productions.

With the intention of becoming a psychiatrist, young Walter enrolled in Grinnel College in Iowa, but later transferred to the University of California at Los Angeles, graduating with a degree in psychology.

While in college, he had performed in summer stock in Vermont and decided he really wanted an acting career after all. Upon graduation he enrolled at the Neighborhood Playhouse in New York. Two years later, he returned to the West Coast and won his first acting job, the part of Irving Da Dope on *Day In Court.*

His acting career has included guest-star roles in *Columbo, Medical Center, Ironside, Mannix, Alfred Hitchcock Presents, Mr. Novak, Ben Casey, The Untouchables* and *Combat.* He's also another graduate of Gene Roddenberry's earlier television series, *The Lieutenant,* and a leading role in that series eventually led to his being cast in *Star Trek.* He was featured in the motion picture, *The Deadly Honeymoon* and costarred in *Six Characters in Search of an Author* among his off-Broadway stage appearances.

On the Los Angeles stage, he played three roles—a priest, a Nazi, and a Jewish refugee in *The Deputy.* Other stage productions have seen him starring in *Night Must Fall, Steambath, The White House Murder Case, Girls of Summer, Blood Wedding, La Ronde* and *Make a Million.*

Since *Star Trek,* he has devoted more time to writing, authoring several teleplays, and currently is working on his second novel. He wrote and produced the low-budget film exploration of three struggling actors, *I Wish I May,* and directed three plays, *Hotel Paradise, American Hurrah,* and *Becket* for the stage in Los Angeles.

Serious-minded Walter especially enjoys teaching and the opportunity it affords to integrate his acting, writing and directing abilities with his knowledge of psychology. He instructs classes at the California School of Professional Psychology, UCLA, and Sherwood Oaks Experimental College in Hollywood.

At home in North Hollywood, Walter devotes his time to his wife, actress Judy Levitt, whom he married in 1965; their two children, Joshua and Danielle; and his passion for his unusual hobby—collecting comic pinback buttons and "Big-Little" books. He has just completed a diary of his experiences during the filming of *ST—TMP,* entitled *Chekov's Enterprise* (Pocket Books, 1980).

* * *

Nurse Christine Chapel may not have realized her dreams of melting the Vulcan heart of Mr. Spock, but she's succeeded in achieving an even more meaningful dream—and *Star Trek—The Motion Picture* sees Majel Barrett returning as silky dark-haired *Doctor* Chapel. Naturally Majel was delighted with both the promotion and the fact that she wouldn't have to ruin her hair as she did in the television series by dying it blonde. And she's given Christine, the doctor, more depth in the movie than would have been possible for a nurse. Her characterization is based, in part, on this description in the *Writers'/Directors' Guide:*

DR. CHRISTINE CHAPEL—Introduced in Star Trek I as Nurse Chapel, her medical degrees have been accepted by Starfleet, and she has returned to the U.S.S. Enterprise to serve as McCoy's associate. She is second in command of the ship's medical section, and McCoy seems to enjoy passing on to her every duty he finds too boring, irritating or annoying to himself. Yet outside of Captain Kirk, she is probably McCoy's closest confidante. An expert in psychotherapy, she has unusual ability to teach patients how to use the healing powers of their own bodies.

Doctor/Nurse Chapel is really the second *Star Trek* character portrayed by Majel. In 1964, after being "discovered" in Gene Roddenberry's *The Lieutenant* series, she was featured in the first *Star Trek* pilot episode, playing the part of "Number One," the second in command of the starship *Enterprise.*

She was born Majel (pronounced "May'-gel") Lee Hudec on February 23 in Columbus, Ohio. Her first name is American Indian, but she is actually Bohemian by nationality. She grew up in Cleveland, where she graduated from Shaker Heights High School and attended Flora Stone Mather College for Women at Western Reserve University. Graduating as a theatre arts major, she entered University of Miami Law School for a year, but decided to make acting her career and moved to New York. Her start came during eleven weeks of stock in Bermuda, followed by a play that closed in Boston before it could reach Broadway, and a nine-month tour in *The Solid Gold Cadillac.*

Turning to California, Majel appeared with Edward Everett Horton in *All for May* at the famed Pasadena Playhouse, then began studying with Anthony Quinn. The actor, impressed with her talent, took her to Paramount, where she appeared in three motion pictures, *The Buccaneer, Black Orchids,* and as costar in *As Young As We Are.*

More study followed, first drama with Sanford Meisner, then comedy with Lucille Ball. The latter led to a year's contract with Desilu. Since then, she has been free-lancing, appearing in such motion pictures as *Sylvia, Love in a Goldfish Bowl, Guide for the Married Man, Track of Thunder, Westworld,* and *The Quick and the Dead.*

Her numerous tv appearances have included guest roles in *The Next Step Beyond, The Eleventh Hour, Dr. Kildare, Bonanza, Pete and Gladys, General Hospital,* and *The Wackiest Ship in the Army.*

She and *Star Trek* producer Gene Roddenberry were married in 1969. They have a son, Gene Roddenberry, Jr., affectionately called "Rod," and Majel divides her time between husband, son, dogs, cat, tropical fish breeding, and a passion—and skill—for golf. She is also "boss lady" of a busy promotion-mail-order corporation. And she still has one acting goal—"I'd like to be the captain of a starship!" From nurse to doctor to *captain?* Why not?

* * *

Grace Lee Whitney returns to *Star Trek—The Motion Picture* in the role of Transporter Chief Janice Rand, a promotion for her character from that of yeoman in the first season of the *Star Trek* television show, in which she played the captain's yeoman, a job which included being everything from Captain Kirk's secretary to his personal valet. There was little doubt but that Yeoman Rand was also in love with her captain. However, by the second season the network insisted that the good captain should have many girl friends and romances, all to be provided by a succession of female guest stars, so Yeoman Janice faded from sight. (Roddenberry stated many times in the intervening years that he had been mistaken in yielding to network pressure, and should have retained Grace Lee Whitney and Yeoman Rand on the series.)

With the decision to make the movie, it was decided to include Grace Lee again as Janice Rand, now chief of transporter operations. There is no description given in the *Writers'/Directors' Guide* for the transporter chief, so Grace Lee was left on her own in developing this character. But this was not too difficult, for the talented actress and singer had always remained close to *Star Trek,* delighting fans at conventions with original songs about Yeoman Janice Rand's adventures aboard the *Enterprise.* She and Janice are old friends.

Grace was born in Detroit, Michigan on April 1. After moving to

Chicago, she began singing with a band when she was 17, and four years later made her Broadway debut in *Top Banana*.

Upon reaching Hollywood, she became widely known as the mermaid in the Chicken of the Sea commercials. This was followed by her first role in a tv series, a part in *Mickey Spillane*. Soon she landed roles in motion pictures, including *Some Like It Hot* and *Irma La Douce*. Among the many tv shows in which she has appeared are *The Next Step Beyond, The Bold Ones, Batman, Bewitched, Name of the Game, Mod Squad, The Outer Limits, Twilight Zone, Cannon, Mannix, Bonanza, Gunsmoke, The Virginian,* and *The Untouchables*.

Next to acting, music is her greatest joy, and she and husband, Jack Dale, have composed many of their own songs around a *Star Trek* theme. Grace writes the lyrics, Jack the music, and the two of them, along with their group, called Star, have recorded such songs as "Disco Trekkin'," "Star Child," "Spaced Out Pilot," "The Enemy Within," and "Charlie X." Other numbers include "Wait, Don't Spoil It, Baby," "Fire Drill," and a number of new disco tunes including "U.S.S. *Enterprise*" (a disco number), and "Ilia's Theme." Ten of the songs are being readied for a soon-to-be-released album.

She and Jack share their house and backyard recording studio with their Great Dane, Citizen Kane. Grace has two sons by a former marriage; one of her boys, Scott, appears as a Vulcan extra in the rec deck scene.

11

Spray-and-Wear Clothing

It is three centuries from now. You have an important function to attend, and naturally, you haven't got a thing to wear. Not to worry—simply step into your shower, relax as the gentle spray of the sonic mist not only cleanses your body, but at the mere touch of the right button, disintegrates your tired old clothing for recycling into new duds.

Throwaway clothes, Gene Roddenberry believes, is the future of the clothing industry, and the idea was incorporated into *Star Trek—The Motion Picture*. When the Ilia-probe materializes au naturel in the was denoted by the color of the shirt worn by a crew person, in the charmingly brief leisure outfit forms around her. Gone (theoretically) are all the seams which would be visible in our old-fashioned cut-and-sewn clothing. (If "Ilia" had wished to change clothing, her old costume would dissolve away, to be reprogrammed into a new costume, very similar to the way a person's molecules are broken down and reassembled in the transporter.)

Unfortunately, all this is only theory, and *Star Trek—The Motion Picture* had to find other means of designing and fabricating the more than seven hundred costumes worn in the picture. For this reason a 20th-century choice had to be found—an experienced and creative costume designer by the name of Robert Fletcher.

Costume designer Robert Fletcher poses with some of his more elaborate creations.

Fletcher came to *Star Trek*—his first motion picture assignment—well equipped to meet its heavy demands. He is considered one of the American theatre's most successful costume and scenic designers, and in a varied career going back more than thirty years, he has designed costumes for major ballet and opera companies across the United States in addition to ice shows, television specials, and the New York stage.

His first ambition was to become an archeologist. Before graduating from Harvard, however, the native of Cedar Rapids, Iowa, had become an aspiring actor in campus productions. He later made his bow on the New York stage with Ethel Barrymore in *Embezzled Heaven*. His last acting role was with Orson Welles in *King Lear,* for which he also designed the costumes. By this time, Bob was hooked on costume design, and his career eventually brought him to *Star Trek*.

Bob had a tough act to follow. William Ware Theiss has become very well known as the man who created the original *Star Trek* television series costumes, and the starship crew's uniforms were practically synonymous with the program in the eyes of the fans. Some of his alien costumes are still considered science-fiction classics. As for Theiss's Starfleet uniforms, it is generally agreed that they were perfectly adapted to the television medium—not only their cut and flair, but also their bright reds, blues, greens and other hues so exciting when seen on the relatively small television screen. When Bill Theiss was unavailable for the movie, due to another major film assignment, Bob Fletcher was asked to do something entirely different for the film version. Fashion tastes had changed since the sixties—the miniskirt female costumes, so exciting ten years ago, would almost certainly be condemned in the seventies as sexist. Fletcher also agreed with the producer and director that the outstanding brightness of the television show's uniforms would work against believability when seen on the wide screen. His first task, then, was to design totally new uniforms for the *Enterprise* crew—uniforms which would meet the director's requirements of not detracting from the action, and which would allow the audience to focus attention on the relationships between the people up on the screen, rather than on what they were wearing.

Some vestiges of the television show were allowed to carry over into the movie in the form of the identification patches on the crew's uniforms. Whereas in the tv series the division of ship's assignments were denoted by the color of the shirt worn by a crew person, in the movie these color codes are now found in the patches on each person's uniform. All of the identification patches in the television series were a metallic gold, etched in black, with a logo in the center designating the branch of starship duty to which the wearer belonged—command, science, medical, engineering, and so on. In the movie, there is only one logo—the insignia originally used to designate "command." This now serves as the identification for *everyone* serving aboard the starship *Enterprise*. It is shaped exactly as in the television program, and is *superimposed over a circle of color* sewn to the uniform directly below the left shoulder. The *colors in the circle* (rather than the color of the uniform itself) now serve as an indication of the crewperson's area of service.

white	— Command
red	— Engineering
orange	— Science
pale gold	— Operations
green	— Medical
gray	— Security

There are a couple of other changes from the tv series evident here. Since Mr. Spock is one of the most important principals in the film, prominent in nearly every scene, director Robert Wise felt that the former *blue* color of science wouldn't be a good choice, since it would not show up well on the grayish-blue uniform usually worn by the science officer—hence the orange patch for the science division. (Blue is also a difficult color to work with since it can create problems when working with the blue screens commonly used in optical effects work.) Medical was also blue in the television series, falling under the aegis of the science section. In the movie, Doctors McCoy and Chapel and other medical personnel have a color patch of their own—*green*, which is often associated with that profession.

Fletcher not only devised uniforms for all the crew, but, as with most military services, there are also several classes of uniforms.

Dress uniforms are worn only on formal occasions and at Starfleet Headquarters. The best example of this can be seen in Admiral Kirk's uniform worn at the beginning of the movie, with Bill Shatner wearing the crisp loden green and white uniform.

Class A uniforms are double-stitched in gabardine and have gold braid designating rank. Some of them have open necklines or other variations, as is true in the military services of our century. Rank designation became a point of confusion because of a decision made years before on television series uniforms. It was felt that the traditional *four gold stripes* of ship captain's rank was too blatantly "militaristic"-looking for a 23rd-century paramilitary starship. Accordingly, the captain was held to a couple of stripes and lower ranks to even less. It was decided to continue this way for the movie. But many of the new *Star Trek* staff (and even Bob Fletcher himself) kept getting the 20th and 23rd centuries confused. Finally, Jon Povill prepared the following memo:

INTER-COMMUNICATION

TO: Bob Fletcher   DATE: August 3, 1978

FROM: Jon Povill   SUBJECT: Uniforms

Rank insignias are as follows:

        Ensign   .... — — — —

        Lieutenant   ....   ————————

        Lieutenant Commander   ....   — — —)
) Distance between
        Commander   ....   ————————) stripes is the same

        Captain   ....   — — —
                                            ————————
        Rear Admiral ....   ————————) Double width stripe
                                            ▬▬▬▬▬▬▬

Rank designation on epaulets should be the same as on the sleeve.

Ranks of officers are as follows:

Ensign	Lt.	Lt. Commander	Commander	Captain
Rand	Chekov	Sulu	McCoy	Kirk
	Chapel	Uhura	Decker	
	Ilia		Scott	
			Spock	

In this manner it will be possible to determine the rank of
fellow officers simply by glancing at their uniforms. It is not
necessary to salute.

JP/ra

cc: Gene Roddenberry   Walter Koenig
     Robert Wise   Majel Barrett
     William Shatner   Grace Lee Whitney
     Leonard Nimoy   Persis Khambatta
     DeForest Kelley   Stephen Collins
     James Doohan   George Takei
                             Nichele Nichols

The next day, he noticed that he had made a slight error with Rand's
costume:

TO: BOB FLETCHER   DATE: AUGUST 4, 1978

FROM: JON POVILL   SUBJECT: RAND'S COSTUME

I was in error. Rand is not an ensign. She is a transporter chief. This
means there should be no sleeve stripe on her costume.

Sorry about that, Chief.

cc: Robert Wise
     Gene Roddenberry
     Grace Lee Whitney

Class B uniforms utilize shirts which look similar to evolved T-shirts.
These are white, beige, and pale brown, and use shoulder boards to
indicate rank and service division (through color designations).

Uniforms worn on the bridge are of three general classifications. All
command officers generally wear the blue-gray uniforms (Kirk, Spock,
Decker, Scotty, McCoy); other bridge officers like Sulu and Chekov
wear beige; crew personnel who are usually never on the bridge except
for emergencies wear brown.

Each costume also had the *shoes built into the pant leg,* one of Bob
Fletcher's innovations, since he was after a futuristic look that could
not be found in your local stores. The shoes were designed by a noted
Italian shoemaker who has been decorated by the Italian government
for making the models for most of the famous Gucci line of shoes. Bob

admits that making the trousers and shoe all in one was very difficult and expensive. Each shoe was individually sewn in by hand after being fitted to each principal actor. The shoemaker marked the anklebone inside and out, and the pants were cut longer than the floor in order to be pulled down over the shoe form. Adding to the difficulty is a leg pleat just above the shoe. Problems arose when they didn't allow enough material; sometimes a leg would end up too short, making it impossible for an actor to stand up straight.

There was also the difficulty of communicating with the Italian shoemaker, who spoke limited English. This had a disastrous effect on at least two of the cast members—Nichelle Nichols and Majel Barrett. To his Italian ear, the names *Nichelle* and *Majel* sounded very much alike, and he confused their shoe orders as well as their names. Tall, willowy Majel tops out at five nine; Nichelle is a petite five two. For this reason, Majel ordered her shoes with two-inch heels, while Nichelle asked for height-extending five-inch heels. The shoemaker goofed—and the shoe mixup the first day on the set resulted in an embarrassed Majel, looking more like a center for the Los Angeles Lakers than a newly commissioned ship's doctor. She spent most of the day sitting backstage or hiding out in her dressing room, hoping that her scenes would be delayed so she wouldn't have to play her role on her knees! Fortunately for her, the scenes were delayed, and the error was quickly corrected for the next day's shooting.

In addition to these uniforms, there are *jump suits* in white, brown, beige, gray, and sage green (this color worn in Earth scenes only). These are a kind of work suit, and have the only pockets of any *Star Trek* costumes, since these outfits are designed to be utilitarian. The jump suits are also designed to fit like a second skin, moving and bending with the person wearing them. Bob chose a special heavyweight spandex, which he admits was hell to sew, and required the use of a special ballpoint needle to penetrate the material.

Other costumes included *leisure wear, field jackets* (these are worn in the final scenes at the site of *Voyager 6*) and *space suits*. Since all of the costumes were created before most of the featured actors' parts had been cast, many parts had to be filled on the basis of size and height as well as acting ability. Casting director Marvin Paige and his assistant Skitch Hendricks often found themselves searching for tall actresses or size-forty-two actors who could not only act but also fit into the awaiting costumes.

Fletcher prefers natural materials to man-made fabrics, finding that natural fabrics not only sew better and last longer but are self-renewable. "Sheep keep producing wool, and cotton and flax keep growing. Deliver me from the -*ons!*" he pleads, in speaking of synthetic fabrics such as orlon and nylon. "They are horrible! They may wash and wear beautifully, but they certainly don't tailor, and they don't sew or dye well."

For the civilian Earthlings in the film, whom we glimpse in the opening San Francisco tram sequence, he leaned toward a greater freedom in dress. Much of the material for these more casual clothes was found in old storerooms on the Paramount lot, and an amazing amount of fine old silks, crepes, suedes, and leathers was located. Many of these materials had been locked away for decades, some left over from earlier Paramount films dating back to the days of Cecil B. DeMille epics. One such bolt of material bore a tag on it identifying it has having been hand picked by DeMille in 1939. It was in perfect condition, and Bob quickly appropriated the red, black, silver, and gold brocade woven with leopards and falcons and real gold and silver wrapped around silk thread. The costume he created is doubtless the most valuable costume ever worn by a Hollywood extra, the fabric alone estimated by Bob to be worth at least $10,000. Twelve yards of the precious material went into a costume worn by a seven-foot-tall Betelgeusian chief ambassador. Bob estimates that the material probably cost about $150 to $200 a yard forty years ago, and if it could be found today, it would most likely have to be imported from Florence, Italy, at nearly *five* times that cost.

In addition to designing all of the costumes, Bob Fletcher, long a science-fiction fan, took his talents a step further. Along with makeup artist Fred Phillips, Bob created many of the dozen different alien types seen in the film, not only naming these creatures but, with the approval and guidance of Gene Roddenberry, providing complete backgrounds for each. Here are brief descriptions of these *Star Trek* aliens, in Bob's own words:

ALIENS

(As seen in San Francisco sequence and, in some cases, in recreation deck sequence):

AAAMAZZARITES—Therbians from planet Aaamazzara. They generate their own clothing from out of own mouths, like bees making hives. They manufacture everything they use from their own chemistry, from inside their own body, from clothing to furniture. Costumes for film modeled in clay, cast in sheets of foam rubber.

KAZARITES—Like shepherds, from planet still in stage of raising great herds of beasts. But their society is technologically sophisticated. They have certain powers of telekinesis. Can transport selves mentally. Have mental communication with all animals on all planets. Have been imported into Earth system to take care of animals, fish, and bird life. Really 23rd-century ecologists. Little bags hung around them are for food—pellets which they mix with water to produce a yeastlike food.

BETELGEUSIANS—Name taken from the real star. All tall, seven feet and over. Humanoid with characteristics combining eagle and leopard. Derived in evolution from giant leopardlike birds, have claw and bone structure like condor but walk upright like leopards. Costumes: materials found stored in Paramount for as long as forty years. Jewelry made of fabric, but electro-plated.

ARCTURIANS—A militaristic race of great armies. All are identical—they clone each other, can only tell apart by color of uniforms. Provide infantry for Federation. Planet is enormous and population enormous, subject to any amount of expansion; 100 billion population, army of 20 billion ready overnight. Costume—contains leather and linen. Boots are separate. (Bob wanted woven metal tubes for metal rope decorations; found in obsolete plumbing equipment in an old hardware store; silver-plated it for bandolier [jewelry] and for decoration on shoulders and elbows, denoting rank and regiment.) Briefcase made of plastic, belt buckle of cast metal and resin.

ZARANITES—Can't breath oxygen, so must wear breathing mask on Earth; pack on back generates fluorine gas which they breath. Costume: old suedes found in Paramount storage, left over from DeMille's *The Ten Commandments*. Jewelry: hornlike in appearance, supposedly made of horns of one of the most widely cultivated Zaranite animals, the Berbbotjahaa. Actually made from fabric and liquid plastic. Represents family totem. Top part (necklace) designates family, lower is personal designation.

K'NORMIANS—From planet K'norm. Similar to Earthlings but have additional brain structure. Additional part of brain performs functions we aren't capable of, mainly for long-distance communication. They have an eighth sense, can deal with time and space dimension.

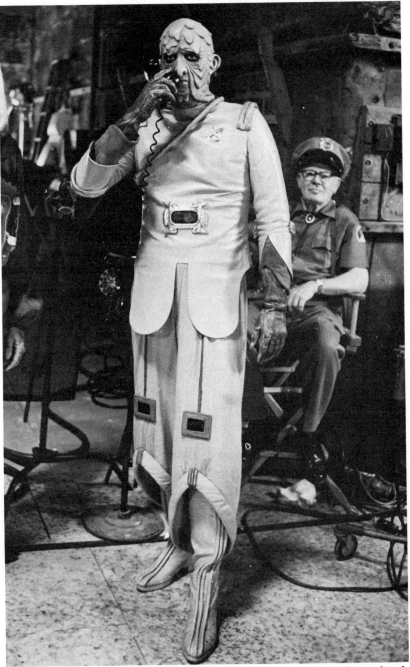

"How are things back on Arcturus?" *Enterprise* crew member takes a break
backstage as studio guard Richard Thompson looks on.

RIGELLIANS—Descended from race of saber-toothed turtles, learned to walk upright. Range from five nine to seven feet and over. Unisex. Lay eggs. Real power is with attendants who serve, feed, and care for them. Costume of draped wool. Hands and feet of sculpted rubber. Wear ceremonial helmet and half-armor. Armor sculpted in studio craft shop, molded Fiberglas and chrome-plated.

RHAANDARITES—From star system Rhaandaran. Simple, gregarious people. Women as big and strong as the men. Long-lived. Are like children, don't mature until 150 years old. Can grow to eight or nine feet with full height when about 200 years old. Crew member on *Enterprise* bridge, played by Billy Van Zandt, is young, about eighty-five. Extremely faithful, good at carrying out commands, not at giving them. Little visual sexual difference. Women designated by a spot on forehead of aluminum and black resin. Costume: silver and black lamé. Necklace: used for communication. All-purpose jewelry with machinery built in, of resin, dark gray plastic. Toy parts used for machinery that can be seen inside jewelry.

SHAMIN PRIEST—From O'Ryan's planet, discovered by Paddy O'Ryan in 22nd century. Costume: made of fabric and liquid plastic, solidifies, turns into another kind of material. Bob developed this process more fully for the movie. All gold objects of this process. Rag parts of costume specially woven on hand loom.

MEGARITES—Quite humanoid, but body has similarity to rhino hide. Four lips, with straining mechanics similar to baleen of whale, in mouth of whales. Live by marine life found in waters of their planet, difficult to live away, have to provide artificial means of keeping alive in other environment.

Federation scientists have found way by intravenous injection of proper nutrients capable of sustaining them for a week. Poetic people, communicate with songlike sounds, musical poems in own language, through four lips. Most of planet made of jade—houses, artifacts, etc., carved from jade. Much of clothing comes from sea animals. Costume: sleeve, cast from plastic, simulates graphite steel. Traditional on planet to wear many ornaments of graphite steel or jade. "Jade" plaque on costume collar made of fabric and plastic, looks like jade. Hood of fabric lined with sheet foam rubber to give body sculptured effect. Costume of indigo blue wool, from studio warehouse.

SAURIAN—A lizard person, very able, excellent space officers. Learned to communicate in Earth tongue, have complicated vocal language of own. Have upright, direct posture. Intelligent. Can breathe a number of gases. Valuable in exploration of new areas because of enormous strength due to four hearts. (Note: in rec deck scene only.)

DIPLOMATIC SERVICE—In San Francisco scene, may be Earthlings or aliens. Interpreters, translators. Have three-unit machine through which can speak or hear any foreign tongue. Can set machine for any language. Right side of jacket has miniaturized components which measure nuances in language translators. Portable computer on left arm. Helmet allows to hear and make sounds during translating.

DELTANS—Hairless people from Planet Delta 4. Deltans are great jewelry makers. Their jewelry is sold throughout the galaxy and is very popular. Male Deltan wears traditional caftan with Deltan symbol on sleeve. Made of gabardine. Ilia costume, as probe, wears leisure outfit of off-white jersey with shaped collar of brown jersey.

VULCANS—(from tv series)—Observed in movie as Mr. Spock, others among crew, and Masters on Vulcan planet scene. Unemotional, scientific people, their culture based on cold logic, reason and control. One of the Federation's most advanced races. Vulcan is a ruby planet, thus ruby jewelry and the red-booted giant figure in Vulcan scene. Great part of the planet is desert, with occasional weathered stone formations. Vulcans are mostly tall, slender, beautiful people, with strong sense of honor. Physically distinguished by upswept eyebrows and pointed ears. Their green blood is copper-based.

ANDORIANS—(from tv series)—Blue-skinned, with white hair and small-knobbed antennae (sensors) out of forehead. Can communicate over great distances. Very musical people, fairly combative. By heritage, a race of savage warriors, with strength masked by soft voices and slender builds. Ladies' costume: hand-painted; adorn sleeves with pieces from planet, used sliced geode framed in brass for ornaments and in hair. Men's costume: has belt and carries Flabbjellah, a combination musical instrument and weapon, carried by most males. Costume of old suede which was stored at Paramount since *The Ten Commandments*.

KLINGONS—(in Klingon space cruiser scene only)—The old foes of the Federation. Warlike. Spine comes up over head and down forehead (different from series). Hair on side of head as though trying to cover spine. Costume: mixed silver powder into fabric and liquid plastic for bright trim on armor. Used surgical tubing dyed black for other trim.

12

Put On an Alien Face

There is something faintly unnerving about seeing rows and rows of disembodied alien heads staring down at you from several shelves on the wall. But if you had paid a visit to the stage 10 headquarters of *Star Trek*'s makeup artist, Fred Phillips, this is the first sight that would have greeted you. His rogues' gallery of alien full-head masks looked more like a collection from some very mad scientist's little shop of horrors. However, once the heads of the alien creatures were united with the bodies of extras, plus the costumes created by Bob Fletcher, there was an exciting transformation. No longer looking like a bizarre trick-or-treat mask, Rigellians, Betelgeusians, and Saurians seemed to have been given the gift of life.

Fred Phillips and his staff produced a total of fifty face masks and full heads for the many aliens seen in the San Francisco and rec deck scenes, designing some himself, making others from Bob Fletcher's sketches. But giving life to his alien creations was only a part of Fred's work as makeup artist on *Star Trek—The Motion Picture*.

To tens of thousands of *Star Trek* fans, the name Fred Phillips was already a household word, something few makeup artists can claim. The reason for the fame of this congenial, youthful seventy-one-year-old man's popularity extends back to the 1960s, when Fred and Gene

Fred Phillips' "rogue's gallery" of alien masks.

Roddenberry puzzled over the proper size and shapes for Mr. Spock's Vulcan ears. After many screen tests, Fred came up with the pointed ears, which were seen in *Star Trek*'s television pilot, "The Cage," and became Mr. Spock's trademark. Freddy also worked on all three years of the television series, and with the exception of Gene Roddenberry and some of the original cast, he has been involved with *Star Trek* longer than anyone else. *Star Trek* marks Fred's 450th screen assignment, and his other recent films include *One Flew Over the Cuckoo's Nest* and *When You Coming Back, Red Ryder?* A milestone was passed during the production of the *Star Trek* movie when Fred produced his 2000th Spock ear. This proliferation of pointed ears was necessitated by the fact that although in the television series the ears could be used again and again (up to four times, since slight nicks or tears didn't show up on the small screen), in the film version, Leonard Nimoy went through *an average of nearly three sets per day!*

Several days before Leonard's first scene, the actor reported to

makeup in order to have molds made of his ears, enabling Fred to produce the perfectly fitted latex appliances. Although the makeup artist had saved the molds from the television series, Leonard's ears had grown in a few places during the interim years, and the old molds were useless. From these new molds (two of each ear) Fred Phillips whipped up his latex mixture each day. Six ingredients were carefully measured and weighed to the exact gram requirement, then blended together, according to a special recipe, in an ordinary kitchen mix-master. Fred insisted that the temperature of stage 10 be kept no hotter than 70 degrees or these ingredients and other makeup would be ruined. Two sets of ears were poured and baked each day in Freddy's special oven for six hours, and any excess ears were stockpiled for emergencies. And sure enough, an emergency occurred. Over the 1979 New Year's holidays, the cast and crew were off from Friday until Tuesday, and before leaving for the long weekend, Freddy mixed up a batch of Spock ears and put them in the oven to bake. He was assured by a studio nightwatchman that the oven would be turned off in five and a half hours, when the ears would be thoroughly cooked and ready. But the guard apparently had too much holiday cheer, and forgot all about the oven. Four days later, Freddy returned to find the oven was still on, and the molds had blown up! New impressions of Leonard's ears had to be cast, and Freddy had to work around the clock to produce new molds in time for Spock's next scenes.

Fred did quite a brisk trade in pointed ears during the motion picture. Not only did Mr. Spock keep him occupied, but the Vulcan Masters also had to be properly fitted with the pointy appliances. It is a biological fact that human's (and presumably humanoid's) ears and noses grow throughout their lifetime. Since the Vulcan Masters are very old, even by Vulcan standards, which consider two hundred fifty years an average lifespan, these wisened leaders would naturally have much larger than average ears, and you will notice that Fred allowed for this growth when you look carefully at the actors in the scene on Vulcan.

An important part of Freddy's job as makeup artist is to be a good psychologist, relaxing a tense actor who may arrive at 6:30 in the morning not having slept well or may have other problems on his mind. If there is any tension in a face, not only won't the makeup go on smoothly but the actor may be tense all day on the set, which can have disastrous effects on his scenes.

Leonard Nimoy's first visit to Freddy's makeup chair, after ten years, found it a happy reunion for both, although there were a couple of minor problems in transforming him into Mr. Spock. Fred had become a bit rusty from lack of practice in applying pointed ears, and together he and Leonard struggled through that first session. For example, Fred had forgotten that the first step was to glue Leonard's own ears back, which Leonard suddenly remembered about halfway through the session, when he began looking like the Vulcan version of a hobgoblin. Leonard agreed he felt a little strange having the ears put on him again after all those years. He had never expected this would happen again when he became Mr. Spock for what he assumed was the last time on the day the final television episode was filmed in 1968.

Leonard Nimoy was usually the first to arrive and settle into the makeup chair. He has always been Fred's special responsibility, and the two men have built up quite a good rapport during all these years. One morning, after the movie had been in production for about five months, DeForest Kelley arrived earlier than usual and settled into the chair, ready to be made up as Dr. McCoy. Fred, conditioned to put ears on the person who was always in the chair at that hour, didn't bother looking up from his powders, creams, and spirit gums, assumed it was Leonard who has just seated himself, and began putting ears on DeForest! The actor was startled, but didn't say anything, wondering what Fred was up to. Finally, the makeup artist downed some of his morning coffee, opened his eyes a bit wider, and realized what had happened. He had turned Dr. McCoy into a Vulcan! Much to DeForest's relief (and no doubt the good doctor's, as well), the ears were quickly removed.

Freddy was also responsible for the final look of the upswept eyebrows which further characterize Mr. Spock and other Vulcans. For the movie, the eyebrows had to be applied hair by hair each day, and often Leonard was kept in the chair for nearly two hours, more than twice the amount of time needed for the television series makeup.

After Leonard's makeup was completed each day, Fred and his assistant, Charles Schram,* turned their attention to the more routine makeup of other cast members, while his daughter, Janna, worked on Steve Collins (a routine application of facial makeup) and Persis

---

*Fred and Charles have worked together since the Thirties, and Charles is credited with creating the formula for Spock's latex ears.

Khambatta, whose bald dome had to be freshly shaved every day, then given an application of makeup to avoid any possibility of glare from the hot lights on the set. You will recall that Fred did the original shaving of Persis's head, a job which was not only traumatic for Persis, but touched him quite deeply as well. When Janna was a child, she had baby-fine platinum hair which grew like wispy cotton. It was recommended that her head be shaved so that newer, coarser hair could grow in its place. Fred admits he hated to do it, but he finally had to shave his little girl's head, and when he was doing the same to Persis many years later, he relived that sad moment in his life all over again. (Janna's hair did grow in stronger, so the "operation" was a success.)

At first Persis had no qualms about having her head shaved. But when her once lovely hair today was gone tomorrow, she started worrying about whether she'd have to spend the rest of her life looking like a distant relative of a honeydew. When she brought a request for a Lloyd's of London insurance policy to Gene Roddenberry, he sent the following memo to Paramount's executive in charge of the *Star Trek* production:

TO: JEFF KATZENBERG   DATE: JULY 19, 1978
FROM: GENE RODDENBERRY   SUBJECT: PERSIS KHAMBATTA

I have a request from Persis Khambatta ("Ilia") that we consider insuring her against shaving of her head causing any kind of permanent hair damage. She made the request herself on a personal level rather than legalistically through agent or attorney, being that kind of gentle person.

I think we should look into this for a couple of reasons. First, when we faced a similar concern over shaving Leonard Nimoy's eyebrows over three years of series we were told by a reputable doctor that it could not possibly harm hair regrowth. Thus the price of any such insurance might very well be negligible. Second, it would have the advantage of reassuring Persis and making her feel more comfortable during her role. Third and finally, if the price does turn out to be negligible, John Rothwell, our publicist, assures me that we would probably get many times the cost back in publicity about the insurance.

If you agree it should at least be looked into, would appreciate your placing this matter in the proper hands.

The idea was kicked around awhile, but the policy was never taken out. It turned out to be *very* expensive, since insurance companies queried believed that there could be difficulty in proving whether the hair grew back *exactly* the same way as the original. A compromise was reached. Persis visited the renowned Georgette Klinger Skin Care Salon in Beverly Hills, specialists in maintaining skin and scalp. Since she had to have her head shaved daily, followed by *three* coats of thick makeup, the salon experts recommended that she receive six facials and scalp treatments during the course of production, and that she follow a prescribed program of scalp treatment, suggesting that she included these products in her routine:

1. Cleansing bar in place of shampoo (shampoo is too harsh on scalp when there is no hair).
2. Brilliantine lotion to be used as moisturizer for scalp after washing.
3. Conditioner to be used once a week (left on for two hours) to soften and condition.
4. Makeup remover.
5. Cleansing lotion.

The studio did agree that these products were necessary, and Persis spent the next six months following the salon's tedious but necessary instructions for scalp care, which eventually did result in the healthy regrowth of her hair.

Fred's daughter, Janna, had no idea when she was a child that she was a prototype for a Deltan, although there was really never any doubt as to her future career. The pretty blonde grew up surrounded by a family of makeup artists. Fred's father, F. B. Phillips, began the makeup dynasty sixty years earlier, and in 1927 organized the Motion Picture Makeup Artists Association, the first group of makeup artists in the United States. Fred and his two brothers, his two nephews, and his ex-wife all took up the art of motion picture makeup. Janna became involved with the business as a teenager, when Fred was designing Mr. Spock's television ears. Her job at the time was to help her dad pour and mix rubber at home for Leonard's ears.

Janna still spends a lot of her time acting as her father's guinea pig, and the things he's tested on her include everything from Andorian antennae and blue facial makeup to alien appliances and masks. Janna even had an impression of her throat taken so that the special effects department would have a model to test potential throat buttons for the Ilia-probe, as later worn by Persis. When Janna wasn't making up Steve or Persis, or serving as test model for her dad's experiments, she was on the *Star Trek* set helping with touch-ups which are needed on actors' makeup throughout the shooting day.

Another of Fred's assistants was Ve Neill. Ve's biggest project each day involved making up Billy Van Zandt, the Rhaandarite alien on the bridge. This *prosthetic* makeup (makeup which involves appliances which must be attached to the actor's face or head) included an oversized brain structure, covered with Billy's own hair, followed by a lacy gray hairpiece wig to make him look eighty-five years young. The whole process took anywhere from forty-five minutes to a full hour. His character also called for him to wear contact lenses, which had black centers surrounded by yellow and orange. These made it virtually impossible for him to see, and most of Billy's scenes were done by touch alone. The enlarged brain appearance of this alien creature earned it the name of "Bumphead," and for a long time before the invention of a true generic name, Billy Bumphead became quite well known around the lot. Of course, there were exceptions, as when visitors to the studio, unaware of the excellent makeup job, wondered about the poor fellow with the malformed cranium who probably didn't have long to live!

Ve was also charged with making up Bill Shatner, and his sense of humor often kept her on her toes, especially during touch-ups on the set. Bill loves to while away the time between takes by chewing bubble gum, and one afternoon his passion for the sticky stuff nearly destroyed Ve's own sense of humor. On the day the travel pod sequence was being filmed, Bill was blowing his biggest bubble on record, when, without warning, his bubble burst—all over his face.

While Bill put on his best little boy pout, Ve chastized him while removing the pieces which were stuck all over his face. As she picked at the gum, Bill began perspiring uncontrollably under the hot lights, causing the gum to adhere even more. Finally, Ve grabbed the remaining wad of gum from Bill's mouth and used it like a magnet to blot up the remaining bits while the rest of the production crew looked on, laughing.

Hair styles of the future were another challenge to the makeup department. Usually, it involved creating strange alien hairdos, but *Star Trek*'s hairstylist supervisor, Barbara Kay Minster, claims her most challenging job was to style Persis's hair on the morning of the famous sheering. She spent quite a bit of time getting each curl on Persis's head to look just right for the "before" photos, then watched sadly as her handiwork ended up in a box that Persis used to save her shorn locks. (The actress still has them at home in a drawer.)

As production hairstylist, Barbara was responsible for creating the hairstyles of nearly everyone in the cast, as well as touching up wayward wisps and cowlicks that arose on the set. Most of these styles didn't present much of a problem, as the *Star Trek* "look" that Roddenberry and director Wise wanted was a simple, unadorned militaristic one. Bill Shatner's hair has a natural curl to it, and it had to be blow-dried each morning to make it match the previous day's scenes exactly. Since Shatner's hair has a tendency to curl under the hot lights, nearly every break between takes found the hairstylist running over with her comb to smooth his hair back down again. On the other hand, Leonard Nimoy's hair and Mr. Spock's bangs were sprayed down with so much lacquer that even a hurricane couldn't move them. Nichelle Nichols's "natural" seemed likely for the 23rd century, and she required just a touch of Afrosheen and a pat or two to keep it in place. No one was allowed to have long hairstyles, and the other ladies in the cast, Majel Barrett and Grace Lee Whitney, both had their hair put up in twists.

The challenge of making a science-fiction film is evident in the unusual hairdos which had to be created for the San Francisco scene. Among the most difficult wigs to design were the ones for the Andorian females. These very striking white wigs involved a lot of backing with starchy material, and wire, and were covered in cotton along with real hair. In all, twenty ladies' wigs were created for that scene. It is a good example of science-fiction costumes, makeup, and hairstyles all blending together into believable people doing believable things, in a place that is not yet in existence, in a year that has not yet arrived.

13

Property of Star Trek

The easiest way to get property master Dick Rubin's attention is to holler "Back!" The word has nothing at all to do with props, but everyone who knows this dean of Hollywood propmen greets him with some form of the word: "It's nice to have you *back!*" "Rube's *back!*" "Get *back,* here comes Dick Rubin!" Jerry Lewis, a close friend, once ordered some personalized stationery for Dick which said "From the Desk of Richard Rubin, Creator of Back." Actor Jack Lemmon offered to buy Dick a "personalized" license plate with the letters B A C K. (He politely declined.)

It all started fifteen years ago when Dick was returning a telephone call to a certain company, and was informed that the party he wished to speak with was out. Dick replied, "Would you please have him call Mr. Rubin back?" To which he received the reply, "Yes, I'll have him call you, Mr. Rubinback." After that, he began receiving calls for Mr. Rubinback. His coworkers teasingly called him Rubinback, which eventually was shortened simply to "Back." Now, wherever he goes, he is likely to be greeted by a resounding chorus of "Back!" The *Star Trek* crew took the joke one step further. Someone spotted the Back Motel on Olympic Boulevard in Los Angeles and had a giant blowup made of it. The entire production crew then autographed the photo with some choice phrases, most of which can be left to the imagination.

Prop man Dick Rubin *(left)* **explains the new communicator to Bill Shatner.**

Dick "Rubinback" takes all this in stride. He has been in the business so long and is so skilled at his craft that a newspaper columnist once wrote, "Half of the propmen in Hollywood have worked for Dick Rubin at one time or another, and the other half wish they had." It's not difficult to understand why Dick's talents are always in demand. He began working with props in the heyday of the old RKO Studios. He worked on the first pictures of Gregory Peck, Frank Sinatra, and Jack Nicholson. For eight years he was propman on all of Jerry Lewis's pictures, and the two have a continuing close friendship. He also did six pictures with Barbra Streisand, plus numerous other films, including, *Straight Time,* with Dustin Hoffman, *Who'll Stop the Rain?* and *Dog Soldiers.** Rube's no stranger to science fiction either. He worked on fifty-five *Outer Limits* television episodes, and on the feature film *Marooned.* †

---

*Another case of production company overlap—Richard Kline, *Star Trek's* cinematographer, also worked on *Who'll Stop . . .* and *Dog Soldiers.*
† Overlap here included first A.D. Danny McCauley.

From this last movie, he claims he gained an insight into space films. One of the things he learned is that there's no dust in space, so everything on a set depicting outer space must be entirely dust-free. Since one of the prop person's responsibilities is to coordinate the physical look of the set with the set dresser, it was up to Rube to have the set dust-free before the shooting company arrived each day. For his cleanup crew, he devised a special chemically treated mop which would magnetically pick up the dust. You won't notice any dust aboard the *Enterprise*—there is none, thanks to Rube, who checked the sets for dust the way a snoopy old aunt does when she runs her finger across the coffee table looking for telltale signs.

Each morning while Bill, Leonard, and the others were in makeup, Rube could be found in his "office" (a makeshift room constructed in the far northwest corner of stage 9) preparing what he called his "day sheet." This handy reference, based on his breakdown of the script for that day's scenes, indicated how many people were working, and the number and kind of props that would be needed. These were put on his "hot cart"—a mobile cart Dick loaded with the day's props, then wheeled to the set. He also would remain on the set throughout the day's shooting in the event that a prop might break and need replacement, or should an actor use a prop incorrectly—as in the case of Bill Shatner wearing his wrist communicator backward the first time he used it.

A *prop* may be defined as something used by an actor in connection with his work. It must be utilized in some way by the actor, or it falls in the realm of set decoration. This fine line of distinction is very important in the trade, since the studio unions are sticky about their members crossing over into another's territory. For example, a book lying on a table is set decoration, but if in some scene an actor picks up that book and reads it, the book is actually a prop, and would be selected and placed by the person in charge of properties.

Rube's philosophy as property master on *Star Trek* was that nearly every actor or extra ought to have something in his hands. On a busy ship like the *Enterprise,* no one should be just walking around or standing idly by. Therefore, he devised and had fabricated approximately three hundred fifty props for *Star Trek,* fifty-five of which were used in one scene alone—the San Francisco air tram sequence. Many of the props were redesigns of ones created for the *Star Trek* television series, but the changes weren't at all arbitrary. As with changes in sets or costumes, these too were natural progressions from further advances in our own scientific technology over the last fifteen years.

Almost all of the props were of new design. There was, however, one prop used in the television series that was also used in *Star Trek—The Motion Picture.* As communications officer, Lieutenant Uhura must often listen to all kinds of subspace communications that may be going on. There couldn't be a speaker on her console because it would blare incessantly and interrupt other dialogue. When Uhura notifies the captain that "something is coming through from Starfleet," she's receiving the message via a wireless earpiece that fits in her ear. It is practically a part of her image. Uhura without her earpiece is almost like Spock without ears. Yet, except for those few people who had worked on the show before, no one seemed to remember this device. On Nichelle Nichols's first day of shooting, she settled into her seat at Uhura's console and immediately began searching around for her earpiece. There wasn't any. When Nichelle asked, "Where's my earpiece?" Bob Wise turned to Gene and said, "What's that?" Dick Rubin was called over and asked to come up with an earpiece within the next ten minutes! Normally, it takes several weeks to create a prop, and there certainly wasn't time to make anything which would look good on the big screen on such short notice. But sure enough, ten minutes later, Dick had produced not one, but *two* earpieces. The Creator of Back was now also proclaimed a magician. Actually, Jon Povill and Dick went to the basement of the old Paramount prop building, located a box of dusty leftover odds and ends from the original *Star Trek* series, and found a pair of well-preserved earpieces, the only original props used in the motion picture.

Other props in the movie include the following:

PHASER: Phasers are handheld weapons that emit a beam capable of doing many things to an adversary, ranging from simple *stun* to *disintegrate.* Although the television series sometimes used heavier types of phasers, the only one used in the film was the pistollike hand weapon. It was decided that the old phaser seemed to require some refinement to meet wide-screen needs, and it also seemed logical that Starfleet might change the design of its weaponry as new products and new methods came about. Thus Rubin was asked to submit a prototype phaser. The model eventually used was entirely self-contained, with its own circuitry and batteries and four-color blinking lights on top, plus a ray of light emanating from the front. It also had a $4,000 price tag. The multicolored lights were dropped, reducing the size of the phaser by a third and thus lowering the cost of the additional phasers, a total of fifteen of which were made up for the film.

COMMUNICATOR: Gene Roddenberry knew at the time that the original television series communicators were designed that they were far too large; even in those days miniaturization was common, and microminiaturization was certainly on the horizon. But he felt that because this wasn't a reality at the time, the general public would better understand a communicator that could be more easily seen. But by the late seventies, when computers had shrunk to the size of credit cards, it had become obvious that they couldn't continue using the old-style communicators. Gene had all sorts of ideas. Perhaps the people of the 23rd century would have implants, but someone pointed out that it would look a bit funny to see someone talking to their elbow! It was finally decided to try for a wrist communicator design, providing it looked far different from the ones Dick Tracy had been using in the comics for decades. The new Star Trek communicator, unlike the Tracy device, had all of the mechanism on the *inside* of the wrist and was designed to do many other things, including a direct contact with the main computer on the U.S.S. *Enterprise*—a function that will have to wait for any sequel movies, since it was never used in this film.

Like the phaser, the prototype of the communicator also bore a healthy price tag—$3,500. This was battery-operated and was used for "insert" shots—close-ups of a communicator actually lighting up, which are later inserted into a scene when the film is edited. In all, there were about two hundred communicators, but most of these were dummies. The ones of top quality were worn by the principals in closer camera angles.

TRICORDER: This is a device used to take scientific, medical, and other readings. The biggest objection to the tricorder used in the television series was the over-the-shoulder strap, which Dick Rubin was afraid would look today like Saturday afternoon at Disneyland with the old family super 8 movie camera. The strap was scrapped, and the tricorder was reduced in size over the earlier version. There were twenty made for the movie, ten of which were actual working models with battery-operated lights. The tricorders, as well as most of the props, were made of plastic, as it was Dick's belief that in the future, most things will be of man-made materials rather than metal.

BELT BUCKLE: These were actually designed by Bob Fletcher and are worn with each uniform. There were five hundred buckles made, in three sizes. The buckles are supposed to monitor bodily functions and report biofeedback information, but no working models were designed since the function never appeared in the film script (although it does appear in Roddenberry's book, *Star Trek—The Novel*).

SCANNER AND SONIC ANALYZER: These are used in the engine room to test tensile strength, detect excess heat or structural defects. There were approximately forty different types of these test instruments made.

TEMPERATURE TIMER: This was used by Scotty in engineering to test for stress points, and has a strobing mechanism.

COMPUTER CLIPBOARD: Pens, pencils, and paper are never seen aboard the *Enterprise*. Instead, electronic clipboards which are touched with electronic stylus when used for note-taking, or they can be tied in with the ship's computer. Dick designed two dozen different computer clipboards, representing different departments of the ship—sickbay, engineering, and so on.

14

Take My Advice...

Electronic doors that sense the presence of an individual. Talking computers. Hypodermic injections that don't break the skin. Weapons that stun, rather than kill. Personal communications devices. These are just a few of the many ideas introduced in the original television *Star Trek* that have become realities a decade later. Much of *Star Trek*'s successful prediction of these modern-day realities is due to the insistence of *Star Trek*'s creator, Gene Roddenberry, that all such things in the program be based on established scientific facts or theories. In television, and to an extent even in movies, *Star Trek* was a forerunner of a whole new form of entertainment which tried to combine science-fiction adventure with believable ideas and some respect for the intelligence of the audience.

From the first, Roddenberry had insisted on top-quality technical advice, which led ultimately to contacts with prestigious science research organizations. The television show received input from groups such as the Rand Corporation, from Jet Propulsion Laboratory at California Institute of Technology, and others. So it is not surprising that the *Star Trek* motion picture received advice from an assortment of experts which included NASA, JPL, Massachusetts Institute of Technology, a former U.S. astronaut, and numerous other firms and individuals, including the distinguished biochemist/science-fiction writer, Isaac Asimov.

Initial research came from a private company located on the Paramount studio lot—Kellam deForest Research, and those familiar with Stephen Whitfield's *The Making of Star Trek* will recall their research work during the television series. With the motion picture, they were involved on a script continuity basis; the script was checked for previously established *Star Trek* concepts, as well as for possible conflicts with known character names or well-known facts. Some of the things their researcher Joan Pearce noted in an early script version were:

Commander Will Decker: Who's Who lists a William* Decker, a New York businessman born in 1900. Do not consider usage here presents a conflict.
Dr. Christine Chapel: Character established previously. We find no current listing for a physician in the United States with this exact name.
Commander Ronak: No conflicts, but this is an unusual name for Vulcan. Most Vulcan names have begun with an "S" sound.†
U.F.P. vessel . . . U.S.S. Aswan: The Egyptian Navy has a minesweeper with this name. Do not consider usage here presents a conflict.‡
linguacode: We find no proprietary of trademark usage of this term.
Navigational deflectors: This is new equipment for the Enterprise.

Star Trek—TMP's greatest amount of technical advice came from the National Aeronautics and Space Administration (NASA), whose own space program has received much support from the Trekfans turned space fans.§ The reverse is also true, and many of NASA's scientists are also *Star Trek* fans, as in the case of Jesco von Puttkamer, the man furnished by NASA as technical advisor on the film.

Jesco (pronounced "Yes-co") first met Gene Roddenberry in 1975, when they were introduced by a mutual friend—Fred Durant III, Assistant Director of Astronautics at the Smithsonian Institution in

---

*Decker was later given the first name "Willard."
†Ronak later became "Sonak" in the movie.
‡The scene was later dropped from the script because of length.
§NASA assistance was provided under the same conditions and restructions by which NASA (and other government agencies) provides assistance to any other film or artistic project which is determined to be in the public interest and where technical assistance results in no extra costs to the taxpayers.

Washington, D.C. A short time later, Jesco was a guest speaker at a mammoth *Star Trek* convention in Chicago. His report and evaluation of *Star Trek* fandom impressed the folks back at NASA, and Jesco couldn't resist sending a copy of these comments to Gene. As a friendship developed, Gene realized this was the man he wanted as technical advisor on the *Star Trek* movie, and an arrangement was worked out.

This strikingly handsome man in his mid-forties with white hair, jet black mustache and German accent as thick as the foam on a stein of Lowenbrau has a list of credentials even Mr. Spock would envy (if he were capable of emotions). His NASA title alone is three lines long:

Gene Roddenberry *(left)* **and NASA technical advisor Jesco von Puttkamer check the complex wiring behind Spock's science station.**

Program Manager of Space Industrialization and Integrated Long-Range Planning Studies in the Advanced Programs Office of NASA's Office of Space Transportation Systems (OSTS). His job entails developing and directing major new studies of advanced economical space activities for NASA, and he is responsible for NASA's long-range program studies in space flight, particularly for new applications of the Space Transportation System and concepts of permanent occupancy of space by humans. He holds a bachelor of science degree in general and mechanical engineering, and a master of science degree in aerospace engineering, both from the Technical University of Aachen, Germany. In 1961, he joined Dr. Wernher von Braun's rocket development team in Huntsville, Alabama, and later became involved in the Saturn/Apollo Lunar Landing Program, the Skylab Space Station program, and in the early development of the new space shuttle. He obtained his U.S. citizenship in 1967.

Jesco has always had an interest in science fiction, and published ten science-fiction novels in Europe to help pay his way through college. He has translated many of noted science fiction writer A. E. van Vogt's books into German, and had the pleasure of guiding Mr. van Vogt around the *Star Trek* sets during production. He has also written some *Star Trek* fiction, and recently had one of his stories published in an anthology of *Trek* stories. And he recently completed the English-to-German translation of Gene Roddenberry's *Star Trek—The Novel*. *Star Trek* particularly interested him because it showed a regard for true science, and because it gave people a vision of what the realities of space could be. In fact, he feels that *Star Trek* did this in some ways which NASA could not. For example, NASA's own Apollo moon shots never gave the impression of great speed in spite of the fact that they traveled thousands of miles an hour. Jesco was impressed with the initial *Enterprise* fly-by in the television show opening, which gave a feeling of the tremendous speeds the ship can reach. This was just the sort of thing NASA needed to get the interest and support of the general public. Jesco was probably the first person at NASA who really came to grips with the fact that *science fiction* does more to interest the public in supporting science and space exploration than all of the real events which *actually happen* in science and in space. He was immediately drawn to the original *Star Trek* series, and took great pride and care in the advice he later supplied for the production of the movie.

From 1976 until the completion of the *Star Trek* film over three years later, Jesco supplied the writers, producer, and director with memos on everything technical in the script(s), from *Enterprise* bathroom facilities, black holes, and matter implosion theory, to story continuity, equations for monitor readouts, and wormholes. Working evenings, weekends and vacations, he sent 61 memos, for a total of 276 pages. That is without counting hundreds of magazine, newspaper, and technical articles, photographs, bibliographies, and other information supplied both in person and via telephone. The following is an excerpt from a typical memo from Jesco:

WARP DRIVE EFFECT   4/10/78

This whole area is of crucial importance: let's not forget that the main star of the show is the starship itself!

Basically, the Enterprise has two propulsion systems, both of which are way beyond anything we can do in the foreseeable future. One is the rocket-type system of the "Impulse Power Engines," using thrust forces produced by jet action and nuclear fusion processes—for emergency situations and slow flight well below the speed of light. The other is the famed Warp Drive using energy realized by total matter/antimatter annihilation, the ultimate energy source. It provides 100 times more energy per unit mass than nuclear fusion, turning one kilogram antimatter into 14,000 million kilowatt-hours (5×10^{16} Joule). Today, antimatter particles are created in high-energy accelerators, amounting to about half a millionth gram per year yield total. This is a million times too low for useful propulsion application. But things will have improved 200 years from now (one hopes). On the Enterprise, the antimatter is kept in storage in high-gauss magnetic fields in the two warp engine pods in the rear.

We are talking about a combination of two different way-out ideas: While the matter/antimatter annihilation system as an energy source is already a mind-boggler of high-energy physics in itself, the principle of the Warp Drive adds an even more exotic feature of advanced relativistic physics on top of it. Rather than using the energy to produce propulsion by the thrust of emitted particles (ideally: photons), we manipulate the structure of space itself to free ourselves from the shackles of Einstein's General Theory of Relativity which restricts us to sub-light velocities in this Universe.

With the Roddenberry Warp Drive, there are no jets, no exhaust trails. When going "into Warp Drive," the warp engines in the two propulsion pods create an intense field which surrounds the entire vessel, forming a "subspace," i.e., a space curvature closed upon itself through a Warp, a new but small universe within the normal Universe (or "outside" it). The field is nonsymmetrical with respect to fore-and-aft, in accordance with the outside geometry of the Enterprise, but it can be strengthened and weakened at localized areas to control the ship's direction and apparent speed.

Because of its non-symmetry about the lateral axis, the subspace becomes directional: The curvature of its hypersurface varies at different points about the starship. This causes a "sliding" effect, almost as a surf-board or a porpoise riding before the crest of a wave. The subspace "belly-surfs" in front of a directionally propagating "fold" in the spacetime structure, the Warp—a progressive, partial collapse of spacetime caused by the creation of the subspace volume (similar to but not the same as a Black Hole). Just like a surfboard, the geometric shape of the subspace is of paramount importance in this mode of traveling, and since it in turn is determined by the geometry of the Starship, the outside shape of the Enterprise is of major significance. (Klingon ships produce different warp geometries, of course.)

By banking against the hyperspace it rides upon, the Enterprise can turn as an aircraft does, not as a rocket braking (but only on Warp Drive). It would have little or no momentum (it better not!) and only a small speed with relation to the local space around it. To the Universe outside in "normal space," the speed would be huge—warp speed.

In considering all of the above and recalling the inconceivable energies necessary to warp space and to go into Warp Drive, I feel strongly that we should show appropriate optical effects, particularly in the moment of "breakthrough" (Warp One), when the ship goes trans- and then superphotic. The effect should not be firework-type lights but more a dimensional, geometric warping and twisting, an almost stomach-turning wrenching of the entire camera field-of-view.

Once broken through and during traveling shots showing the Starship going by at superphotic speeds, you may want to stay away from outside effects if they would disturb the photographic cleanliness of the picture. If asked, I would prefer to see a continuing, but subdued, unobtrusive rippling effect only alongside the two warp engine pods, again purely geometric—like a rippling mirror or fluttering flag (because the warp effect is basically gravitational; any flashes, lights, heat and noise effects would suggest incomplete conversion of the ship's power into gravitational force, i.e., a somewhat wasteful process).

At one point, NASA's involvement caught the attention of the press, and an article printed in a weekly newspaper *The Star* claimed that NASA, JPL, and Boeing had loaned valuable equipment to the *Star Trek* production, and had hired the FBI to protect this equipment. This prompted at least one constituent to write to her senator, complaining that (as misquoted in the article) NASA had no business loaning electronic equipment, paid for at taxpayers' expense, to any Hollywood movie company. The senator promptly initiated an investigation (Congressional Inquiry N317805). Since the production was being shrouded in secrecy, an amused Gene Roddenberry could well understand that newspaper mistakes could occur, and he had already sent the following note to Jesco:

September 11, 1978

Mr. Jesco von Puttkamer
NASA
Washington, D.C.

Dear Jes,

Thank you for the incredible news clipping about my hiring the FBI to protect Star Trek and the mind-boggling electronic equipment from NASA, JPL, Boeing, etc. If we have all this stuff, why hasn't someone told me about it? I suppose it comes under the category of "creative" news writing. Our closed-set policy is resulting in a lot of mystery being built up about our film, and I think we can expect some pretty wild rumors over the next year. As a matter of fact, next week I will be talking to Paramount's New York head of publicity and intend to suggest to him that we release a bit more publicity from time to time so that news reports will not have to turn to rumors.

Dailies continue to look good.

Best wishes,

Gene Roddenberry

During the rewrite of the final scenes, there was a running discussion between Gene and the studio executives over the script's ending. The main problem was that the executives didn't believe in the possibility of a living machine. They decided to call in a consultant. The man they selected was Dr. Isaac Asimov, a well-known science-fiction writer and scientist who has written over two hundred books. If this man felt that intelligent machine consciousness was possible, then the script's ending could stay. It seemed a strange question to pose to a man who practically invented the concept of robots and who developed the "Three Laws of Robotics"—the prime directives to which all independently thinking robots must adhere. Naturally, Isaac loved the ending. He agreed with the story's ending and its moral—that meaning for all of us comes out of the "divine restlessness of the human spirit," and he was quick to point out the parallels which should be drawn between Spock and V'ger. He was instrumental in clarifying the true meaning of the ending, stating: "V'ger is not immortal. It and Decker die and become new species. What V'ger's transcendency offers us is mortality with change. It is better that the individual die in order that the species can advance. It is better that the species die in order that a new species be born. And it is better that, perhaps, life itself die so that something greater can exist." At last, the studio bought Gene's ideas, finding only one small area of contention:

TO: GENE RODDENBERRY/BOB WISE   DATE: OCTOBER 23, 1978
FROM: JEFF KATZENBERG   SUBJECT: ISAAC ASIMOV COMMENTS

As I mentioned to you Isaac Asimov has read the latest draft of Star
Trek and he feels that, with the possible exception of the wormhole, the
science fiction community will readily accept what is currently in our
script.

The generally accepted theory by the science-fiction community is
that a wormhole is the area between a black hole and white hole. It is
assumed that one could not enter a wormhole without having first
passed through a black hole. Since this is not the case in our script it is
Isaac's feeling that a small fraction of the sci-fi community could take
exception to this.

Isaac suggested that if it is possible to change this one word, in the
post-production of the film, then we should. However he feels that the
number of people that will pick up on this inaccuracy is small. Isaac
feels it would be more accurate, as well as acceptable to the sci-fi fans, if
we call it a "temporal tunnel." (The vague definition of which is a time
tunnel in which travel and time are distorted.)

Given the above data, I think we should make the effort to correct
this, if possible, during post-production.

During the years since the original television series, Gene Roddenberry had maintained his friendship with several contacts at Cal
Tech's Jet Propulsion Laboratory, the organization that had been so
helpful in supplying technical aid for the program. In addition to some
of the monitor film which JPL supplied for the *Enterprise* bridge in
ST—TMP, Gene felt that it would be of great value to have an
authentic model of the *Voyager* spacecraft designed and built by that
company, a_sd outlined his needs in the following letter:

October 25, 1977

Mr. John Casani
Outer Planets Project Manager
Jet Propulsion Laboratory
4800 Oak Grove Dr.
Pasadena, CA 91103

Dear John:

As we discussed on the telephone, I am writing to request the loan of
JPL's mock-up of the Voyager to be used in the filming of our opening
two-hour movie of the new Star Trek II television series. The Voyager
mock-up will be used as part of a set that will represent the interior of a
gigantic spaceship—a representative of a highly advanced machine
society from a distant planet in the galaxy. As developed in the story,
the society is the outgrowth of a union between an older, decaying
machine civilization and the wandering Voyager. It was the Voyager

which inspired the civilization with a strong sense of purpose that led to incredible advances in their technology.

As you know, Star Trek has consistently held a highly optimistic view of mankind's future, and our new series will continue with that view. We are saying that three or four hundred years from now, man has achieved harmony with himself and the planet. War, pollution, disease have been overcome. Large portions of the Earth have returned to their natural state. Man is free to go on to challenge the new frontiers of space. As always, Star Trek will maintain a respectful and supportive attitude toward NASA and the space program.

If the loan of the mock-up can be arranged, we will be needing it on our stage at Paramount around November 12th. (Our final production schedule has not been set yet, so I can't give you specific dates at the moment.) We will need the mock-up for a total of five days: two days to transport it to Paramount and set it up on the stage; a day or two for the shooting; and another day to return it to you. We, of course, would supply you with the necessary insurance papers, and would, of course, return it in exactly the same condition in which you gave it to us.

I would be most grateful to you and JPL if the arrangements can be made. I'm looking forward to hearing from you.

Best regards,

Gene Roddenberry

Several telephone calls followed, and at one point things looked good for getting a loan of the *Voyager* backup model, but it was decided in the long run that the *Star Trek* production could not make appropriate guarantees as to the model's safety. In the end, it became clear that it would also probably cost less if an original model were built from scratch. However, John Casani and JPL scientists Richard Green and Bill Koselka were most cooperative in supplying numerous diagrams, which became a valuable aid to the *Star Trek* art department. Based on this information, the department was able to recreate an authentic three-quarters scale model of the actual *Voyager* spacecraft.

The "spacewalk" scene in which Spock and later Kirk don space gear for an extravehicular visit to *V'ger* was actually filmed *twice*, and although the first attempt at this scene (filmed by Robert Abel) was eventually scrapped in favor of Douglas Trumbull's version, an attempt was still made at true *Star Trek* authenticity. This aborted scene had *Apollo 9* astronaut Russell Schweickart coaching the actors from the sidelines on the proper way to stroll in a vacuum. Looking like a European skiing champion, this lean, blond man in his turtleneck sweater actually spent most of his time advising Leonard's and Bill's doubles, who did most of the long shots in the scrapped and also the actual footage which was saved. Rusty is science adviser to California governor Jerry Brown and is well versed in all aspects of science—including space walking, something only he and a handful of others on this planet have done. The actors and/or doubles were suspended in midair with special rigging and piano wire, and exhibited a natural tendency to move in this simulated weightless condition in a swimming motion. Rusty was quick to point out that this was not the proper way to move in space, and advised the actors on the correct positioning of legs and arms, plus very complex descriptions on body pitch and yaw, angle of bend for the knees and arms and so on. Although the scene was finally shot differently, the change had nothing to do with the expert advice supplied by Rusty Schweickart, and his contribution, along with those of all the many others who advised *Star Trek—The Motion Picture,* was vital to the director, producer, and others who worked to maintain *Star Trek*'s tradition of scientific accuracy.

15

It's Not All Done With Mirrors

When Alex Weldon goes to the supermarket, his shopping list might be very similar to yours: a box of steel wool pads, several cans of evaporated milk, maybe a roll or two of aluminum foil, some household ammonia. But he's also very likely to pick up *a quarter ton* of dry ice!

As supervisor of special effects* on *Star Trek—The Motion Picture,* Alex frequently uses common household items such as these, and he's a whiz at creating new and unexpected uses for everyday things. Even when he's not working, he loves to tinker around the house, often spending afternoons "fiddling around in the garage, doing odds and ends." A young-appearing sixty-five, Alex had planned to retire from special effects work after forty-two years in the business and hoped to play a lot of tennis, his favorite pastime. But his wife urged him to take the work on *Star Trek* because she thought he didn't have enough to do. He quickly discovered how right his wife was: There was *plenty* to do on this technically complex film.

Construction for the 1977-planned tv show was semicomplete when Alex was hired. Many effects were well under way, including much of

---

Special effects are done *live* during actual filming, as opposed to *optical effects,* which are done in postproduction, after completion of principal photography.

the initial wiring of the bridge consoles. A good foundation in bridge effects had already been laid under the supervision of Jim Rugg, special-effects supervisor for the proposed tv show, who had also served on the original *Star Trek* television show. Now it was up to Alex to complete the task for the much higher budgeted and more complex motion picture.

The first step in preparation called for an analysis of the script in terms of special effects. Before Alex could do his shopping, he had to be aware of all the effects he would be expected to produce. Together with the other members of his special-effects team—Darrell Pritchett, Kris Gregg, Marty Bresin, and Ray Mattey—Alex worked out all the possibilities for pulling off the effects convincingly.

Much of *Star Trek* involved intricate wiring, and many *thousands of miles* of wiring were used in lighting up the consoles on the bridge and in producing chase sequences (lights which burn in a controlled sequence and pattern).

On the *Enterprise,* Weldon discovered that the plastic buttons at the bridge station consoles were melting. He solved this problem by lowering the voltage of the light bulbs beneath the plastic console buttons from 25 watts to 6 watts.

Many of the panels at the bridge stations are touch-activated. Based on the same principle as the buttons in modern elevators, the controls are heat-sensitive and react to body warmth from the crew person's fingertips. Graphic artist Lee Cole prepared a complete book on the proper touching sequence, and each actor was required to know his or her station's panel. Spock's station was even more complicated (which is only logical!). Leonard Nimoy could activate his console's monitor screens (8mm rear projectors) with a mere touch of the proper fingertip panel. Spock's redesigned station also had rollout auxiliary consoles which neatly contained all the science station circuitry—sort of the "works in a drawer," as opposed to the television series, which saw Mr. Spock crawling underneath his science control board, lying on his back, appearing to be fiddling around under the "dashboard" of the *Enterprise.* These new consoles were rigged for hydraulic operation, and could be rolled back toward the walls (like closing a drawer) when not in use. But when it was discovered to be easier to work them by hand, the hydraulic system was disconnected.

The bridge has an additional elevator in the motion picture, for a total of two bridge "turbo-lifts." The doors were easily parted by an off-camera person who opened them by means of a pully, very much like the drapery pulls you might have in your living room. But sure enough, as in the television show there were occasional accidents. Both Bill Shatner and Majel Barrett were victims caught in too quickly closing elevator doors.

The core of the engine room had its own special-effects lighting which was handled by a very unique team, as we'll discover shortly.

Alex found Lt. Cleary's explosion scene in the engine room the perfect opportunity for the brillo pads. The scene calls for a flare as "something shorts out at the mechanism where Scott and Decker had been working." Alex carefully hid the steel wool inside the console and rigged an arc welder to operate by remote control when the actor pulled a wire. The arc welder was specially rigged to create a spark instead of actually welding, causing the steel wool to burn and make sparks. So effective was this plan that one of the cast members became startled each time by the flare-up and the scene had to be retaken again and again. It's not easy to work when sparks are happening a few feet in front of your face!

Special effects are at work to make this explosion in the engine room happen on cue.

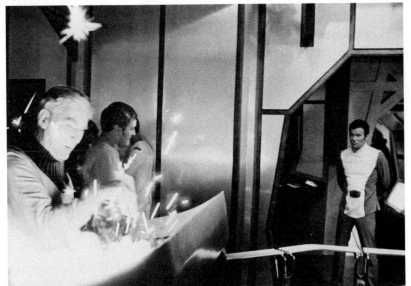

If you recall seeing Captain Kirk and others riding up and down on those one-man elevators in the engine room, you'll remember how easily and naturally they seemed to move along the three levels. That's because each elevator was rigged with an air winch with a two-thousand-pound capacity, and cables were hidden just out of the frame of the picture. Unseen also was the air winch operator, who awaited the rider at the top level of the engine room.

Chekov's burn scene was even trickier. Although the entire incident takes only a few minutes in the film, it took Alex many hours of preparation. First, a piece of aluminum foil was placed around actor Walter Koenig's arm. Then a protective pad was added and his uniform sleeve was pulled down in place. Alex prepared a compound of ammonia and an acetic acid solution. At the right moment, this was touched to Walter's sleeve, the interaction of the chemicals causing it to smoke. There were difficulties, and the procedure had to be repeated through ten takes. It was especially uncomfortable for Walter, whose arm was slightly burned when, despite precautions, some of the solution leaked through to his arm. His screams were *not* entirely acting!

CAUTION: *There is potential danger in any of these effects, and no one should attempt to duplicate these tricks themselves.*

Persis Khambatta found herself and her character, Ilia, involved in several special-effects scenes. One scene resulted in her developing a severe case of tonsillitis, which kept her at home for several days, forcing Bob Wise to rearrange his shooting sequence while she recovered. The scene is the one where the Ilia-probe materializes, unclad, in the real Ilia's sonic shower. Persis's strict religious beliefs and conservative Indian upbringing were not in keeping with the script's call for her to be totally nude behind the shower door. In India, people don't even kiss on screen. What would her family think? She finally agreed to wear a thin skin-colored body stocking, and the impression on film is virtually indistinguishable from the real thing. Nevertheless, she did manage to catch cold as the result of the special effect that produced the sonic mist. To make the mist, Alex dropped dry ice (frozen CO_2) into warm water, causing a steamy vapor to form. This steam was funneled into the sonic shower by a hidden tube. As the extremely cold vapors filled the shower, they sank heavily to the floor, chilling Persis's feet and eventually her whole body. She also had to leave the shower frequently for breaths of fresh air, as the carbon dioxide vapors are poisonous, and too much cannot be breathed for any length of time. At least five hundred pounds of dry ice were used in getting this scene filmed.

The Perils of Persis continued in yet another special-effects scene. The script describes the scene:

260   MEDICAL OFFICE DOOR   260

with the METAL BUCKLING, TEARING—and a single hand slicing the steel door like paper. It is the Ilia-probe, her face absolutely impassive, her whole manner incongruously benign. . . .

How do you slice through metal like it were paper? The best way is for the door to actually *be* paper. Alex made *eight* sets of doors in all. Some were made out of corrugated cardboard, two or three layers thick, covered with sheets of aluminum foil on the outside to give the appearance of shiny steel. Other doors were made from quarter-inch cork covered with aluminum foil. Alex had the doors scored (weakened) with a razor blade so she could easily slice on through. But not all went well. On the first try, Persis kept hacking away at the door, but it refused to give way. When it finally did, she stumbled through. *Take two.* This time, the doors gave way much too easily, and she practically strolled through and burst out in a huge grin. *Take three.* Persis forgot to press forward through the doors and instead pulled them back, cutting her finger. *Take four; five; six; seven.* Only one specially prepared set of doors remained, but at last the take was a success.

Throughout all the time Persis appears as the Ilia-probe, she wears an illuminated button in the hollow of her throat, the one distinguishing mark between the real Ilia and the probe—the link to *V'ger.* In order to activate the 12-volt light bulb in this button, Persis had two tiny hair wires which went across her throat into two little clips, then continued down her arm connecting with a battery on her back. Hidden inside her sleeve was the on-off switch, which she used to control the light. Although she turned off the light between takes, the heat of the bulb was enough to cause a slight burn to her neck, leaving a tan mark. Calamity Persis took it all in stride, by this time getting

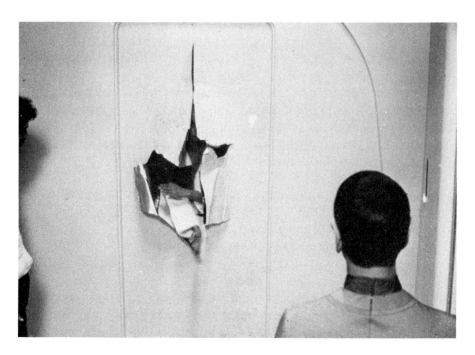

"Ilia" attempts to slice through the "steel door like it were paper"—which it is.
When the door parts too easily, Persis bursts out in a huge grin.

used to the idea that in order to become an American film star, one has to experience any number of discomforts and injuries.

One of the briefest, yet most interesting, special effects was nicely executed by several of Alex's assistants, particularly Marty Bresin. It involves the antigrav device that seemingly floats along, unaided, outside the engine room just prior to Kirk's initial appearance there. To achieve this effect, Marty built a circular track that had the same shape as the corridor, suspended the antigrav on four very small wires which connected to the track from a special unseen two-foot-long carrier. The wires were rendered invisible by use of special "wire acid," which oxidizes instantly and turns the wires a dull gray. The camera doesn't pick up these gray wires unless the background is white—and since the corridor lighting here was a deep blue, it is virtually impossible to detect any means of support, no matter how many times the scene is watched.

Wires were also used in the cargo deck scene to make the antigravity cargo boxes appear to float through the zero gravity deck. These boxes were made out of a light balsa wood so that the very fine wires used would not show.

Alex's most spectacular effects were prepared in connection with *ST—TMP*'s only exterior set built at Paramount—the planet Vulcan. Location scenes had already been shot at Yellowstone, and it was up to Alex to find a way of duplicating the swirling pools of milky steam with a look of authenticity. Both dry ice and steam machines were used. The steam given off by the combination of these two came bubbling to the surface by means of hidden tubing. To match the appearance of the swirling pools of water in the real Yellowstone, Alex used evaporated milk and white poster paint, mixed with water and poured into the set's pools. The pressure of the steam caused just the proper amount of movement in the pale white whirlpools and eddies duplicated in this enormous outdoor set.

Alex and his staff achieved some remarkable things in the way of *Star Trek*'s special effects. Some equally remarkable accomplishments were also done by two young men who turned out to be real finds. They were discovered by associate producer Jon Povill, almost by accident.

In the course of any motion picture, the production offices are inundated with all sorts of proposals from nearly everyone who has a skill or talent to sell. Jon's office was swamped with scores of demo video-tape cassettes, and part of his job involved evaluating each of these for someone who might be of potential service on the film. Some were interesting; most were routine. Rarely was one of any value. Not so the tape submitted by Samuel B. Nicholson and Brian Longbotham. The day Jon first ran their tape, he was so impressed that he immediately called in everyone who was free for a few moments to see this different tape. "A great deal of Sam and Brian's work was absolutely, totally unlike anything I'd ever seen before," says Jon. At the time, director Bob Wise was extremely concerned with what kind of lighting might be used in the engine room. Experiments with lasers had proved disappointing; something new and exciting in the way of lighting had to be found. Jon was sure that Sam and Brian could find the solution.

The team had been working out of Sam's house in Venice, Califor-

Sam Nicholson and Brian Longbotham adjust lighting on the V'ger set.

nia, a peaceful community of smaller, almost cottage-type houses. For about a year the two had been working together, primarily doing experimentations with abstract visuals on video tape and film. Prior to that, Sam, who holds a master of fine arts degree from UCLA, was a free-lance abstract artist, working with both painting and photography. Brian had worked for three and a half years in advertising and radio and television broadcasting, with a particular interest in the area of video tape and film. They met at a party and decided to combine their talents to produce video-tape and film effects which had their origins in abstract art. When they submitted their tape to the associate producer, they hoped for a chance to do some postproduction effects or maybe a few monitor films.

As soon as Robert Wise saw the tape, he called them in. Could they do what was on the tape "live," on an enormous scale? They said they could. Bob explained that this was *not* to be a postproduction or film effect; the problem was that he needed something for the engine of the *Enterprise*, and time was growing short. They immediately returned to Venice and began working on ideas that same afternoon.

Sam compares their experience of developing their engine room lighting concept to the Wright brothers in the process of learning to fly. Indeed, Sam and Brian soon began gathering as much curiosity about their mysterious work as, no doubt, did Wilbur and Orville. They began in the garage, building a mock-up of the *Enterprise*'s engine, testing various light systems. Bigger and bigger prototypes were built, and one day it simply became too big for the garage, and they had to move the latest model into the house. To make room for the now house-sized behemoth, most of the furniture was hauled out to the garage. Sam moved his plants into the one furnished room, the bedroom, so they'd stay alive while he blacked out all light in the rest of the house.

One night they were working on an eight-foot prototype utilizing a gaseous material, when the strange smoky vapors were noticed by a neighbor. The potentially helpful neighbor called the fire department, and when the fire fighters arrived, they were greeted not by a fire, but a matter/antimatter engine in the middle of these obviously crazy guys' living room! In weeks to come, Sam and Brian became neighborhood celebrities as they would try out new lighting techniques. Lights would flash out all over the street, different rooms flashing in different colors, some in time to music they used to help create the mood. Neighbors stopped going to the local disco; this show was free—and better.

With guidance and input from Gene Roddenberry, Bob Wise and NASA's Jesco van Puttkamer, five prototypes were prepared before the final design was accepted for *Star Trek*'s engine room. The challenge was to develop a replica of the matter/antimatter source of energy which has to go from extreme slow motion through various engine speeds to white-hot, and even to "emergency power" where it looks as if it is unbalanced and ready to explode. The real problem with the engine was that the set had already been built, with no consideration given to the new type of light that was needed for the engines. Since no access was planned underneath, Sam and Brian had to invent a way to have crawlspace. Working down from the top of the thirty-foot tube was something else, and they had to be hoisted up via a crane.

They are reluctant to talk about the lighting system they invented, realizing that they have something that is new in an industry that constantly needs more and more imaginative and inventive special effects and film techniques. Their imaginations see many possibilities for their new system of kinetic lighting.

They began by observing light as it reflects through water to the bottom of a swimming pool, watching the patterns that form when sunlight strikes a pool and makes kinetic patterns on the cement bottom. How could they get that kind of light movement *out* from the pool and *into* a thirty-foot column on stage 9? According to Sam, "You look for similar things that occur in nature that everyone else would overlook, like the pool reflection. You substitute other things for the water in the pool, and *voilà*!" In the case of the engine room, they substituted different color gels (thin transparent sheets of colored plastic with a consistency of cellophane), crumpled mylar, light bulbs, and a complex mechanical system that moved the light around, scanning over reflective surfaces to give it its character.

Sam and Brian suggested an experiment similar to their process which can be done at home. Take a wineglass and fill it with a liquid. Place it in a sunny window. The image you see on the opposite side from where the sun enters the glass will be very close to what was in the engine. Experimenting with different kinds of light produces different effects.

Director Robert Wise was delighted with the job Sam and Brian had done for the engine room, and they were equally delighted to be a part of the *Star Trek* production. Both are admitted Trekkies, ages twenty-five and twenty-six respectively, and when they had set their sights on being involved with the production months before, they really never dreamed it would happen. Sam, more or less the spokesperson for the two, refers to *Star Trek* as "a Cadillac, a Rolls Royce, not just any space movie." They felt that *Star Trek* had helped give them inspiration. As further situations arose, they continued to impress Wise and the rest of the production people. Soon, if there were problems, their assistance was eagerly sought. For example, when more monitor footage was needed, they quickly replied to Jon Povill's request with a typical "We'll do our best," managing to supply about seven thousand feet of monitor footage in all. Notable were the scenes they created of *V'ger* absorbing all of the material from the *Enterprise*'s computer. They relied on their imaginations to help them create what they felt would be the proper visual representation of the film's unusual happenings. They also created visual impressions of the high-speed messages coming in from *V'ger* to Mr. Spock's station. As with the engine lighting system, they worked out of their living room, creating the monitor footage by using rented equipment to film interactions of static electricity, neon lights, high frequency electricity, lots of gels, glass, oil, water, mercury, and tin cans.

By now the two had formed Spectrum Productions—still in Sam's living room. They had built a good rapport with production designer Harold Michelson and the entire art department, which was deeply involved in the plans for the *V'ger* set. Sam and Brian, still anxious to continue inventing, spread an underground rumor that they could provide the special lighting needed. This was originally to be done by Robert Abel and Associates, but they were behind schedule on things long overdue, so Bob Wise decided to let "the boys" have a go at it. Once again, Sam and Brian fulfilled Bob's expectations.

Lighting is vital to the movie's climactic moments, when the *Enterprise* officers are in the very brain center of *V'ger*—the site of *Voyager 6*. As the scene progresses, *V'ger*'s anger and moods are exhibited by the kinetic light changes. Bob Wise admits the *V'ger* sequences were the most difficult scenes in the entire picture, much of the complexity arising from the difficulties of lighting the set.

The set was built in nine sections, on a platform framework that allowed plenty of room for Sam, Brian, and their now *twenty-five assistants* to operate the lighting devices from underneath the set.

Plexiglas windows allowed the light from below to pass through. Beneath the set they placed drums that looked like an enormous foil-wrapped ham with a hormone problem being barbequed for a luau. There were eighteen of these wrinkled, rotating mylar-covered oil drums which worked on the same principle as fake fireplaces. These were flooded with light from below—up to 10,000 watts on each drum. Colors were created by the use of ninety gels, which took only five minutes to wash out from ultraviolet radiation emitted by the lights. (However, the lights *did* help to give everyone a healthy-looking suntan.) Fresh gels were constantly being prepared by every available crew person to replace the faded gels as quickly as possible. At times, the colors *V'ger* was emitting had to change abruptly, and Sam and Brian orchestrated this from below like a football game card stunt section. Taking their cue from Robert Wise, utilizing a bullhorn somewhere up above, they would direct their crew in gel changes: "One-two-three-four-CHANGE!" To further complicate matters, the same thing was happening above where cinematographer Richard Kline was directing the color changes that were occurring simultaneously on the actors, while electrical gaffer Larry Howard coordinated the surface light definition of the set and the actors under Dick's direction.

To further carry out *V'ger*'s lighting, Sam and Brian rented as much equipment as they could—just about all the hot lights in Hollywood. They used xenon, hmi (helium-mercury-iodine), arc lights, strobe lights, quartz and incandescent lights. The lights required more AC current than had ever been used in one studio on the Paramount lot. No doubt the Los Angeles Department of Water and Power was grateful to Sam and Brian too. All this juice taxed the power cables to the limit, and at times the stage smelled like a burning rubber factory. Shorts were common. One morning, an electrician named Tiny Zimmerman was nearly electrocuted when he tried to connect up two lights and became a ground instead. He shuddered, unable to let go or cry for help, as most of the crew looked on, thinking that he was only struggling with the lights. Unaware that electrical current was passing through the lights and Tiny, electrical best boy (head electrician) Larry Freeman came up behind him to help with what he thought were just extremely heavy lamps. Larry became stuck also, a scene that fortunately caught the eye of one of the grips (on-stage carpenters) who immediately sized up the situation and made a flying tackle.

This brave act probably saved two lives, as the two were finally separated. Tiny suffered a broken shoulder from the impact. Better than being electrocuted, however.

One unusual light Sam and Brian secured was a helicopter light. This was needed in the final scenes when Decker and "Ilia" fuse with V'ger. They also designed a system of overhead lights that reflected off mirrors. Some tricks, it would seem, *are* done with mirrors.

Whatever the means Sam and Brian used to create their outstanding lighting effects, these gifted young men, who refer to themselves simply as "visual entertainers" and "musicians of light," are sure to do some astonishing things for the motion picture industry in years to come.

16

Welcome to Vulcan; Please Don't Feed the Bears

The next time you're planning a vacation trip, you may want to consider the planet Vulcan. You won't need a space suit or even a starship—the family car will do. Simply follow your map till you reach the southeast corner of Montana. You'll recognize Vulcan when you see it. It looks just like Minerva Hot Springs in Yellowstone National Park. Don't expect to see Mr. Spock there, though. He left to re-up with Starfleet and hasn't been seen since.

Vulcan wasn't always located at Yellowstone. For a while, no one seemed to know just where on Earth one might expect to find this ancient harsh, thin-aired, 140-degree desert paradise Mr. Spock calls home. During the months of pre-production on *Star Trek—The Motion Picture,* director Robert Wise and his sketch artist Maurice ("Zuby") Zuberano combed through various books depicting natural wonders and/or ruins (which the scene on Vulcan called for) in exotic far-off places such as Afghanistan, Tibet, and Turkey. At one point it seemed certain that Vulcan would be located by some ancient temple ruins in a remote area of Turkey. But the budget for such a venture was prohibitive, and an even better selection of terrain was discovered in one of America's own scenic wonders—the northwest corner of Yellowstone.

John James, who later became optical coordinator, was assigned the job of location coordinator, and together he and Zuby flew to West Yellowstone, Montana, for a quick reconnaissance of the area. They took pictures from every possible angle at Minerva Hot Springs, the chosen site, and set about securing the Parks Department's permission to film the Vulcan scenes, no easy feat in a National Park at the height of the summer tourist season. The Parks Department acquiesced, but crew setups had to be limited to the boardwalks, because of the danger to the delicate geological formations. Anxious to cooperate, the Parks Department later built an additional platform to the art department's specifications.

From Zuby's photos it had become apparent that there was only one angle from which to properly film the scene. Mike Minor of the *Star Trek* art department made a fast trip up there also, then created a large painting of how the scene might look. Mike and production designer Hal Michelson worked out an idea that involved using miniatures in the foreground combined with the actual filming of the hot springs background. They built a three-piece model of the temple stairs, composed of two-by-two-foot modules bolted together into one two-foot-deep by six-foot-wide foreground miniature representation of the stairs. In the movie the bottom third of the frames shot at Yellowstone were actually composed of the miniature stairs, plus some rocks, broken bits of red glass and a miniature version of an Olmec-like Vulcan statue head. The center of the frame has Mr. Spock—note the sunlight on his face—and a bit of the park surrounding him. The top third of the frames in these scenes are a matte painting. This shot was part of one of the most complex shots of the movie.

On August 8, 1978, the day after *Star Trek* production began at Paramount, an eleven-person second unit took off for Yellowstone to capture that jigsaw piece of the Vulcan scenes on film. Among those making up this location unit were Matt Yuricich, the matte artist on *Close Encounters* who would eventually be doing the matte painting in these Vulcan scenes; Mike Minor; Jim Lyles, second unit camerman; John James; Joe Viskocil, in charge of location special effects, and, of course, Leonard Nimoy, ready to shoot his first Mr. Spock scenes of the picture.

During the three days the crew took to film the sequence, they found time to relax by doing some river rafting and a bit of sightseeing. But the park's real tourists were enjoying a different kind of sight-

Spock meditating at Yellowstone.

seeing than they had anticipated, and many of these vacationers had the unexpected experience of seeing an actual movie being made. Some were able to guess immediately that it was *Star Trek,* since not only is Leonard Nimoy's face easily recognizable, but there just aren't too many people with pointed ears in front of the cameras unless they're playing the part of a Vulcan. Even the kids working for the summer in the hotel cafeteria were enthralled with the idea of having a movie company staying at their hotel. They raided the kitchen for aluminum foil, from which they manufactured their own version of pointed ears and wore them all day in Mr. Spock's honor while serving curious, unaware vacationers.

Once these scenes were in the can, the art department found themselves faced with the problem of the other jigsaw pieces which would match with what had taken Mother Nature millennia to construct: somehow Yellowstone had to be duplicated on the studio lot. Reverse angles were needed, along with the temple ruins Spock is facing. The best studio site for this exterior (outdoor) set turned out to be down in the B tank, an actual tank approximately 110 by 150 feet which can be flooded with millions of gallons of water to represent the South Seas *(Return to Gilligan's Island),* San Francisco Bay *(Barbary Coast)* and other large bodies of water.

Since the sun had been on Spock's face up at Yellowstone, the proper angle for building this huge set had to be determined. Mike Minor took one of the set designers' quarter-inch mock-ups down to the B tank about a month before construction began, set it down on the cement tank floor (which was luckily empty at the time), and watched to see where the shadow fell. He knew from his previous experience the exact angles at which it had to fall across the set and out of the frame. He made measurements and determined the final position for the set's construction. He also had to remember his basic astronomy, taking into account the sun's position a month from that day.

Construction was innovative. Using the set designer's plans, a plywood base was built on metal platforms to give the general silhouette of the stones. Then chicken wire was added for support. Under the guidance of the Los Angeles Fire Department, polyurethene foam was blown over the framework with a machine similar to a spray-painting machine, a kind of reverse vacuum cleaner. For a while, Vulcan's landscape was very pink, since this is the color of the foam when it dries. Later it was painted to resemble the actual

Yellowstone counterpart and a sixteen-foot-high Fiberglas foot was added, representing the bottom part of the ruined statue of yore. Yellowstone's steam was provided by the special-effects team.

Shooting the scene at the studio saw problems that made the location shooting seem much simpler by comparison. To match this reverse angle, the sun had to be in the west, behind the set. But first it had to shine! Three afternoons of clouds and unseasonal sprinkles didn't help any, and production got farther behind schedule.

Then there were difficulties with the cast involved, those who played the stoic Vulcan Masters. What could account for their un-Vulcanlike nervousness? Leonard Nimoy, puzzled by this reaction from his fellow performers, brought the question to Gene Roddenberry. Gene did a bit of investigating and discovered that the actors were in awe of Leonard—he had become that much of a legend as the Vulcan Spock.

In spite of all this, however, the Vulcan scenes were finally completed. Should sequel movies wish to return to Vulcan, they'll have to go somewhere else on that planet other than to the abode of the Masters, since nothing was saved of the B tank set. It was torn down so that the tank could be used for the remainder of the summer—as a parking lot. Only in Hollywood can you park at the bottom of a former San Francisco Bay that used to be the planet Vulcan.

17

All Hands on Deck

The signs posted outside the *Star Trek* stages proclaimed the disheartening news to would-be sightseers: CLOSED SET, NO VISITORS. If you ignored the sign and were not authorized for admittance to the sets, a uniformed guard, awaiting you the moment you stepped inside, would politely, but firmly, usher you right back outside again.

Part of the reason for so much security was the hoped-for secrecy of *Star Trek*'s plot. Great measures had been taken to maintain this secrecy. Scripts had been numbered, and a list was kept of the person who received each copy. The press was told nothing in the way of the story, and only a few undetailed stills were allowed to be published. Everyone on the production staff and crew was warned not to divulge the storyline.

Earlier in the year, a young man who had been visiting stage 9 while the bridge was still under construction decided to take home a contraband souvenir—a set of blueprints. He also decided to sell duplicates of them, illegally of course, to any fans who would pay him $75 a set. Paramount officials reported the matter to the FBI. After initiating an investigation, the FBI turned the case over to the Los Angeles Police Department. Hollywood detectives followed up and arrested the man, who was convicted and fined $750. Later it was learned that the blueprints that had been stolen weren't even the final ones of the movie's sets.

The media was by now without much news at all on the production of *Star Trek*, which had just gotten under way. They seized this story as a long-awaited "scoop." Headlines in supermarket checkout line weeklies read: FBI RAIDS STAR TREK SETS! and FBI CALLED IN TO GUARD STAR TREK STAGES! None of this was true, but the phones rang for days with calls from gossip-thirsty Trekkies looking for confirmation of this oasis of news.

The studio was getting a bit nervous. The front office created a system of badge identification for all set visitors. Badges were to be controlled by either studio executive Lin Parsons' office, or Gene Roddenberry. A memo went out to all personnel even remotely connected with the film:

TO: ALL CONCERNED   DATE: SEPTEMBER 5, 1978

FROM: GENE RODDENBERRY   SUBJECT: VISITORS—
                                          STAR TREK STAGE

The situation on Star Trek stages require that we immediately tighten our security arrangements. Effective immediately, all visitors to the Star Trek stages will have to wear a visitor's badge in order to gain admittance past the security guards. This includes even those visitors personally escorted by management, producer, production staff, actors, crew or anyone else connected with the show. These badges can be checked out from either the Star Trek production office or Lin Parsons's office after approval of the visitor by either of these offices. The name of visitor and sponsor will be logged and sponsor will be responsible for the return of the badge(s) at the end of the visit.

We hope you will understand that this inconvenience is dictated by the extraordinary press, fan and public interest in our production. It is to our mutual interests that we protect story and other information vital to proper publicity at the time of film release.

Still, on visiting the stages, one might wonder what it would have been like if this *hadn't* been a closed set. Everywhere there were people standing around, proudly wearing these little laminated clip-on badges as though they were some sort of status symbol. Every day, for a hundred and twenty-five days, nearly all of the eighteen badges were in use. It got so crowded that if one had a guest to bring to the stage, reservations had to be made in advance in order to be assured of getting a badge.

Who were these lucky visitors to this very restricted filming of *Star Trek*? Many were press, there to do the few permitted interviews, closely shepherded around by publicists John Rothwell and Suzanne Gordon. Others were scientists, writers, family and friends of the production crew. Some were important fan leaders and organizers who had given of their own time and effort during the past ten years. Some were people already on the Paramount lot who were involved in other films. Clint Eastwood, Tony Curtis, Robin Williams, Henry Winkler and Mel Brooks all dropped by during filming, some even exhibiting Trekkie tendencies themselves.

Had you been fortunate enough to have visited the set, your visit would have been both exciting and informative. Guided tours for prominent visitors were conducted routinely by those working in the production offices. Michele Billy (Harold Livingston's secretary), Rosanna Attias (Jon Povill's secretary), and Susan Sackett often took turns showing the VIPs through the sound stages, giving a descriptive spiel of everything in sight, from Kirk's shower ("It works on sound waves—you know, like jewelry cleaning devices?") to the unusual grating in the *Enterprise*'s flooring ("I'll bet you wish you hadn't worn those spiked heels!")

If you were really lucky, you might have had a chance to talk to some of the behind-the-scenes people on stage. Chances are you'd first check in with Elaina Vescio, stationed backstage near the entrance. Elaina was Lord of the Badges—if you weren't on her badge list, you didn't get past her and onto the set. So efficient was this Paramount Studio guard, that she was nicknamed "Spike" by the rest of the crew, partly as a joke, partly because she knew how to be tough with trespassers. Once, she went just a bit too far. It was very early in the production, and she spotted a strange-looking man in old clothing, a half-smoked cigar protruding from his unshaven face. When she asked him if she could help him (obviously he was lost), he answered, "That's okay honey, I can find my way." He didn't seem to be getting the message. Elaina politely insisted that he leave at once. The man politely refused. After all, he was Harold Livingston, who was totally involved in the all-vital task of rewriting the script—he ought to be allowed on the set without a badge. Elaina turned crimson and, smiling weakly, ushered him through.

Once Elaina cleared you, you were a member of the elite—you had made it home free! The *Star Trek* stages beckoned unrestricted. The next person you were very likely to meet was Jimmy Chirco. Remember Sergeant Bilko, the television character of the fifties who owned all the concessions in his motor pool? Well, *Star Trek* had its own version of the enterprising (ouch!) Bilko. Jimmy Chirco (usually just "Chirco" to everyone on the set) was in charge of craft services. His job was to keep fresh coffee, donuts, soups, and other items on hand for the crew, and generally to keep the cast members happy with whatever they might need along those lines. While not fixing the coffee, Chirco organized. He organized the baseball and football pools, and each week's charts were an autograph hound's dream. Scribbled in the ninety boxes on each sheet containing the points were the signatures of virtually the entire cast, crew, and production staff at one time or another. Everyone liked to get in on these pools.

Chirco organized the softball team and scheduled all the games. Stephen Collins was captain, Walter Koenig pitched, and nearly everyone else in the cast and crew was involved with the team. Even the secretaries learned a few cheers and made a few feeble attempts as pom-pom girls.

But Chirco, like Bilko, also has a heart. A personal friend of national Muscular Distrophy Association chairman, Jerry Lewis, Chirco has always felt a strong desire to be helpful in raising funds for this charity. He organized several *Star Trek* softball games, and the proceeds were contributed to MDA. So was a percentage of *Star Trek—TMP* T-shirt sales of his own design. Chirco even arranged for a local MD poster boy to tour the sets. All of the cast took turns posing with this youngster in the wheelchair, his smile outshining even the brightest klieg lights.

Another very important person backstage you might have encountered was Michael Avisov, the transportation captain. He was charged with the very difficult task of always anticipating the needs of the entire production company so that delays could be avoided. He had five permanent drivers on his staff, and if something was needed on the set, one of these people could get it there in moments. Sometimes they had to drive some important visitors to the set and back to the offices. Often they were asked special favors by cast members, and Michael and his staff were always happy to oblige. These drivers knew a lot about all sorts of vehicles, including trucks, motor homes, and where to get good prices for parts or full repairs. Mike liked the idea of doing favors for people such as cast members. He knew that keeping them happy kept morale high. He would gladly handle minor repairs for their cars; if the actors' cars wouldn't run properly, neither could the production.

Backstage, but a bit closer to the set, you next might have come across a man sitting behind a wheelchair full of equipment. This was the man who nicknamed *Voyager 6* "the microwave wok" and who also ran the lost-temper pool for Robert Wise. Tommy Overton used the wheelchair to house all of his sound-mixing equipment because of the ease and mobility this afforded. As sound mixer, Tommy, at the other end of the microphone, recorded the dialogue of each take. When Bob Wise called for action, Tommy rang a bell *once,* signaling silence, then hit a switch which turned on several revolving red lights, both inside and outside the sound stage. Visitors were cautioned that these two actions meant they were to freeze in their tracks immediately and not make another sound (since this could easily be picked up by the sensitive mikes and ruin the take) until they would hear *two bells,* signaling all clear after Bob Wise had said "Cut."

Associate producer Jon Povill, who was on stage most of each day throughout production, had a typical introductory experience with the rule of strict silence. During the first week of shooting, a bell rang and cameras were rolling. Jon had just taken a swallow of fruit juice which had gone down the wrong way, and was suddenly consumed by an urgent need to cough. Suppressing it just made him choke more. He tried to run down the nearest corridor of the *Enterprise* to get away but couldn't because that was where the scene was being filmed between Kirk and Decker. Finally, Jon managed to locate an off-camera area of corridor to run through so he could get out of microphone range and cough. But he'd choked so silently for as long as his body would permit. Jon had barely begun to run down the corridor when he could contain the cough no longer. *Cut. Two bells.* Poor Jon blushed, coughed and apologized profusely. Everyone told him to relax—they'd all been there themselves. Jon's initiation had been completed, but later that afternoon it was his secretary Rosanna's turn when she walked in front of the blue screen during a take. When Bob Wise yelled "Cut!" and congratulated her on just having completed her first screen test, she too turned bright red.

Not all sound problems were created by humans. According to sound boom man Dennis Jones, and his assistant, second sound boom man Winifred ("T") Tennison, there were many extraneous noises on the set that were often picked up during dialogue recording. The seats on the bridge, when operating their automatic safety devices, raising head rests, etc., did not produce sound effect that was wanted. Neither did the pulley-operated elevator doors. These sounds would have to be covered with a separate track later, one with the proper sound effects. Some of the noises in the background were not so easily eliminated later. On the V'ger set, the many lamps had to be cooled with fans, since they quickly overheated. The *whir* sound of these fans could not be controlled, and the dialogue later had to be "looped," the exact words and timing repeated in postproduction by the actors involved.

The dozens of other people working backstage made up the heart of the production crew. These vital people included the camera operator and assistant cameramen; electrical gaffer, best boy, and other electricians; the key grip and the other grips—those who do needed carpentry on the set and help with camera movements; the men's and women's costumers, as well as men's costume supervisor Jack Bear and women's costume supervisor Agnes Henry; hairstylist, makeup and special effects people; set painter-supervisor Sam Giardina and his tireless crew of painters, and still photographer Mel Traxel, there to capture everything going on, both in front of the cameras and behind the scenes.

Cameras themselves are probably the most important items of any film company, and *Star Trek* was fortunate in having one of the finest cinematographers in the business, Richard Kline. Dick has done about fifty films, having been a director of photography now for eighteen years. An extremely polite and modest man, it takes some coaxing to get him to admit that he has been nominated for the Academy Award *twice*—once for *Camelot* and the other nomination for *King Kong*. However, he does exhibit a bit of pride about his membership in the American Society of Cinematographers, a select group of feature cameramen. (It is listed in *Star Trek*'s opening credits—Director of Photography, Richard H. Kline, A.S.C.)

Dick describes his work as director of photography on *Star Trek* as a collaboration with the director. Zuby would sketch out concepts, Bob Wise would look at them and decide if they were on the right track. Then Dick and Harold Michelson (and Alex Weldon, if special effects were involved) would discuss the look they wanted. Each scene and sequence was "storyboarded" (sketched in advance) by Zuby. It was then up to Dick to execute it, discussing with Bob Wise the type of

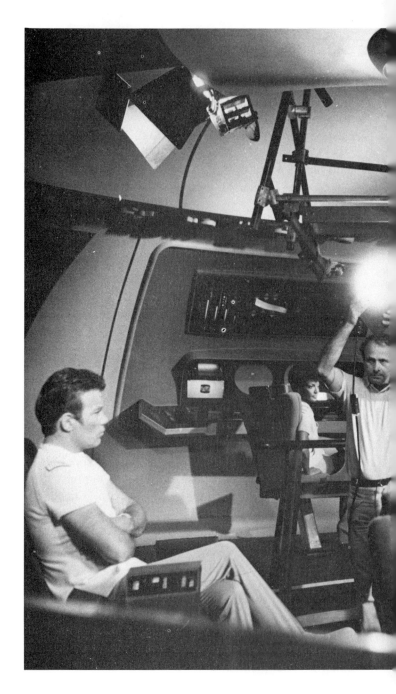

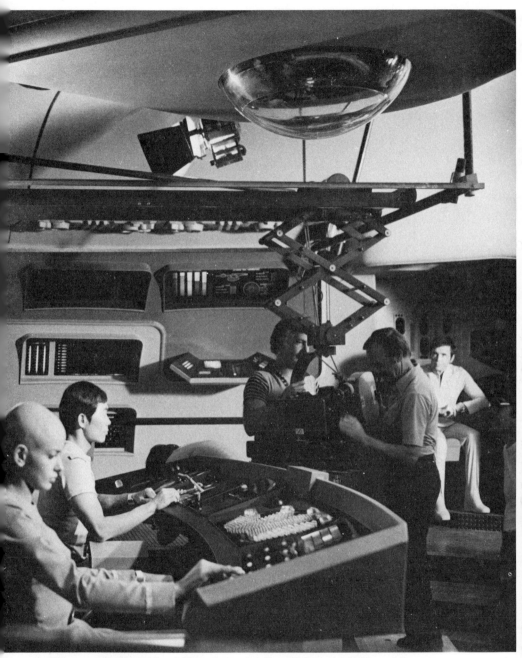

Cinematographer Richard Kline *(center)* Adjusts lighting on bridge while camera operator Al Bettcher *(far right)* and key grip John Black set up camera for close ups.

lighting desired, angles, variations, colors, and textures required by the scene in order to get the desired dramatic look. "That is the cinematographer's function," says Dick Kline, "—how to interpret this preplanning and make it indelible on film. It's a way of everybody being on the same wavelength." He was ultimately responsible for light setups and exposure, setting the mood for the scenes to be shot. On the bridge Dick worked with low lighting, quite the opposite of the brightly lit bridge required by television's needs during the original series. There were a couple of reasons for much lower lighting now. First of all, the low density of light helped the monitors (small console viewers) show up better. Also, the light conditions on a ship should normally be dim enough so the crew would be able to see the readouts. This is true of the actual lighting aboard modern-day self-contained vessels such as submarines.

The actual printing of *Star Trek* film was also of concern to Dick Kline. At each day's rushes, he'd watch carefully to see if the camera caught what he'd expected, especially noting lighting, print quality, and color. He photographed mostly in 35mm anamorphic, although scenes which were to have opticals added in postproduction (about a third) were shot in 65mm spherical. The entire picture was released in both 70mm (65mm plus 5 for soundtrack) as well as 35mm for smaller houses.

Kline worked as cinematographer with Bob Wise on *The Andromeda Strain* and believes that Bob's gift for organization may be the reason *Star Trek* was completed despite the many problems that constantly arose. "There wasn't an easy shot on this picture," Dick said in retrospect. "There was always some kind of crazy consideration that served as a challenge, whether it be the fact that we couldn't quite get the camera exactly where we wanted it, or we got the camera there but the lens wouldn't focus close enough. The various floor levels on the bridge were an example. You could never just shoot a shot—you always had to lay track or devise some method of shooting over a rail or under a rail, or move a chair to get a certain spot. It just wasn't a 'parlor, bedroom and bath show,' so to speak. On the bridge you had to fight reflections—the crew would appear in some of the monitors, or the shiny grillwork on the floor caused reflections of light.

He describes *V'ger* as probably the most ambitious sequences to shoot in the entire film, primarily because of the scope and the many light changes and color values these changes brought with them.

Physically, it was difficult too. Several of the *V'ger* shots found Dick and camera crew on catwalks forty feet above the stage, or perched atop a long crane, or balanced on a specially constructed twenty-five-foot-high platform. Fortunately, Dick had had practice. On an earlier film he'd been required to get close-ups of that notorious ape, King Kong, and Kong stood well over *fifty feet tall* in his hairy stocking feet!

Wherever Dick Kline and Robert Wise were to be found, you could usually count on finding a good-natured lady bedecked with a stopwatch and open script. Bonnie Prendergast, script supervisor for *ST—TMP*, put in one of the longest work days of anyone involved with the production. During the daytime Bonnie was on the stage, usually within breathing distance of Bob Wise, taking copious notes which would be written up later that evening, after the company had broken for the day. It was up to Bonnie to see that the actions of the actors matched in the same scene from different angles, making sure that the wardrobe matched each time, checking to see that the props were in the right place, and so on. For example, if an actor had had one of his sleeves pushed slightly up, or held his hands in a certain position during the take, Bonnie would note and remember each detail. Several minutes often passed between takes, and it was up to Bonnie to remember even the minutest of details that would be necessary in resetting the shot.

Bonnie was further charged with watching and listening for wrong words in the dialogue or changes in dialogue. If an actor ad-libbed or changed a couple of words, she noted it. She also kept track of all the slates, noting the scene number, take number, length of each take, and which takes were selected by Bob Wise to be printed. This and other vital information would then be presented to film editor Todd Ramsey, who relied heavily on all the information Bonnie accumulated each day. According to those who were involved, Bonnie did a terrific job, loading her shooting script with voluminous notes, a complement to her computerlike mind which she crammed with details.

Robert Wise was also aided on stage by first assistant director Danny McCauley. Danny could easily be spotted since he was the only member of the crew who always wore a hat, indoors or outdoors, rain, shine, morning and evenings. Danny was never without his lucky hat, a fresh cigar, and a friendly hello. His job was monumental. During preproduction, he and unit production manager Phil Rawlins broke down the script into a shooting schedule form. This is done on what is referred to simply as "the board." It looks like a giant mutated backgammon set, a large wooden board hinged into two long halves. Each film sequence is written on a strip of paper which fits into slots in this board. The strips, about three millimeters wide, contain the scene numbers, the cast members' numbers (Kirk is "1," Spock is "2," etc.) and number of pages for each scene. They are then arranged into the most economical shooting order, taking into account the availability of sets and actors. The strips can be shifted around on the board to accommodate any last-minute changes in shooting order.

Danny's responsibilities on stage were also vital to the production's smooth operation. He is the one who checked to see that everyone was in position, calling for quiet and for cameras to roll, followed of course by Bob Wise's call for "Action!" As assistant director, Danny was the organizer of the set and it was his job to keep the company moving as fast as possible. The importance of this can be understood when you realize that each hour on stage cost the *Star Trek* budget about $4,000.

Finally, Danny was charged with selection of extras, the no-dialogue actors who people the crowd scenes. Danny coordinated these groups with the wardrobe personnel, making sure there was a costume for each. He also placed the extras on the set, giving them their initial direction before Robert Wise would take over.

Scurrying about the stage, helping Danny in his efforts for efficient organization, was Doug Wise, the second assistant director. Besides helping Danny with his responsibilities, Doug was responsible for making out the "call sheet" for each following day, based on the progress of daily shooting. He and trainee Kevin Cremin had to notify all cast members of their next day's call time. A sample of a call sheet and the follow-up production report can be found in chapter 1. These show what cast were required, what crew were needed, etc., during the very first day of shooting.

The complexity of such a production requires considerable coordination, including people who keep an eye on efficiency and expenditures. The studio had several executives assigned to the *Star Trek* project. Some of these people, such as studio executive in charge of production Jeff Katzenberg, were directly concerned with expediting every stage of the movie, seeing that there was smooth progress from the writing of the script to the premiere of the film. Jeff's involvement was *total*—if something went wrong, it was up to Jeff to see that the situation was remedied quickly, efficiently, inexpensively, and in as artistically and managerially sound a way as possible. He worked closely with the studio's overall production manager, Lindsley Parsons, Jr., who held the budget reins as tightly as was possible in keeping with the film quality that Paramount had wanted.

Helping to keep costs down was *Star Trek*'s own unit production manager, Phil Rawlins, who constantly revised the budget in accordance with front office requests from Lin Parsons and Jeff Katzenberg. Phil was the third person to come on the show after producer Gene Roddenberry and director Robert Wise, and his responsibilities were as vital. The owner of a working cattle ranch about thirty miles north of Los Angeles, tanned and muscular Phil is a very unlikely-looking production manager. The six-foot three-inch wrangler would just as soon show you his rope burns from last weekend's cattle roundup as he would the most current *Star Trek* budget sheet. But he is equally at home in both worlds. In fact, Phil was more at home on *Star Trek* than most, since he's one of the few people who was involved with both *Star Treks*—the original television series, *and* the motion picture. He worked as first assistant director on the second season of the tv series.

Following his work on tv's *Star Trek,* Phil went on to become assistant director on *Adam 12,* eventually directing several of the episodes of that series. He was also director of the popular program *The High Chaparral* for two years, and was production manager on the feature film *California Suite.*

Phil's first job on the *Star Trek* movie was to break down the show into schedule form. He determined how long it would take for the company to prepare for shooting and utilized this information in hiring the rest of the crew. During production his office functioned as the hub of the entire production, handling the many everyday problems that continually arose. His troubleshooting involved injuries, insurance claims, paper work, servicing the production company on power and equipment requests, meeting the needs of the director, calling in the extras for Danny McCauley's selection, signing all the bills, and generally accounting for every penny spent on the film. His office phones constantly emitted a chorus of jingles as he and his assistant, production coordinator Anita Terrian, tackled each day's myriad problems. The two of them often put in the longest hours of anyone during production, many twelve- and fourteen-hour days, beginning as early as 6:30 or 7:00 A.M. and winding down long after the last crew member had departed for the evening. Anita's job was especially difficult and one which she handled with a good deal of public relations expertise, always managing to keep calm in the eye of some latest hurricane. Their office was also given much needed help by Phil's six-foot four-inch son, Lex Rawlins. Lex was probably the most versatile "gopher"* who ever worked on any film. He spent most of his time running errands for his dad and Anita, as well as others on the production crew. He also holds a Screen Extras Guild card, and his height made him a perfect extra whenever there was a need for a tall alien or a model to test a space suit.

Later, in postproduction, he worked as a film loader at Douglas Trumbull's shop where the opticals were being filmed. For all of his nineteen years, young Lex has had more experience in the motion picture industry than most have in a lifetime, thanks to having a father there first. Son, like father, is as at home on a sound stage as he is on a cattle ranch.

---

*A "gopher" is some who runs errands—i.e., "go fer this and go fer that."

18

It's a Wrap

The last week of production seemed to take months. Every kind of problem imaginable happened during the final week of principal photography. The red gels kept appearing orange in dailies. Three people were almost electrocuted. Lighting problems wreaked havoc with a very exhausted cast and crew.

On January 26, 1979—125 days after it all began—*Star Trek—The Motion Picture* did finally wrap. Applause, laughter and slaps on backs greeted the final takes for Bill Shatner, Leonard Nimoy, and DeForest Kelley (the "Three Musketeers," as Bob Wise had affectionately nicknamed them) when the three leads delivered their final lines at 4:50 that afternoon. Many staff and crew members grabbed pieces of paper or 8-by-10 glossies and began collecting autographs of the cast. Quite a number of the grips, technicians, artists, and even secretaries had become fans of *Star Trek* and the actors, and now they wanted these souvenirs of their involvement over the past five and a half months.

Before the company could go home, however, there still remained one scene to capture that afternoon—the climactic scene where Decker fuses with *V'ger*. Note the script's emphasis on lighting:

391   VARIOUS EFFECT SHOTS—DECKER BEING FUSED—   391
                                    V'GER TRANSCENDING

> For just an instant nothing happens—and then a
> BLINDING SHAFT OF LIGHT STRIKES Decker. The color
> becomes BRIGHTER AND BRIGHTER, begins spiraling
> through the room. "Ilia" steps toward Decker, is caught in
> the LIGHT, and instantly VANISHES in a BRILLIANT
> WHITE GLOW.
>
> We SEE Decker seeming to grow larger—as if his
> molecular pattern is expanding. A SPECTACULAR SERIES
> OF VISUALS, the SPIRALING LIGHT enveloping the entire
> area.
>
> All this emanating from Decker's body, becoming
> LARGER—also BRIGHTER AND BRIGHTER until now it is
> almost transparent. And the SPIRALING now expanding
> in all directions, and the room itself starting to dissolve,
> vanishing into nothingness—and all commencing to slip
> into the new dimension.

Special highlights on Stephen Collins as Decker were created with tiny dabs of cotton carefully glued along the outer edges of his jacket, capturing and emphasizing the backlighting to create a body halo. Brilliant lamps of 4,000 watts, helicopter lights, and wind machines were used in creating the effect of his fusion with the mighty *V'ger* and ultimate departure from this dimension.

Unfortunately, the first attempts at this backlighting on Steve became a nightmare on film. The lighting caught the millions of ordinary dust particles, which are always present in the air, but usually go undetected by nearly everyone but chronic allergy sufferers. The scene had been taken earlier in the week, and the next day in dailies it looked like *V'ger* and Decker were caught in a blizzard. Crews mopped and dusted the set constantly during the retakes that week, and it took hard physical and technical work to eliminate the presence of this dust in the final cut of the film.

The harsh lighting caused still another problem, this time to Steve and Persis, who remained to complete the above scene, that last day after the other cast had gone home. As the Ilia-probe, Persis had perfected her character's fixed stare and could go for several minutes at a time without blinking. During the scene, she and Steve stood opposite each other, she open-eyed, he blinking normally, as they revolved on a turntable. Although she could have gotten in a fast blink each time she was turned from the camera, Persis stayed in character and continued her blank stare. They continued shooting until 10:00 that night, by which time everyone on stage was having problems with aching eyes, and both Steve and Persis were nearly unable to see. The next morning Persis awoke in great pain due to the harsh light during the fusing scene. Steve, too, reported discomfort the next day, but fortunately the damage, while painful, was only temporary, and both cast members recovered nicely.

Two weeks later, the entire cast and crew, along with studio executives and just about anyone who had lent a hand with the making of the film, got together for the traditional wrap party.* Some four hundred people attended the bash, which took over Liu's Chinese Restaurant and the adjoining Chez Moi Disco on world-famous Rodeo Drive in Beverly Hills. These same people who had spent the last several months together as a production "family" now munched egg rolls and boogied the night away, knowing that this was the last time the entire group would ever be together. There was a touch of wistfulness here and there, but most were relieved that this complex film was behind them.

Although Gene Roddenberry and Robert Wise had almost a year's work ahead of them, they both took time out following the wrap to catch their collective breaths. Gene had undergone a tremendous strain during production as well as the nearly four years at Paramount which had preceded it. Mental and physical exhaustion had finally caught up with him. During that time, he began a program of diet and exercise, eventually regaining his health.

Robert Wise was in better shape, but was nevertheless grateful for this first opportunity in months for some time off, and spent a week vacationing in Vancouver, Canada.

---

*The largest part of production had officially drawn to a close, although there still remained three live-action scenes to film during postproduction: the San Francisco tram sequence, with its many aliens, saw Bill Shatner's return to the lot a month later; the Klingon bridge sequence, with Mark Lenard as the Klingon Commander (his third alien role in *Star Trek* history, having played a Romulan and a Vulcan in the television series), and the Epsilon 9 tracking station sequence, which featured the long awaited appearance of David Gautreaux (the young man who had been signed to play Lieutenant Xon in "In Thy Image"). It was also the debut of Michele Ameen Billy, Harold Livingston's former secretary, who received her "big break," a dream come true after years of dramatic study.

Bill Shatner immediately began rehearsals for a new play, *Otherwise Engaged,* which opened to critical acclaim and ran for several months at the Solari Theatre in Los Angeles.

Leonard Nimoy toured the country with his one-man show *Vincent,* based on the life of Vincent Van Gogh as seen through the letters of his brother. Leonard wrote, produced, directed, and starred in the play.

The world seemed to be returning to normal for everyone. Now it was up to the postproduction team to finalize *Star Trek—The Motion Picture,* a monumental task that had to be accomplished by Christmas at the very latest.

_____(Person's Name)_____

and your guest
are cordially invited
by
Paramount Pictures
to celebrate
the "Wrap" of

"STAR TREK—THE MOTION PICTURE"

Saturday, February 10th
8:00 PM
LIU'S CHINESE RESTAURANT
and CHEZ MOI DISCO
140 South Rodeo Drive
Beverly Hills

R.S.V.P.—468-5000, Ext. 2315

(Please present this invitation for admission)

19

After the Trek Is Over

The *Enterprise* was in darkness. The bridge that had only recently been a calliope of sound, light, voices, and footsteps now was silent, the consoles draped with heavy cotton covers. The engine room, sickbay, transporter room, and Kirk's quarters all were empty. No one was in sight in the corridors. She had become a ghost ship.

The crew and most of the staff had been gone within two weeks after principal photography was over, with only a handful of people involved with the film remaining on the lot. Stage 9 had the loneliness of an amusement park after the crowds have gone home for the night. The sets had been put under wraps, like a Christmas tree in January—all the bright lights and shiny ornaments were stripped away and stored.

Now the work could begin, work that would cover more than twice the amount of time spent thus far in the filming process. Most on the *Star Trek* production team were gone, and new faces were appearing. The producer and the director would stay, and of these two, Robert Wise would be by far the busiest. He had directed the film, and it was his mind that held the reasons for the choices he had made. It was the time for the postproduction specialists—those experts who could take thirty or more hours of what seems a repetitive puzzle on strips of celluloid and turn it into a motion picture.

In the nearly one year that elapsed between the last principal take and the premiere of *Star Trek,* this motion picture had to go through the processes of editing, adding final optical effects,* music composing and scoring, sound effects, looping, and final sound dubbing.

Editing, of course, had been an ongoing process ever since the first day of shooting. Each morning film editor Todd Ramsay and his story. During this, Todd Ramsay and his assistants would go over any day's footage in the form of separate sound track and picture. By finding the exact place where the "clapper" closed, they would then synchronize the picture and sound track, and with the aid of Bonnie Prendergast's script notes showing the number of angles shot of each moment, they would build this, reel by reel, into the unfolding of the story. During this, Todd Ramsey and his assistants would go over any notes received from Bob Wise or others on this film. Todd would run the footage a number of times to familiarize himself with the various nuances and angles. Soon he had formed in his head a general pattern of how the various shots within a scene should go together, and how those scenes fitted with still others. This process had gone on all during the shooting of the picture, each day's photography slowly being pieced together bit by jigsaw bit with others. Long before the entire picture was photographed, Todd and his assistants had already put together "rough cuts" of various sequences for viewing by Wise, Roddenberry, and others. Even at these early stages, there were already discussion and plans for the sound effects, music, and opticals that would all be added later as completed. Meanwhile the editor would be using temporary sound effects and music, as well as photographed sketches and printed information showing whatever optical effect would be inserted at these points in the completed picture. Todd Ramsey is one of those experienced film editors who wants his rough cuts of a picture to carry as much of the final look and sound as possible so as to constantly provide both others and himself with an accurate "feel" of the film's progress and direction.

Todd is another example of Robert Wise's efforts in giving a chance to young people with talent. Todd, who is himself an aficionado of science-fiction films and literature, had seen almost all of the *Star Trek* television series episodes. In a *Star Trek* trivia contest, he might not know Mr. Spock's mother's maiden name, but he would sur-

---

*Covered in the next chapter.

pass even the most devoted Trekkies and Trekkers in knowing what angle Kirk was speaking from, or what the background music was in key scenes from those episodes. Quite understandably, he wanted very much to work on *Star Trek—The Motion Picture*.

He had worked with Bob Wise as an assistant editor on *The Hindenburg,* and hoped that this meeting plus his extensive background in opticals would lead to an editorial job on the *Star Trek* film. As Todd was about to send a letter he had just written to Bob Wise, he received a phone call from the director asking if he'd like to interview for the job of film editor. (Talk about timing!) Todd is always quick to point out that Bob Wise gave him his first big break—his first feature film.

Todd found that Bob Wise's own early experience as an editor helped him tremendously in his cutting tasks. Bob shoots his film very economically with a clear indication of how it will go together. He's actually the first architect and designer of the film, and Todd claims that this made his work especially enjoyable. According to Todd, "Bob's style makes the story become the most important aspect. He doesn't draw attention to the filmmaker and doesn't intrude upon the story. He's extremely conscious of tempo and doesn't have to shoot every scene from every conceivable angle."

During postproduction editing, Todd also received some suggestions from producer Gene Roddenberry via a memo to Bob Wise. The memo ran for eleven pages, and included the following ideas, which all agreed to incorporate into the final cut:

TO: BOB WISE   DATE: APRIL 19, 1979
FROM: GENE RODDENBERRY   SUBJECT: CURRENT STAR TREK CUT

Suggest we strongly consider looping the Vulcan ceremony scene into Vulcan language. Among many arguments for this is the fact we will be doing Klingon language in the Klingon scenes and it may feel something like a "cheat" to do the Vulcan scene in King James-type English. It will take considerable work to invent a Vulcan language, but Nimoy is the only character whose voice we know, and then on the woman and the others we can use any professional voice that can handle the invented Vulcan language.

Reel 6, in the heated exchange between Kirk and Decker, I miss McCoy looking on and watching how these two men are reacting toward one another. That is, after all, why he invited himself into Kirk's cabin, i.e., to make an estimate of Kirk's apparent emotional condition and ability to command.

I have objections to Chekov repeating "Red alert." Until now, we've usually handled that type of thing via a computer voice of some sort, and it seems to me awfully 20th century that Chekov must use his time to give this vocal warning to everyone else.

When Spock makes the statement that they have been contacted but why have they not replied, it seems to me we need a cut to Uhura. After all, she is communications officer and there is at least an implication in Spock's statement that she has somehow failed to pick up a message being transmitted to them. It seems that at least she should seem surprised when hearing Spock's statement.

Do we want Kirk to ask Spock for an analysis of the weapon streaking toward them? Or do we simply want Spock to do what he should be doing, i.e., give the captain that analysis the instant he has it ready?

Regarding Spock's comments confirming that the intruder has been trying to communicate, it seems to me we again need a quick cut to Uhura, who has to have some feeling about learning this.

Would we be better off if we dropped Decker's line saying that V'ger is 78 kilometers long? The other lines seemed to cover its immensity much more dramatically.

What happens to Decker and Ilia is very exciting, even in this rough form!

cc: Todd Ramsay

After most of the footage was "in the can," Todd continued to polish and improve the film as he began to trim the picture to its best running length. Scenes moved faster as he cut out unnecessary moments, but only if those cuts would not jeopardize character or story development or short-change the visual sweep, giving importance to all three of these elements, "the pyramid on which this film stands," as he calls it. During the final cut of the film, Todd said that he kept in mind the fact that "a film is a living thing, an organic thing, and it has to grow. It can't be constrained by a previous conception. Things have to be flexible and able to change."

During postproduction Jerry Goldsmith began work on his elaborate music score for *Star Trek*. Early in the summer of 1979 there was enough footage in the rough cut for Jerry to work with in composing the music, and the Academy Award and Emmy Award winning composer-conductor worked for several months completing his score. At the time he began his work a science-fiction movie called *Alien* was breaking box office records, and the reviewers had nothing but the highest praise for Jerry Goldsmith's music. The *Los Angeles Times* said that it outdid "his earlier excellent work in its effectiveness and in its sheer musicality. The opening statement, all woodwinds and flutes, is beautiful . . . enhancing the moments. The music is symphony-sized and on occasion thunderous. More often it is restrained, an urgent shimmering in the strings, a quick savage blast of brass. It's a thrill to hear."

It is rather unusual for a motion picture reviewer to rave about music, but then Jerry Goldsmith does create praiseworthy scores. He first gained recognition composing and conducting for television in its early days, including such programs as *Hallmark Hall of Fame, Playhouse 90, Studio One, Climax, Twilight Zone, General Electric Theatre, Gunsmoke,* and *Doctor Kildare.* It was in the late fifties that he scored his first feature film, and shortly after, in 1960, *Lonely Are the Brave* brought his first critical attention. Two years later he received his first Oscar nomination—for *Freud.*

In 1976, Jerry earned the Oscar for Best Original Dramatic Score for *The Omen.* He has been nominated for the Academy Award nine other times—for *The Wind and the Lion, Chinatown, A Patch of Blue, The Sand Pebbles* (directed by Robert Wise), *Planet of the Apes, Patton, Papillion, Freud,* and for the song "Ave Santani," from *The Omen.*

He is a three-time Emmy winner, for *Babe,* the six-hour *QB VII,* and the Bell System Family Theatre's *The Red Pony.* He also was nominated for *The Waltons, The Man From U.N.C.L.E.* and *Thriller.*

Among his other outstanding music scores, representing a wide range of moods, are dozens of films, including *Lonely Are the Brave, The Mephisto Waltz, Seven Days in May, The Blue Max, Patton, Logan's Run, Islands in the Stream, MacArthur, Capricorn One, Coma, The Swarm, Damien-Omen II, The Great Train Robbery, Magic, The Boys from Brazil,* and *Alien. Star Trek—The Motion Picture* marks the eighty-fourth film score composed by Jerry Goldsmith.

During principal photography there were several occasions when the original recording of dialogue was inaudible or technically unacceptable for some reason, often due to unavoidable background noise interference. Some of this was mentioned here in earlier chapters—things like the monitor rear projectors on the bridge, the electric fans used to cool the hot lights on the *V'ger* set, and the motors that operated the chairs on the bridge. When the dialogue must be replaced, or "looped," the actor is called back during postproduction. Looping is usually done in a small room with recording facilities. The scene is put on a film loop and played back for the actor over and over again. He or she wears an earpiece through which he hears his own voice. He delivers his lines, trying to match the lip movement in the film. Skilled actors and editors can achieve almost perfect synch, and good sound technicians can record it in such a way that it is virtually impossible to tell which line was an original one and which was looped.

The final assault on the *Star Trek* film took place on the dubbing stage at Samuel Goldwyn Studios in Hollywood, after all other editing had been completed. There were many separate reels used in this final mix. Separate sound effects tracks contained everything from footsteps and door openings to equipment background noises, engines and phasers, and even the sound of actors breathing where needed for reality. The music was delivered on several different tracks for use in a stereophonic theatre system. There were many separate dialogue tracks. In all, there totaled more than *fifty different tracks,* which had to be mixed down into *one* sound track. It is no wonder that Todd described this final phase of the film as "as massive a logistical undertaking as a military invasion." During this dubbing process, which lasted for three months, Todd organized a team of editors—dialogue editor John Hanley, who had worked on the original television episodes; head sound editor Richard Anderson; music editor Ken Hall—and under Todd's supervision, they completed the final mix. It was the last great hurdle of the film, with many days spent working around the clock as the release date of *Star Trek* loomed closer.

20

Optical Optimism

At the time the first draft script, "In Thy Image" was being prepared for a two-hour television special, it was realized that the quality of the special optical effects in the just-released *Star Wars* and those being prepared for a film called *Close Encounters of the Third Kind* would be reflecting the latest in new optical techniques and advances. It was also realized that once the public had seen this level of opticals, the new *Star Trek,* even though then planned as a television movie, could hardly settle for the outdated tv opticals of ten years earlier. Post-production supervisor for the new series was Paul Rabwin, and Gene Roddenberry asked him to begin a search for a top optical firm who could handle the task. It was discovered that many studios were suddenly interested in science fiction, and most of the established firms and key optical talents were already busy. Rabwin recommended that a firm named Robert Abel and Associates be considered, and the studio began checking them out. One of the people they talked to was Douglas Trumbull, whose Future General Corporation is a subsidiary of Paramount Pictures. Film director Doug Trumbull, whose experience in opticals dates back to *2001: A Space Odyssey,* agreed that Abel and Associates appeared to be the best choice available. Doug pointed out that opticals were part of a strange never-never land of mixed art and science where the best laid plans often went awry. On the other hand, the firm's president, Robert Abel, and his people had done a number of visually spectacular television commercials such as the unusual "Little Trademark" for Levi-Strauss (which has the highest surveyed audience recall of any advertisement in the history of television*), plus a number of other visually intriguing commercials. They were inventive and some of their key people had interesting backgrounds, one of them having been associated with Trumbull in creating opticals for major science fiction films.

When the tv movie evolved into *Star Trek—The Motion Picture,* the number and complexity of optical effects increased accordingly. Abel and Associates bid approximately $4,000,000 for doing all of the film's optical effects, and Paramount accepted the bid, assigning that firm to the film. By May of 1978, with the film still in preproduction, more optical effects had been added to the film, and the Abel group revised their bid three-quarters of a million dollars upward to cover this. Given the increasing complexity and costs of the film's optical effects, Gene Roddenberry recommended that Paramount's front office find an optical effects expert to look into optical costs, schedules, and other related concerns.

TO: MICHAEL EISNER   DATE: JULY 24, 1978
FROM: GENE RODDENBERRY   SUBJECT: STAR TREK
                                          OPTICAL EFFECTS

Robert Wise and I have an idea of where we are on every area of filming except opticals—in the optical area we are planning and operating too often by guesswork and by promise.

Our problem lies in the fact that the current state-of-the-art in optical effects has grown so technically complex and specialized that normal or even superior filmmaking experience is not a sufficient background for many of the optical effects decisions required of Star Trek's producer and director.

What I am questioning is whether we can afford to continue making far-reaching decisions on optical effects scenes, techniques, costs and schedules without being guided by a Paramount optical effects technical expert—someone capable of fully understanding and evaluating our optical effects plans, problems and needs and helping us to work with Abel and Associates on that basis. Paramount's stake in the optical effects area is such that it seems to me only sound business

---

*ABC Evening News, March 15, 1979.

management to move quickly to protect our investment and reduce our risks via either Dick Yuricich, someone else, or some combination of experts working for Paramount. At the moment, without this kind of skilled advice and assistance, I cannot predict with any certainty that the optical effects part of this film will be completed and delivered in 1979 even by spending the additional $220,700 to expedite those effects. Indeed, we may not have heard the last of optical expediting expenditures. It is possible we could also have other expenditures in dollars and delays on optical techniques, systems and equipment which do not work out as planned. Major optical effects of this type carry many hazards under the best of circumstances, and the director and myself have an urgent need to make decisions on them from something more than an "it sounds reasonable" basis.

cc: R. Wise
     J. Katzenberg
     L. Parsons
     P. Rawlins

Eisner responded immediately to Roddenberry's memo. Dick Yuricich (mentioned in the memo) was assigned to the show. A series of meetings began to explore the optical situation. Paramount vice-presidents Jeff Katzenberg and Lindsley Parsons, Jr., were assigned to give more and more of their time to the project.

By Christmas of 1978, there were considerable creative differences between Abel's company and Paramount's production team. At the same time, Doug Trumbull had just become available, and Paramount brought him in immediately.

By mid-February, 1979, Paramount and Abel's company had agreed that their creative differences were irreconcilable, and principal responsibility for the *Star Trek* film's optical effects was given to Doug Trumbull. In March, 1979, a meeting was held in which the studio offered Trumbull virtual carte blanche if he would get the work completed by December of that year, a film release date to which Paramount was committed, having accepted advances from exhibitors on promising delivery for the Christmas holiday market. Trumbull seemed fairly confident that the work could be done without the quality suffering. By this time the optical effects budget figure had grown to approximately $10 million.

At only 37 years of age, Doug Trumbull has climbed to the top of the special optical effects ladder and has an international reputation for inventiveness and excellence in his work. In 1964 he worked on a film called *To The Moon and Beyond* in Cinerama 360 for the New York World's Fair. The film caught the attention of Stanley Kubrick, who hired young Doug as one of a team of four special effects supervisors for *2001: A Space Odyssey* (others were Wally Veevers, Con Pederson and Tom Howard). The film won the best special effects Oscar in 1968.

In 1969 Doug created the special effects for Robert Wise's *The Andromeda Strain*. A year later, in 1970, he wrote and directed the highly imaginative space film *Silent Running*.

In 1974 he formed Future General Corporation as a subsidiary of Paramount Pictures Corporation for the purpose of research and development of innovative entertainment concepts. In 1977, Paramount made Doug and Future General available to Columbia Pictures for *Close Encounters of the Third Kind,* and Doug received an Oscar nomination for special photographic effects.

From the beginning, Doug had been involved with *Star Trek* in a consultative capacity, but even after he had taken over there was minimum publicity about it. Part of this was his own wish not to have his name constantly associated with optical effects only. The *Star Trek* film may in fact be his last involvement with someone else's motion picture. "I think of myself as a filmmaker in my own right. I'm not a special effects man. I'm trying to develop Future General and my own things, my own projects which I'd like to direct. It's been really hard for me to break the public image mold of being a special effects man. That's only a small part of what I do. It's been very frustrating for me to have made my own movie in 1970 and not to have had a chance since to make another one."

But he *is* a master of special optical effects, which is why he was so needed on *Star Trek*. Doug's tasks on the film were not easy ones. Hundreds of opticals were required—matte paintings, "gags" or trick sequences such as explosions, model and miniature photography including all shots of the *Enterprise* itself, design and photography of *V'ger,* animation sequences such as the transporter effect and malfunction, and the energy probe. Nearly one-third of the film involved optical work of some kind.

One of Doug Trumbull's key people was Richard Yuricich. Dick had had a long association with Doug, having been involved with him on films on and off for the past eleven years. He refers to himself as "one of the graduates of the Class of *2001*," since he spent six months photographing mattes of stars on that film. He also worked with both Trumbull and John Dykstra on *Silent Running*. Prior to *Star Trek*, Dick served as Director of Photography for Photographic Effects on *Close Encounters of the Third Kind*, for which he received an Academy Award nomination.

Trumbull and Yuricich formulated a plan which involved a crash program of re-assembling the equipment and crew for *Close Encounters of the Third Kind*, modifying the Future General facilities and adding more cameras, printers, electronics, stage space, equipment and personnel—with a large budget but very little time.

Time was to be the enemy, and Dick Yuricich had the job of designing more optical printers and cameras, laying out floorplans for three new buildings, cajoling cameramen, engineers and artists to drop everything to expedite work on *Star Trek*. Trumbull developed ideas to improve, yet simplify, lighting and photography of the dry dock, the *Enterprise* and other miniatures, while planning how to create thousands of pieces of artwork, shoot thousands of exposures onto single shots, and deliver in nine months *twice* the amount of effects in *Close Encounters* or *Star Wars*, both of which had taken over two years to complete. Trumbull and Yuricich were confident that significant work could be accomplished, and "maybe" the completion date would be met if virtually nothing stood in the way of expediting every detail.

At the time this book was being written (in the summer of 1979), Doug Trumbull was still in production on *Star Trek's* optical work. He was supervising the photographing of the *Enterprise* in dry dock on one stage, while several of his other stages were given over to filming the other models—the space office complex, the work bees, the travel pod and the Vulcan shuttle.

Many of the models used in *Star Trek* were built by another Paramount subsidiary, Magicam, under the supervision of Jim Dow. The Magicam company began as a video system initially invented by Trumbull and eventually branched out into building models and miniatures as these became required for their photographic system. One of the best examples of their expertise in this area is the model work Jim did for Doug on *Close Encounters*. Back in 1977, Magicam had built a dry dock, an office complex and *V'ger* model for *Star Trek's* "In Thy Image" tv movie. However, these models had not been designed to meet motion picture quality standards, and when STAR TREK became a motion picture, these models were put on the shelf and Magicam began designing new ones.

The Enterprise and the dry dock are the two most spectacular models used in the film. The "Big E" herself is eight feet long, with a scale of one-tenth inch to the foot (one inch equals ten feet). It took fourteen months to build, at the cost of $150,000. The ship differs from the television starship in several ways. The initial redesign came from the television movie art director Joe Jennings, with input from the designer of the original tv *Enterprise*, Matt Jefferies. Jennings' tv designs were turned over to Magicam, and eventually received further modification from Abel and Associates, and from Jim Dow and others at the Magicam shop. The basic differences include a slightly wider secondary hull, angled and swept back struts supporting the nacelle pods, and an elaborate electronic wiring system to govern the model's various types of lighting.

The model itself used the latest in state-of-the-art techniques, including newer lightweight plastics instead of the standard Fiberglas (the entire model weighs only eighty-five pounds). The biggest problem in building the *Enterprise*, according to Dow, was that its various ship sections and connecting struts had to be enormously strong so that no part would ever bend, or sag, or quiver even when the model was being moved during photography. Special optical effects are photographed so precisely that even the slightest quiver in any part of the model would destroy believability. The completed model can be supported at five different points as required by various photographic angles. There is also a second model of the *Enterprise* which is twenty inches long, used for long shots.

Doug Trumbull found that the lighting in the *Enterprise* model was still not adequate for his needs, and he had the starship completely rewired. He questioned that the *Enterprise* could be traveling in deep space, light-years from the nearest sun or star, and still be flooded with light. It just wasn't logical. Except for lighted ports, the ship should be totally dark. And yet, if the ship was realistically dark, how could the audience appreciate what it was and how it looked? Trumbull conceived of a clever alternative—a concept of self-illumination. Today's jetliners have lights on their tails so that other pilots can see their airplane; ships at sea are lit up the same way. Doug pictured the *Enterprise* as something like a great oceanliner, "a grand lady of the

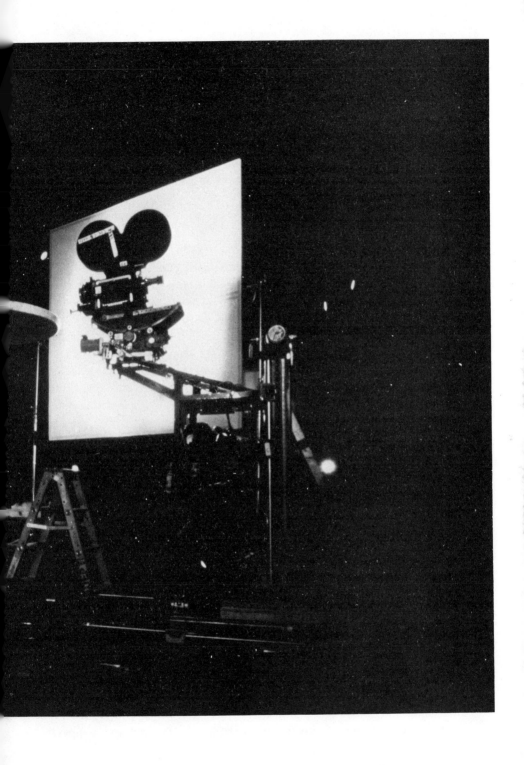

seas at night," and had lights designed into the starship so that it would illuminate itself. He did the same for the Klingon model, which had also been built by Magicam, but this time he pictured it less well lit than the *Enterprise*. He reasoned that the Klingons shouldn't go in for the same clean look of the Federation starships—as the villains they should be more like "an enemy submarine during World War II that's been out at sea for too long." The ship was also self-illuminating, but in a grungy sort of way.

Magicam's other model spectacular was the orbital dry dock in which the *Enterprise* is first seen during the film. It is a remarkable example of model miniaturization, four feet high by ten and a half feet deep by six feet in width. Its fifty-six neon panels required 168,000 volts of electricity, and a separate table was used to support the transformers supplying all this juice. The price tag: $200,000.

The scenes of the *Enterprise* in this Earth orbiting dry dock cover only two pages of script, but Trumbull needed forty-five different shots (averaging about one shot per day) for the travel pod containing Captain Kirk to make its flight from the space office complex to the area where that pod docks with the *Enterprise*. Eventually, double shifts working 24 hours a day were required to complete this optical work on time.

Subcontracted to Doug and Future General was John Dykstra of *Star Wars* fame, plus his Apogee Company. At the age of thirty-two, John already has an enviable track record in the special optical effects field. He spent five years studying industrial design at University of California at Long Beach. Soon he too was involved in Robert Wise's *The Andromeda Strain*. He then went to work for Doug Trumbull on *Silent Running*, where he applied his industrial design training and still photography experience, working as part of a team on model design effects and special effects photography. He later joined a project at the University of California at Berkeley under a grant from the National Science Foundation involving a computer-oriented probe camera which was used for the study of urban and regional planning. Following his work at Berkeley, he joined Graphic Films to do special effects photography on a specialty presentation Imax film called *Voyage to the Outer Planets*. This resulted in his being approached by George Lucas in 1975 to set up and supervise the special effects and visual effects facility for *Star Wars*. His efforts were rewarded with a Class Two Technical Academy Award for the facility, and a separate

Academy Award for the visual effects produced at that facility. Just prior to *Star Trek,* John produced and supervised the special effects for the first five hours of Universal's *Battlestar Galactica,* for which he later received television's Emmy Award.

John and his seven partners at Apogee, Inc., also have the latest equipment, including four optical printers, and the "VistaFlex" system of motion control photography which he developed himself. He employs a staff of sixty people, who like himself, are almost all under thirty-five years old. Despite the pressures of trying to complete his assigned optical work for *Star Trek* in the time available, he and everyone at his complex in Van Nuys, California, seem to enjoy their work tremendously. John himself admitted to wanting more time, especially since he says the studio told him, "We don't want anything that we've ever seen before. You've got eight months to do it, and by the way, we want to keep the price down!"

In addition to detailing out the models for Doug and shipping them out to Trumbull's complex in Marina del Rey, John's firm was charged with preparing the transporter sequences, the whiplash bolt, the photon torpedo firing, the destruction and assimilation of the Klingons, the building of the Epsilon 9 miniature, the wormhole asteroid, *V'ger's* home planet (the machine plant seen in Spock's mindmeld), the maw and exterior of *V'ger.* They also had five men working full time on a redesigned space suit, rocket pack and helmet for the spacewalk scene. Even with hundreds of thousands of dollars worth of the latest optical effects equipment, it was an awesome task. "There was more work in this thing *(Star Trek)* than there was in *Star Wars* and *Close Encounters* put together," John asserts.

Another vital area of optical work involves matte painting, and in this case too, *Star Trek* was fortunate in having one of the best artists in the business. Matthew Yuricich has been doing matte painting since 1950, beginning with Robert Wise's *The Day the Earth Stood Still,* and going on to do work for *Forbidden Planet, Ben Hur, North by Northwest, Logan's Run* (for which he won an Academy Award), and *Close Encounters of the Third Kind* (which earned him the Oscar nomination). Matt worked out at the Marina as part of Doug Trumbull's team, where his brother, Dick Yuricich, directed all photography on the film, including Matt's mattes.

A matte is an optical process by which specially prepared paintings can be combined with live action—an example of this being the

Vulcan planet landscape painting which surrounds the Spock scenes shot at Yellowstone and in the B-tank at the Paramount lot. In *Star Trek*, there were approximately one-hundred paintings used—in scenes such as San Francisco, the cargo deck, from Earth orbit, the wing walk, and so on. The process involves matting or blocking out the unwanted parts of a photographed scene (such as the blue Earth sky in the Vulcan sequence) and replacing this with a specially created painting of what is wanted there instead (the red-hued Vulcan landscape and sky). The matte painting is photographed and then is mated in an optical printer with the live action photography, these two pieces of film becoming one which shows the actors in the desired setting.

Another use of mattes is that of photographing the actors in combination with a specially prepared and carefully lit blue screen. An example of this is the main viewer on the starship's bridge which is photographed as blue screen, with the actual viewer images added later. This is made possible by the fact that the proper blue color can be separated out in the color processing, creating a clear area in the film. Later, the desired viewer images can be photographed and inserted into this clear area in much the same way that painted matte backgrounds are added.

Another talented person added to Doug Trumbull's artistic staff was the well-known space artist Robert McCall. Bob is one of the artists chosen by NASA to document the United States space program, and he was also selected to paint the enormous wall murals which can be seen in the National Air and Space Museum as well as those for the Johnson Space Center in Houston. He is known in the motion picture industry for his original posters for the film *2001: A Space Odyssey*. During the six weeks he worked on *Star Trek*, Bob painted close to twenty huge canvases of conceptualization art to provide Trumbull with possibilities for Spock's spacewalk/mindmeld with *V'ger*, a brief scene which required many weeks of preparation because of its importance as a visually dramatic moment.

An entire book would be needed to properly describe and explain the hundreds of optical effects in *Star Trek—The Motion Picture*, and the publishers plan just such a book.

21

Keep On Trekkin'

It was like being pregnant for ten years. *Star Trek—The Motion Picture* was finally about to be born, and many anxious Star Trekkers felt like expectant parents awaiting the birth of a long, long overdue baby. Millions of others were interested, too—the drama behind the making of the film had caught the interest of the general public.

The months that preceded the premiere of *Star Trek—The Motion Picture* saw an unexpectedly strong resurgence of fan activity. Dozens of conventions popped up to pay tribute to the upcoming film. In other places, fans simply gathered to compare and discuss the official publicity on the film—and sometimes "unofficial" information and photos, as well as the latest rumors (which were often as imaginative as good science fiction).

The fans had been mentally standing in ticket lines before the lines ever existed. As early as February 1979, the *Star Trek* production offices were swamped with requests for premiere tickets to a film that didn't even exist yet. And no one had the remotest idea where the premiere would be held. But that really didn't matter to some fans. Wherever it was held, they planned to get there by car caravans, by bus, by hitchhiking, or even by flying across oceans if necessary.

Paramount's other plans for *Star Trek* went in work long before the film premiere. Contemplated is a series of motion picture sequels much as happened with the *James Bond* movies. Realizing the value of the various *Star Trek* sets, studio production executive Lin Parsons sent the following memo to the studio president:

TO: MICHAEL EISNER   DATE: 5 JANUARY 1979

FROM: LINDSLEY PARSONS, JR.   SUBJECT: STAR TREK

We have reached a point on Star Trek where principal photography will soon be concluded. We have left many sets standing on the stages, have struck some for storage, and are planning the demolition of others due to their lack of value for a series or for a sequel. I have listed below the manner in which we are handling each of these sets, and have made specific recommendations with regard to others, and need your concurrence with our judgment.

STAGE   9:   Enterprise Bridge (to be stored indefinitely)
               Engine room (to be stored indefinitely)
               Kirk's quarters (to be stored indefinitely)
               Medical complex (to be stored indefinitely)
               Transporter room and corridors (to be stored
               indefinitely)

STAGE 17:   Contains the trench for the space walk. We plan on
               demolishing this set after all principal and second unit
               photography is completed.

STAGE   8:   Contains the wing of the Enterprise, a set that is basically
               a series of platforms and really has no residual value. This
               will be struck upon completion of the editing of this
               sequence.

STAGE 15:   Contains the center core of V'ger. After we complete all
               principal photography in this set, we will photograph
               process plates of all conceivable angles in the event that
               any additional close-up photography is needed at a later
               date; and we will also keep the full-scale model of Voyager
               6. All other elements of the set will be struck.

Approximately one month after the completion of principal photography, we will then shoot the San Francisco tram set, and later shoot the interior of the Klingon battle cruiser and the star base Epsilon 9 set. A determination on retention of these sets will be made at that time.

STAGE   2:   Space Office Complex and Officers Lounge (both of these
               sets have been struck and folded and will be moved to
               stage 9 for permanent storage).
               Cargo Deck (portions thereof).

Recreation Room (major structural members which
consist of approximately $\frac{1}{2}$ of original set—balance of set was
unsalvagable due to temporary construction employed thereon).

This stage must be cleared within the next week or two
to make room for model photography by Doug Trumbull of
the Enterprise and later the Space Dry Dock.

It is my feeling that the Recreation Room is too large a
set for television, would cost too much money for them to
light, and be too costly to staff with the necessary extras.
If we are planning a sequel to the feature the value of the
residual elements is about $80,000. The Cargo Deck is also
a very large set that is complemented by a matte painting.
The elements that we have retained are valued at
approximately $30,000. We shall have no place to store
these last two sets under cover, and a decision should be
made to destroy them or to seek inexpensive warehouse
space off the lot for long-term storage. It is my feeling
that the cost of moving and storing these items over a
long period of time may begin to exceed their value. Do
you concur?

Gene Roddenberry did concur with the above, and sent Lin some
additional salvage requests:

TO: LINDSLEY PARSONS, JR.   DATE: JAN. 24, 1979

FROM: GENE RODDENBERRY   SUBJECT: STAR TREK SET STORAGE

On the subject of storage of Star Trek production memorabilia, sketches,
photographs, etc.—I understand the present plan is to store them
somewhere on stage 9. In my opinion, these things should be stored in
a locked room somewhere in one of our buildings, preferably near the
Star Trek offices. These items will be getting considerable use and
research over the next year and perhaps even longer than that in Star
Trek books currently in preparation and probably in Star Trek books
and studies yet to be assigned. Any locked room with a limited key
distribution would be much preferable. It would also have advantages
from a security standpoint.

At the time he wrote the memo, Gene had already been asked by the
studio to begin thinking about sequel stories. One he likes involves the
Klingon Empire, an inside look at their home planet, their culture, and
the reasons behind their love of battle. Gene states that he never really
liked the tv series Klingons much, pointing out that they were invented by one of the first-year television show writers in need of
villains. He believes that the Klingons emerged as too simply the

epitome of evil—the bad guys who always wear black—whereas one of *Star Trek*'s philosophical cornerstones was that there are many forms of truth, and other life forms (or other humans, for that matter) should not be branded *good* or *evil* solely on the basis of our own customs and values.

A return to television? It seems to be less a question of *whether* rather than of *when*. If, following the movie, the *Star Trek* audience seems to believe that *Star Trek*'s proper format is still television, then there could be an early return to a new tv series. It is generally believed that it almost certainly will return to television someday, even if in the far future, with other actors playing the familiar parts, just as many different people have played James Bond, Tarzan, Sherlock Holmes, and other enduring characters. Some predict *Star Trek* may endure for several generations, eventually giving it a quaint Jules Verne-like quality of being perhaps technologically incorrect but nevertheless a charming and enjoyable story.

Star Trek—The Motion Picture ushered in the decade of the eighties, portraying our human future optimistically as a time of hope and prosperity and excitement. Whatever happens to *Star Trek,* it has already turned the attention of millions to the infinitely more important question of our own future. Those who made the movie insist and believe that *the human adventure is just beginning!*

CREDITS

PARAMOUNT PICTURES PRESENTS
A GENE RODDENBERRY PRODUCTION
A ROBERT WISE FILM

Captain James T. Kirk	WILLIAM SHATNER
Mr. Spock	LEONARD NIMOY
Dr. Leonard ("Bones") McCoy	DEFOREST KELLEY
Montgomery ("Scotty") Scott	JAMES DOOHAN
Sulu	GEORGE TAKEI
Dr. Christine Chapel	MAJEL BARRETT
Chekov	WALTER KOENIG
Uhura	NICHELLE NICHOLS
Ilia	PERSIS KHAMBATTA
Commander Willard Decker	STEPHEN COLLINS
Transporter Chief Janice Rand	GRACE LEE WHITNEY
Klingon Captain	MARK LENARD
Chief DiFalco	MARCY LAFFERTY
Alien Ensign	BILLY VAN ZANDT
Bridge Crew	RALPH BRANNEN, RALPH BYERS, IVA LANE, FRANKLYN SEALES, MOMO YASHIMA
Commander Branch	DAVID GAUTREAUX
Epsilon Lieutenant	MICHELE AMEEN BILLY
Epsilon Technician	ROGER AARON BROWN
Transporter Assistant	JOHN D. GOWANS
Lieutenant Commander Sonak	JON KAMAL
Yeoman	LESLIE C. HOWARD
Lieutenant Cleary	MICHAEL ROUGAS
Engine Room Technician	JUNERO JENNINGS
Engine Room Technician	SAYRA HUMMEL
Cargo Deck Ensign	HOWARD ITZKOWITZ
Security Officer	ROD PERRY
Security Officer	JOHN DRESDEN
Vulcan Masters	EDNA GLOVER, PAUL WEBER, NORMAN STUART
Crew Member	PAULA CRIST

217

Chief Ross	TERRANCE O'CONNOR
Airlock Technician	GARY FAGA
Security Officer	JOSHUA GALLEGOS
Computer Voice/Off Camera	DOUG HALE
Woman in Transporter	SUSAN J. SULLIVAN
Klingon Crewmen ... JIMMIE BOOTH, JOEL KRAMER, BILL McTOSH, DAVE MOORDIGIAN,	
TOM MORGA, TONY ROCCO, JOEL SCHULTZ, CRAIG THOMAS	
Stunts .... ROBERT BRALVER, WILLIAM COUCH,	
KEITH L. JENSEN, JOHN HUGH McKNIGHT	
Directed by	ROBERT WISE
Produced by	GENE RODDENBERRY
Screenplay by	HAROLD LIVINGSTON
Story by	ALAN DEAN FOSTER
Associate Producer	JON POVILL
Special NASA Science Adviser	JESCO VON PUTTKAMER
Special Science Consultant	ISAAC ASIMOV
Special Photographic Effects Directed by	DOUGLAS TRUMBULL
Special Photographic Effects Supervisor	JOHN DYKSTRA
Special Photographic Effects Produced by	RICHARD YURICICH
Edited by	TODD RAMSAY
Production Designer	HAROLD MICHELSON
Director of Photography	RICHARD H. KLINE, A.S.C.
Music by	JERRY GOLDSMITH
Executives in Charge of Production .... LINDSLEY PARSONS, JR., JEFF KATZENBERG	
Unit Production Manager	PHIL RAWLINS
Special Assistant to Mr. Roddenberry	SUSAN SACKETT
Assistant Director	DANNY McCAULEY
Second Assistant Director	DOUG WISE
Costume Designer	ROBERT FLETCHER
Art Directors .... JOE JENNINGS, LEON HARRIS, JOHN VALLONE	
Assistant Art Director	JOHN CARTWRIGHT
Set Decorator	LINDA DeSCENNA
Production Kinetic Lighting Effects in	
Engine Room and Voyager 6 Complex by .... SAM NICHOLSON, BRIAN LONGBOTHAM	
Makeup Artists .... FRED PHILLIPS, JANNA PHILLIPS, VE NEILL, CHARLES SCHRAM	
Hair Stylist	BARBARA KAYE MINSTER
Property Master	RICHARD RUBIN
Assistant Property Masters .... CHARLES SHEPARD, RICHARD LEON	
Special Effects (Non-Optical)	ALEX WELDON
Sound Mixer	TOM OVERTON
Supervising Sound Editor	RICHARD L. ANDERSON
Sound Effects Created by .... DIRK DALTON, JOEL GOLDSMITH, ALAN S. HOWARTH,	
FRANCISCO LUPICA, FRANK SERAFINE	
Assistant Film Editors .... RICK MITCHELL, RANDY D. THORNTON,	
DARREN HOLMES, JOHN DUNN	
Sound Editors .... STEPHEN HUNTER FLICK, CECELIA HALL, ALAN MURRAY,	
COLIN WADDY, GEORGE WATTERS II	
Music Editor	KEN HALL
Special Musical Assistance by	LIONEL NEWMAN
Titles .... RICHARD FOY/COMMUNICATION ARTS, INC.	
Special Animation Effects	ROBERT SWARTHE
Mechanical Special Effects .... DARRELL PRITCHETT, RAY MATTEY, MARTY BRESIN	
Graphics	LEE COLE
Senior Illustrator	MICHAEL MINOR
Illustrators .... MAURICE ZUBERANO, RICK STERNBACH	
Set Designers .... LEWIS SPLITTGERBER, RICHARD McKENZIE, DAN MALTESE,	
JACK TAYLOR, MARIT MONSOS, AL KEMPER	

Decorator Lead Man	MICHAEL HUNTOON
Camera Operator	AL BETTCHER
Assistant Camermen	MICHAEL GENNE, ROBERT A. WISE
Sound Boom Man	DENNIS JONES
Second Sound Boom Man	WINFRED TENNISON
Men's Costume Supervisor	JACK BEAR
Women's Costume Supervisor	AGNES HENRY
Men's Costumers	DANIEL CARTWRIGHT, RON HODGE, MICHAEL LYNN, DAVID L. WATSON, HARRY CURTIS
Women's Costumers	ELIZABETH MANNY, PAT BRADSHAW
Wardrobe	CHARLES TOMLINSON, NORMAN SALLING
Wardrobe Modelmaker	KELLY KIMBALL
Electrical Gaffer	LARRY HOWARD
Electrical Best Boy	LARRY FREEMAN
Electricians	JIM PURSELL, ED REILLY, KEITH L. ROVERUD, AL ZIMMERMAN, NORMAN M. STEWART
Key Grips	ROBERT SORBEL, JOHN L. BLACK
Grip Best Boy	JOHN C. HANN
Dolly Grip	BUZZ WARREN
Assistant Director Trainee	KEVIN CREMIN
Craft Services	JIMMY CHIRCO
Script Supervisor	BONNIE PRENDERGAST
Publicity	JOHN ROTHWELL, SUZANNE GORDON
Still Photography	MEL TRAXEL
Accountant	CHARLES A. OGLE
Production Coordinator	ANITA TERRIAN
Transportation Coordinator	MICHAEL AVISOV
Transportation Co-Captain	BOB MAYNE
Dialogue Editor	SEAN HANLEY
Supervising Re-recording Mixer	BILL VARNEY
Re-recording Mixers	STEVE MASLOW, GREGG LANDAKER
Construction Coordinator	GENE KELLEY
Construction Foremen	ROBERT CHITWOOD, JIM KELLEY
Set Painting Foreman	SAM GIARDINA
Casting	MARVIN PAIGE
Casting Assistant	SKITCH HENDRICKS
Extra Casting	CENTRAL CASTING
Assistant to Mr. Wise	ESTHER HOFF
Assistant to Mr. Livingston	MICHELE AMEEN BILLY
Assistant to Mr. Povill	ROSANNA ATTIAS

SECOND UNIT

Cinematographer	BRUCE LOGAN
Camera Operator	GARY KIBBE
Assistant Cameraman	TERRY BOWEN
Gaffer	BOB SMITH
Grip	JERRY DEATS
Wardrobe	BILL SMITH
Assistant Director	DAVID LESTER
Second Assistant Director	JIM BENJAMIN
Script Supervisor	ROSEMARY DORSEY

OPTICAL EFFECTS PERSONNEL

Director of Photography	DAVE STEWART
Special Photographic Effects	RICHARD YURICICH

219

Matte Paintings .... MATTHEW YURICICH
Additional Matte Paintings .... ROCCO GIOFFRE
Miniatures .... GREG JEIN, RUSS SIMPSON, JIM DOW
Special Photographic Effects .... DON BAKER
Cameramen .... PHIL BARBERIO, DON COX, DOUGLAS EBY, JOHN ELLIS,
    DAVID HARDBERGER, ALAN HARDING, DON JAREL, LIN LAW, CLAY MARSH,
        DAVID MCCUE, MAX MORGAN, SCOTT SQUIRES, HOYT YEATMAN
Additional Photography .... JIM DICKSON
Special Photographic Effects Editorial .... JACK HINKLE, VICKI WITT
Special Electronic and Mechanical Design ... EVANS WETMORE, RICHARD HOLLANDER
Production Illustrators .... DAVID NEGRON, ANDY PROBERT, TOM CRANHAM,
                            ROBERT MCCALL, DON MOORE
Special Mechanical Design .... GEORGE POLKINGHORNE
Special Visual Consultants .... VIRGIL MIRANO, GUY MARSDEN
Special Photographic Effects Gaffer .... DAVID GOLD
Special Photographic Effects Grip .... PAT VAN AUKEN
Special Effects Props and Miniatures .... LARRY ALBRIGHT, BRUCE BISHOP,
    AL BROUSSARD, CHRIS CRUMP, LEE ETTLEMAN, MIKE FINK, KRIS GREGG,
    RICK GUTTIEREZ, MIKE MCMILLEN, TOM PAHK, CHRIS ROSS, ROBERT SHORT
    ROBERT SPURLOCK, MARK STETSON, RICK THOMPSON, PAUL TURNER, DON WHEELER
Special Photographic Effects Photography .... THANE BERTI, GLENN CAMPBELL,
                    CHRISTOPHER GOERGE, SCOTT FARRAR, ROBERT FRIEDSTAND,
        ROBERT HOLLISTER, RUSS MCELHATTON, MIKE PEED, LEX RAWLINS,
                    JONATHAN SEAY, STEVE SLOCUM, BOB THOMAS
Animation and Graphics .... DEENA BURKETT, ALISON YERXA, LISZE BECHTOLD,
    MERLLYN CHING, ELRENE COWAN, CY DIDJURGIS, LESLIE EKKER, LINDA HARRIS,
    NICOLA KAFTAN, JOHN KIMBALL, THOMAS KOESTER, DEIDRE LE BLANC,
        LINDA MOREAU, CONNIE MORGAN, PAUL OLSEN, GREG WILZBACH
Special Electronics .... KRIS DEAN, STEPHEN FOG, JOHN GILMAN, JIM GOODNIGHT,
    FRED IGUCHI, ROBIN LEYDEN, GREG MCMURRAY, MIKE MYERS, JOSH MORTON
Special Editorial .... MICHAEL BACKAUSKAS, KATHY CAMPBELL, NORA JEANNE SMITH
Special Photographic Effects Projectionist .... JOHN PINER
Special Photographic Effects Project Managers .... JOHN JAMES, BILL MILLAR
Assistant to Mr. Trumbull .... MONA THAL BENEFIEL
Assistant to Mr. Yuricich .... JOYCE GOLDBERG
Special Assistant to Photographics Effects .... LEORA GLASS, BRETT WEBSTER
Special Optical Consultants .... ALAN GUNDELFINGER, MILT LAIKEN
Special Mechanical Designs .... GEORGE RANDLE CO., PRECISION MACHINE,
                        DIETER SEIFERT, ROURKE ENGINEERING
Special Photographic Effects Sequences by .... APOGEE, INC.
Special Photographic Effects Supervised by .... JOHN DYKSTRA
Special Photographic Effects Project Manager .... ROBERT SHEPHERD
Miniatures Supervised by .... GRANT MCCUNE
Director of Optical Photography .... ROGER DORNEY
Special Photographic Effects Cameramen .... CHUCK BARBEE, BRUNO GEORGE,
        MICHAEL LAWLER, JERRY POOLER, DOUG SMITH, JOHN SULLIVAN
Special Animation Effects .... HARRY MOREAU
Special Electronic Design .. ALVAH J. MILLER, MAT BECK, PAUL JOHNSON, STEVE SASS
Production Illustrators .... MARTIN KLINE, SYD MEADE,
                            JACK JOHNSON, JOHN SHOURT
Special Mechanical Design .... DICK ALEXANDER, BILL SHOURT, DON TRUMBULL
Special Photographic Effects Photography .... COSMOS BOLGER, DENNIS DORNEY,
        ROBERT ELSWITT, PHIL GONZALES, GREG KIMBLE, RON NATHAN
                MICHAEL SWEENEY, DIANE E. WOOTEN
Special Effects Props and Miniatures .... DAVID BEASLEY, JOHN ERLAND,
    JOE GARLINGTON, PETE GERARD, RICK GILLIGAN, RICHIE HELMER, MICHAEL JOYCE,
        DEBORAH KENDALL, DON KURTZ, PAT MCCLUNG, GARY RHODABACK,

220

JOHN RAMSAY, DENNIS SCHULTZ, DAVID SCOTT, DICK SINGLETON, RICHARD SMILEY,
DAVID SOSALLA, SUSAN TURNER, DON WEBBER, GARY WEEKS
Special Photographic Effects Grips .... MARK CANE, MARK KLINE
Special Photographic Effects Gaffer .... CHUCK EMBREY
Wardrobe .... MARY ETTA LANG
Animation and Graphics .... ANGELA DIAMOS, JOHN MILLERBURG
Special Photographic Effects Editorial .... DENNY KELLY, DAVID BARTHOLOMEW,
STEVE KLEIN, STEVE MARK
Special Visual Consultants .... MIKE MIDDLETON, ERIK NASH, PHIL JOANOU
Assistant to Mr. Dykstra .... MIMI MCKINNEY
Assistant to Mr. Shepherd .... ANN M. JOHNSTON
Special Assistant to Photographic Effects .... DEBORAH BAXTER, JANET DYKSTRA,
PHILIP GOLDEN, PROCTOR JONES, TUT SHURTLEFF
Special Optical & Mechanical Consultants .... B/G ENGINEERING,
ABBOT GRAFTON, GERALD NASH
Geometric Designs .... RON RESCH, BOSTON UNIVERSITY
Certain Models Manufactured at .... MAGICAM, INC.
Special Graphics by .... STOMAR ENTERPRISES, INC.

ADDITIONAL CREDITS

Computer Motion Control System for Miniatures .... BO GEHRING
Certain Special Visual Effects
Conceived and Designed by .... ROBERT ABEL & ASSOCIATES, INC.
Project Manager RA & A .... CON PEDERSON
RA & A Designs by .... RICHARD TAYLOR
Medical Computer Displays Courtesy of .... DIGITAL EQUIPMENT CORP.
Technical Assistance by .... POLAROID CORP.
Certain Computer Equipment by .... SUTHERLAND COMPUTER CORP.
Lenses and Panaflex Camera by .... PANAVISION®
Color by .... METROCOLOR®
Recorded in .... DOLBY STEREO